ALMANAC
2022

ALMANAC
2022

A cheetah cub climbs a branch in South Africa.

NATIONAL GEOGRAPHIC
WASHINGTON, D.C.

National Geographic Kids Books
gratefully acknowledges the following people for their help with the *National Geographic Kids Almanac.*

Bryan Howard of the
National Geographic Explorer Programs

Amazing Animals

Suzanne Braden, Director, Pandas International

Dr. Rodolfo Coria, Paleontologist,
Plaza Huincul, Argentina

Dr. Sylvia Earle, National Geographic
Explorer-in-Residence

Dr. Thomas R. Holtz, Jr., Senior Lecturer,
Vertebrate Paleontology,
Department of Geology, University of Maryland

Dr. Luke Hunter, Executive Director, Panthera

Nizar Ibrahim, National Geographic Explorer

Dereck and Beverly Joubert,
National Geographic Explorers-in-Residence

"Dino" Don Lessem, President, Exhibits Rex

Kathy B. Maher, Research Editor (former),
National Geographic magazine

Kathleen Martin, Canadian Sea Turtle Network

Barbara Nielsen, Polar Bears International

Andy Prince, Austin Zoo

Julia Thorson, Translator, Zurich, Switzerland

Dennis vanEngelsdorp, Senior Extension Associate,
Pennsylvania Department of Agriculture

Culture Connection

Dr. Wade Davis, National Geographic
Explorer-in-Residence

Deirdre Mullervy, Managing Editor,
Gallaudet University Press

Wonders of Nature

Anatta, NOAA Public Affairs Officer

Dr. Robert Ballard,
National Geographic Explorer-in-Residence

Douglas H. Chadwick, Wildlife Biologist and Contributor
to *National Geographic* magazine

Susan K. Pell, Ph.D., Science and Public Programs Manager,
United States Botanic Garden

Space and Earth
Science and Technology

Tim Appenzeller, Chief Magazine Editor, *Nature*

Dr. Rick Fienberg, Press Officer and Director of Communications,
American Astronomical Society

Dr. José de Ondarza, Associate Professor,
Department of Biological Sciences, State University
of New York, College at Plattsburgh

Lesley B. Rogers, Managing Editor (former),
National Geographic magazine

Dr. Enric Sala, National Geographic Explorer-in-Residence

Abigail A. Tipton, Director of Research (former),
National Geographic magazine

Erin Vintinner, Biodiversity Specialist,
Center for Biodiversity and Conservation at the
American Museum of Natural History

Barbara L. Wyckoff, Research Editor (former),
National Geographic magazine

History Happens

Dr. Sylvie Beaudreau, Associate Professor,
Department of History, State University of New York

Elspeth Deir, Assistant Professor, Faculty of Education,
Queens University, Kingston, Ontario, Canada

Dr. Gregory Geddes, Professor, Global Studies,
State University of New York–Orange,
Middletown-Newburgh, New York

Dr. Fredrik Hiebert, National Geographic Visiting Fellow

Micheline Joanisse, Media Relations Officer,
Natural Resources Canada

Dr. Robert D. Johnston,
Associate Professor and Director of the
Teaching of History Program, University of Illinois at Chicago

Dickson Mansfield, Geography Instructor (retired),
Faculty of Education, Queens University,
Kingston, Ontario, Canada

Tina Norris, U.S. Census Bureau

Parliamentary Information and Research Service,
Library of Parliament, Ottawa, Canada

Karyn Pugliese, Acting Director, Communications,
Assembly of First Nations

Geography Rocks

Dr. Kristin Bietsch, Research Associate,
Population Reference Bureau

Carl Haub, Senior Demographer,
Conrad Taeuber Chair of Public Information,
Population Reference Bureau

Dr. Toshiko Kaneda, Senior Research Associate,
Population Reference Bureau

Dr. Walt Meier, National Snow and Ice Data Center

Dr. Richard W. Reynolds, NOAA's National Climatic Data Center

United States Census Bureau, Public Help Desk

Contents

NATIONAL GEOGRAPHIC KIDS
ALMANAC CHALLENGE 2022

THE RESULTS ARE IN!
Which plastic-reducing idea won our 2021 Almanac Challenge? *See page 27.*

Want to become part of the 2022 Almanac Challenge? Go to page 27 to find out more.

YOUR WORLD 2022

Forever homes found! Pet adoptions increased during the COVID-19 pandemic as people sought the comfort and companionship of dogs, cats, and other animals.

ANIMALS DURING QUARANTINE

When COVID-19 hit, these headline-making critters got all the clicks.

"Dogtor" Cares for Hospital Heroes

Not all heroes wear capes; some wear collars! Second-year University of Maryland medical student Caroline Benzel and her pet Rottweiler "Dogtor" Loki brought cheer and smiles to the University of Maryland Medical Center in Baltimore, Maryland, U.S.A. They delivered "hero healing kits" filled with tea, skin lotion, lip balm, and more to the dedicated nurses and doctors working tirelessly to care for coronavirus patients. Benzel even arranged for Loki to "visit" patients virtually.

Sea Turtles Get a Boost

When tourism to Thailand and Florida, U.S.A., drastically slowed during the pandemic, leatherback sea turtles leveled up. After all, with fewer people and pets walking on the beaches and over the turtles' nests, their eggs had a much better chance of surviving. Thailand and Florida both saw an increase in successful nests. Sounds like these turtles are really coming out of their shells.

Penguins Waddle Around

What's a penguin to do during a pandemic? When the Shedd Aquarium in Chicago, Illinois, U.S.A., shut down, its resident penguins had free rein to roam. Aquarium employees allowed rockhoppers Eddie and Annie to wander—and waddle—around and check out their finned friends. Another pair, Magellanic penguins Izzy and Darwin, visited SUE the *T. rex* at the neighboring Field Museum.

Goats Go to Town

When residents of Llandudno in northern Wales, U.K., were asked to stay inside during the pandemic lockdown, a herd of wild mountain goats took advantage of the empty streets and sidewalks. They strolled around, grazed on grassy lawns, and feasted on flower beds. Sounds like those goats had it good!

COOKIES *IN SPACE*

Forget freeze-dried ice cream: Astronauts living at the International Space Station (ISS) may soon be able to satisfy their sweet tooth with freshly baked cookies! Thanks to a special zero-gravity oven, astronauts made a small batch of chocolate chip cookies, the first food ever baked in space from raw ingredients. Although the astronauts didn't get to snack on the cookies (experts had to analyze them first to make sure they were safe to eat), it showed what may be possible in the unique environment of the ISS with limited power supply and no gravity. As for what happened to the cookies? They were returned to Earth and preserved so people can one day check out the made-in-space snacks.

MYSTERY FOSSIL
Discovery

Did a tiny lizard with a skull the width of a thumbnail slither around Earth during the age of dinosaurs? That's what scientists suspect after discovering a fossil of the extra-small animal encased in amber at an amber mine in Southeast Asia. After initially believing it to be a birdlike dinosaur, experts now think that the species was, in fact, a type of lizard that lived around 100 million years ago. The reptile weighed just a few grams and is thought to have been a fierce predator that feasted on bugs with its numerous jagged teeth. It also had huge eyes suited for seeking out prey in the trees. As for the difference between dinosaurs and lizards? The two groups of animals actually diverged from one another some 270 million years ago, well before this lightweight lizard lived.

A TINY FOSSILIZED SKULL PRESERVED IN AMBER

PINK
MANTA RAY

Think pink! This rare manta ray—thought to be the only one in the world to boast the bubblegum shade—was photographed swimming around Australia's Great Barrier Reef. Nicknamed Inspector Clouseau after the detective in the Pink Panther movies, the ray has only been seen a few times. At first, experts thought the ray's rosy hue came from a skin infection or from its diet, much like how flamingos get their pink shade from eating tiny crustaceans. But after doing a small skin biopsy, they determined that a genetic mutation actually causes its skin pigment (which is usually black, white, or black-and-white) to be pink. That makes this 11-foot (3.4-m) ray a true standout of the sea!

Ancient Lines Revealed

Did ancient people use emojis? Some archaeologists believe that prehistoric land art discovered in Peru may have been a way for the inhabitants of the desert coastal area to express themselves—or at least what was going on around them. The giant images, some taller than the Statue of Liberty in New York City, are also known as Nasca Lines and were first discovered in the area in 1927. Recently, experts using high-tech scanning gear uncovered even more images etched into the ground in an area south of Peru's capital of Lima. Some theorize that the images—which depict humans, fish, and birds—represent constellations. Others suggest they were part of ancient rituals. But there's no question that these mysterious works of art were a way for the Nasca civilization to tell a story.

AN ANCIENT HUMANOID IMAGE CAPTURED BY A LOW-FLYING DRONE CAMERA IN SOUTHERN PERU

Let the Games **Begin!**

BEIJING NATIONAL STADIUM—
AKA THE BIRD'S NEST

BEIJING 2022

BIG-AIR SKIER

When the XXIV Olympic Games kick off in February 2022, it will mark the very first time one city has served as host of both the Winter and Summer Games. That city is Beijing, China, which also hosted the 2008 Summer Games. To prepare for this historic double, Beijing will once again use its famous Olympic stadium—also known as the "Bird's Nest"—to hold the opening and closing ceremonies. The Beijing National Aquatics Center, nicknamed the "Water Cube" during the 2008 games, will become the "Ice Cube" and will hold the curling competition. And the Capital Indoor Stadium, which hosted the volleyball events in 2008, will now be the site of figure skating and short-track speed skating. As for the outdoor events like skiing, snowboarding, and bobsled? Those will take place in the mountains outside of Beijing. Because the region averages less than eight inches (20 cm) of snowpack a year, the white stuff will be made by machines.

TOKYO ~~2020~~ 2021

The Olympics was meant to be held in Tokyo, Japan, in 2020, for the first time in 56 years. But when it became clear that it would not be safe to bring thousands of athletes and fans to the capital city due to the spread of COVID-19, the games were postponed until 2021. If COVID-19 remains a concern, they will consider safety measures such as rapid testing for the virus, limited spectators, and "bubbles" for athletes.

NOTE: This information is current as of press time.

BOOKSTORE KITTENS

We're not *kitten:* Otis & Clementine's, a secondhand bookstore and café in Upper Tantallon, Nova Scotia, Canada, is one of the most adorable around! What makes the shop so, well, *aww*-some? A handful of foster kittens can often be found hanging out among the stacks and shelves! Otis & Clementine's owner took in the cats as foster pets and let them live in the store with the hope that customers would want to adopt them. But no worries for those who don't want a pet: It's *purr*-fectly fine to just enjoy the free kitten cuddles instead.

THE OWNER'S DAUGHTER, INGRID, HOLDS TWO KITTENS AT OTIS & CLEMENTINE'S.

SlothBot

If you're ever at the Atlanta Botanical Garden in Georgia, U.S.A., look up! You just may spot the SlothBot slowly creeping along a cable above the ground. The bot, made with a 3D-printed shell, runs on batteries powered by solar energy and even locates the sunlight when its batteries need to be recharged. But the SlothBot isn't just there to look cute: It's equipped to monitor info like weather, temperature, and carbon dioxide levels. The SlothBot's developers—engineering experts at Georgia Tech—hope that it can one day be used in places like South America, where it could provide key data that might help monitor orchid pollination or the lives of endangered frogs.

Harry Potter Turns 25!

Happy birthday, Harry! While the fan-favorite fictional wizard will be forever young in readers' eyes, 2022 marks 25 years since J. K. Rowling's legendary book series launched. The first title in the Harry Potter series was published in the United Kingdom on June 26, 1997, with just about 500 copies sent to bookstores and libraries. The book took off, and today, the original Harry Potter series, which includes seven books, has sold more than 500 million copies, and the franchise features eight blockbuster movies, theme parks, a Broadway play, and more.

GOODY TESTS HER NEW FLIPPER.

Sea Turtle Gets New Flipper

When Goody lost her flipper after becoming entangled in a fishing net, it could have been a tragic ending for the olive ridley sea turtle. But thanks to some kind—and crafty—humans, Goody got a second lease on life. After being rescued in Thailand and later fitted with a prosthetic flipper by researchers at a nearby university, Goody is now able to float freely. And although her injury means she cannot return to the sea, Goody's new life is going just, uh, swimmingly.

HOUND HER✪ES

S outh Africa is home to about 80 percent of the world's last remaining rhinos. More than 8,000 rhinos have been poached, or illegally hunted, in South Africa since 2008. To help protect the species, officials came up with a clever idea that was perfect for sniffing out bad guys: Texas hound dogs. These dogs have excellent scent-tracking skills and use their barking abilities to alert their human helpers to where they are at any time. A pack of hounds traveled from Texas, U.S.A., to South Africa to nab poachers. And the approach is working: Before the Texas hounds arrived, rangers were nabbing only about 5 percent of known poachers. But with the new dogs on the prowl, more than half of the bad guys are now being caught. As the hounds in South Africa have puppies, rangers hope that the young dogs can be trained and then sent to other areas of Africa. That way, more rhinos and many other animals will get a chance to roam free.

ANTI-POACHING DOGS DURING A TRAINING EXERCISE

Cool Events 2022

INTERNATIONAL GUIDE DOG DAY

Pay tribute to all of the dogs who work hard to help visually impaired humans.

April 27

INTERNATIONAL KITE DAY

GO FLY A KITE!

This celebration, which began in Gujarat, India, marks the end of the short, cold days of the winter season.

January 14

WORLD REEF DAY

It's never been more important to protect the ocean's coral reefs. Some 25 percent of sea life depends on them.

June 1

INTERNATIONAL DAY OF HAPPINESS

DON'T WORRY, BE HAPPY!

Make it a goal to keep grinning all day long in this observance of everything that brings you joy.

March 20

INTERNATIONAL JOKE DAY

LOL ALL DAY

by telling your best jokes and riddles—and encourage your friends and family to get funny, too!

July 1

WORLD DOLPHIN DAY

Flip out over our finned friends on this day dedicated to dolphins.

April 14

INTERNATIONAL PUZZLE DAY

Exercise your brain by solving a sudoku or get clever with a crossword today!

July 13

WORLD ART DAY

Promote creativity worldwide by painting, drawing, or sculpting something today!

April 15

WORLD LEMUR DAY

Celebrate the lovable lemur while helping to raise awareness for these amazing—and endangered—animals.

October 28

Tortoise Turns 100

Tuki, an Aldabra tortoise living in a zoo in Turkey, recently hit a mega milestone: He turned 100 years old! The centenarian celebrated alongside some llama friends at the zoo with balloons and a giant cake made of lettuce and vegetables. While Tuki's age is impressive, it's not entirely unusual: Aldabras, one of the world's largest land tortoises, can live for more than 150 years!

New Species Name Honors Climate Activist

One tiny mollusk was recently given quite a big name! The .08-inch (2-mm)-long *Craspedotropis gretathunbergae* was named for teen climate change activist Greta Thunberg. Citizen scientists, together with Taxon Expeditions, discovered the snail in a rainforest in Brunei on the island of Borneo. They say this type of tiny critter is sensitive to drought, extreme temperatures, and other hallmarks of climate change. So they chose the name to honor Thunberg's efforts in speaking up about climate change as well as to encourage future generations to continue to fight to protect the planet—and all of the species living on it.

RED PANDAS might be TWO SPECIES

Red pandas are super rare—it's estimated that there are as few as 2,500 in the wild—and now scientists say those left are actually two species. The difference? It's observed that Chinese red pandas have redder fur and striped tail rings, while the Himalayan red pandas have whiter faces. Scientists hope this discovery will help them better protect the animals' habitats and save *all* red pandas from extinction.

Constructed of plastic waste, this art installation in Kochi, India, was created to remind people of the threat plastics pose to marine life.

WHAT IS PLASTIC?

» **P**lastic can be molded, colored, and textured to make, well, just about anything. That begs the question: What precisely is this wonder product?

THE BASICS:
Plastics are polymers, or long, flexible chains of molecules made of repeating links. This molecular structure makes plastic lightweight, hard to break, and easy to mold—all of which makes it extremely useful.

WHERE DO POLYMERS COME FROM?
Polymers can be found in nature, in things like the cell walls of plants, tar, tortoiseshell, and tree sap. In fact, nearly 3,500 years ago, people in what is today Central America used the sap from gum trees to make rubber balls for games. About 150 years ago, scientists began replicating the polymers in nature to improve on them—these are called synthetic polymers.

WHO INVENTED PLASTIC?
In 1869, an American named John Wesley Hyatt created the first useful synthetic polymer. At the time, the discovery was a big deal: For the first time, manufacturing was no longer limited by the resources supplied by nature like wood, clay, and stone. People could create their own materials.

WHAT IS SYNTHETIC PLASTIC MADE FROM?
Today, most plastic is made from oil and natural gas.

WHEN DID IT BECOME POPULAR?
During World War II, from 1939 to 1945, nylon, which is strong and light like silk but made of plastic, was used for parachutes, rope, body armor, and helmet liners. And airplanes used in battle had lightweight windows made of plastic glass, also known as Plexiglas. After the war, plastic became a popular material. Everything from dishes to radios to Mr. Potato Head hit the market. A few decades later, plastic soda bottles became a lightweight nonbreakable alternative to glass bottles, and grocery stores switched from paper bags to cheaper thin plastic ones.

THAT BRINGS US TO TODAY.
Look around: Are you more than a few feet away from something plastic? Probably not! Plastic is all around us.

AMERICANS use an average of ONE plastic grocery bag A DAY. People in DENMARK use an average of FOUR plastic grocery bags A YEAR.

WHERE DOES ALL THE PLASTIC GO?

Only a small percentage of all the plastic that has ever been made has been recycled to make other things. Most has been tossed out and left to slowly biodegrade in landfills, a process that can take hundreds of years. The other option for getting rid of plastic is to burn it. But because plastic is made from fossil fuels, burning it releases harmful pollutants into the air. Here is a breakdown of where all the plastic has gone since people started making it, and how long it takes to biodegrade if it does wind up in a landfill.

9% Recycled

12% Burned, releasing toxins into the air

79% Sent to landfills or wound up in the natural environment (like oceans)

THE LIFE SPAN OF PLASTIC

Plastic that's sent to a landfill doesn't just disappear—it stays there for a really long time. Different types of plastic take different lengths of time to biodegrade.

PLASTIC BAG
20 YEARS

PLASTIC-FOAM CUP
50 YEARS

STRAW
200 YEARS

BOTTLE
450 YEARS

SODA SIX-PACK RING 450 YEARS

FISHING LINE
600+ YEARS

DEADLY DEBRIS

THE INS AND OUTS OF THE (NOT SO) GREAT PACIFIC GARBAGE PATCH

On a map, the space between California and Hawaii, U.S.A., looks like an endless blue sea, but in person, you'll find a giant floating island—made up of plastic. Plastic can be found in all the oceans of the world, but currents and winds move marine debris around in certain patterns that create huge concentrations, or patches, of plastic in some spots. The biggest one is the Great Pacific Garbage Patch. Scientists estimate that there are about 1.8 trillion pieces of plastic in the patch, and 94 percent of them are microplastics. So, don't try walking on it; it's definitely not solid! Some of the patch is made up of bulky items, including fishing gear like nets, rope, eel traps, crates, and baskets. The patch is also made up of debris washed into the sea during tsunamis. A tsunami is a series of waves caused by an earthquake or an undersea volcanic eruption. It can pull millions of tons of debris—from cars to household appliances to pieces of houses—off coastlines and into the ocean. Scientists and innovators are working on ways to clean up the patch, although with more plastic constantly entering waterways, the effort will inevitably be ongoing.

TANGLED NYLON ROPE WASHED ASHORE OFF THE COAST OF PHUKET, THAILAND.

SMASHED-UP SHIPS EVENTUALLY MAKE THEIR WAY TO A SWIRLING MASS OF DEBRIS IN THE GREAT PACIFIC GARBAGE PATCH.

GARBAGE PATCH ZONES

There are five large systems of circulating ocean currents around the world called gyres. Plastic and other trash travel with the currents and get trapped in the gyres. The gyre that the Great Pacific Garbage Patch swirls in is the largest of them all.

Garbage patch area with low concentration of plastics

Garbage patch area with high concentration of plastics

THE GREAT PACIFIC GARBAGE PATCH MEASURES 618,000 SQUARE MILES
(1.6 MILLION SQ KM)

That's about:

3 TIMES THE SIZE OF FRANCE

2 TIMES THE SIZE OF TEXAS

There are **250 PIECES OF PLASTIC** in the Great Pacific Garbage Patch for **EVERY HUMAN** on Earth.

SEA TURTLE RESCUE

RESCUERS SWOOP IN TO HELP A SEA TURTLE THAT SWALLOWED A BALLOON.

A young green sea turtle bobbed along the surface of the water off the coast of Florida, U.S.A. Young turtles usually don't hang out at the surface—that's where predators can easily spot them, plus their food is deeper underwater. But something was keeping this one foot (30.5-cm)-long turtle from diving.

Luckily, rescuers spotted the struggling turtle and took it back to the Clearwater Marine Aquarium, where they named it Chex. Staff placed Chex in a shallow kiddie pool so that the turtle wouldn't waste energy trying to dive. They tested Chex's blood and ran x-rays but couldn't figure out what was wrong. "Then one day Chex started pooping out something weird," biologist Lauren Bell says. The weird object turned out to be a purple balloon and an attached string.

SOS (SAVE OUR SEAGRASS)!

Sea turtles often mistake floating trash for food. "Even some *people* can't tell the difference between a plastic grocery bag and a jellyfish in the water," Bell says. But plastic doesn't just hurt sea turtles: It hurts their habitat.

Green sea turtles often hang out close to the shore near seagrass, one of their favorite snacks. Plastic trash left on the beach or coming from rivers that empty into the sea often ends up in this habitat. When it settles on the seagrass, the rubbish can smother the grass, causing it to die. That can mean trouble for green sea turtles like Chex that rely on the seagrass for food or shelter.

> During one three-hour cleanup on a beach in Virginia, U.S.A, volunteers collected more than 900 balloons.

TURTLE POWER

BALLOON STRING

PIECE OF BALLOON

1 CHEX THE GREEN SEA TURTLE PROBABLY MISTOOK A TWO-FOOT (0.6-M)-LONG STRING FOR FOOD.

2 CHEX RECOVERED AT THE CLEARWATER MARINE AQUARIUM, SPENDING LOTS OF TIME IN A KIDDIE POOL. ONCE THE TURTLE STARTED EATING SOLID FOODS AGAIN, RESCUERS DECIDED CHEX WAS READY TO RETURN TO THE OCEAN.

GREEN SEA TURTLE
Redington Beach, Florida, U.S.A.

ARCTIC OCEAN

NORTH AMERICA

EUROPE

ASIA

PACIFIC OCEAN

ATLANTIC OCEAN

AFRICA

PACIFIC OCEAN

SOUTH AMERICA

INDIAN OCEAN

AUSTRALIA

Seagrass

ANTARCTICA

BYE, BALLOON

After several days at the aquarium, Chex started to improve as the balloon made its way through the turtle's digestive system. Chex eventually passed the entire balloon, plus a two-foot (0.6-m)-long string. A few months later, after aquarium staff had successfully introduced solid food back into Chex's diet, rescuers declared the turtle ready to return to the sea.

Bell stood hip deep in the waves as another staff member handed Chex to her. She carefully placed the little turtle in the water and watched it paddle away. "Chex was like, 'Oh, there's the ocean! Okay, bye!'" Bell says. Chex's rescue is worth celebrating ... but maybe without the party balloons.

POLLUTION SOLUTION: PLASTIC PREDATOR

The ocean is full of trillions of pieces of trash called microplastics that are smaller than the period at the end of this sentence—which makes them really hard to clean up. But the solution might be in tadpole-like creatures called larvaceans (lar-VAY-shuns). These marine animals eat by filtering tiny food particles out of the water and through their bodies. The particles are first trapped in what's called a mucus house—a thin, see-through bubble of, well, mucus that surrounds the larvacean as it travels. Scientists are studying this behavior to see if a similar process could pull harmful microplastics out of the water.

3 BIOLOGIST LAUREN BELL PREPARES TO RELEASE THE LITTLE TURTLE BACK INTO THE SEA.

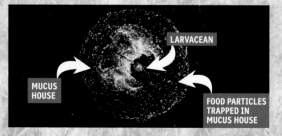

LARVACEAN

MUCUS HOUSE

FOOD PARTICLES TRAPPED IN MUCUS HOUSE

25

OUR AWESOME OCEAN
SHOW & TELL!

NATIONAL
GEOGRAPHIC
KiDS
ALMANAC
CHALLENGE
2022

Earth is sometimes called the blue planet because more than 70 percent of its surface is covered by ocean. Award-winning underwater photographer and National Geographic Explorer Brian Skerry has traveled the world to capture images of some of the oceans' most elusive creatures. From the fiercest fish to the most wondrous whales, Skerry has just about seen everything in the sea. Here, he shares more about life behind the lens, as well as why it's so key we all work together to protect our oceans.

What inspired you to become an underwater photographer?

I grew up in Massachusetts, and my parents would take me to the beach as a young boy. There was something so magical in the ocean. It was a place that was ripe for discovery, and the idea of exploring the ocean really appealed to me. I also loved photography and the idea of exploring the ocean with a camera and telling stories with pictures.

Are you ever afraid of swimming in the ocean or diving with sharks?

I've never been afraid of the water. It has always seemed so natural and comfortable to me. But I do have a healthy fear of predators like sharks. I know there are risks, and I try to do things as carefully and safely as possible.

What is one of your best memories of interacting with sharks?

I have thousands of memories! One of my favorites is swimming with oceanic whitetip sharks, one of the most dangerous species in the world. After 16 days, we only had one encounter, a female. She came right toward me! There I was, spinning around in the beautiful blue water of the Bahamas. She was very curious and swam big, lazy circles around us as I took her picture. I was pleasantly surprised about how polite she was. It was magical.

Besides sharks, what other animals have you worked with?

I love whales, and I recently had the opportunity to photograph multiple species. Through my work, I discovered that whales have a culture that's not that much different than humans'. They have different languages and dialects. Humpback whales have singing competitions. Some whale families even have babysitters! It's so fascinating, and I hope it gives people more appreciation for whales.

Why is it so important that we take care of our oceans?

The ocean is everything. Even though we live on land, we live on a water planet. About 72 percent of Earth's surface is ocean, and 98 percent of where life can exist on our planet is water. Everything from the weather to the air we breathe comes from the sea. The oceans are essential to human life: Our own survival depends on us understanding the ocean and protecting it.

THIS YEAR'S CHALLENGE

Now it's your turn! Help celebrate Our Awesome Ocean by showing and/or telling us all about your favorite ocean animal. There are so many cool animals: whale, octopus, sea turtle, dolphin, sea otter, walrus, seahorse, clownfish, jellyfish, and so many more. Choose the animal and method (show or tell—or both) that's right for you.

Show: Draw a picture of your favorite ocean animal in its environment. Be as accurate as you can about how it looks, so that we can appreciate it as you do. With your drawing, include the name of the animal, where in the world it lives, and one important fact about it.

Tell: Write a short essay, biography, or poem about your favorite ocean animal, including its name, where in the world it lives, basic information like how big it grows and what it eats and why it's your favorite. Be informative and creative in writing about the creature, so that we can appreciate it as you do.

The most creative visual and written pieces will be featured in next year's Almanac!

Find inspiration and details on how to enter at **natgeokids.com/almanac.**

LAST YEAR'S CHALLENGE

Kids proved they can be part of the plastic pollution solution! Last year more than 35,000 kids took the Nat Geo Kids pledge to reduce their plastic waste. And most of them aren't doing it alone. They're involving their families and friends to have an even bigger positive impact on the planet.

The 2021 Almanac Challenge winner is Mary Rose Farinella, age 9, for her entry, Planet Protector: Making a Difference, One Sip at a Time.

Mary Rose inspired her family to recycle more and cut down on their use of plastic straws and plastic grocery bags. But the most significant thing she did was to replace plastic water bottles with reusable metal ones. Nearly one million plastic drink bottles are sold every minute around the world, so choosing a reusable bottle can make a huge difference. Plus, it's something everyone can do! You can read Mary's entry and more at **natgeokids.com/almanac.**

Certificate
of
Heroism

This hereby recognizes

Mary Rose Farinella

as a **PLANET PROTECTOR**, pledging to help save the world by decreasing the use of straws, water bottles, and other single-use plastic items.

GARY E. KNELL
Chief Executive Officer
National Geographic Partners

NATIONAL
GEOGRAPHIC
KIDS.

kids
PLASTIC

10 EASY WAYS TO CUT BACK ON PLASTIC

Encourage your parents to shop with **REUSABLE TOTES** instead of **PLASTIC** shopping bags.

MUNCH ON FRUIT like apples, bananas, or oranges instead of snacks that come in plastic packaging.

SKIP THE PLASTIC BOTTLES AND OPT FOR A **REFILLABLE WATER BOTTLE.**

ENJOY your ice cream in a cone and **AVOID** using plastic cups and spoons.

Encourage your family **to shop for snacks, cereal, and pasta in** bulk and store them in **glass containers.**

Ask your parents to buy products like laundry detergent and milk in **RECYCLABLE CARTONS INSTEAD OF PLASTIC JUGS.**

Stock up on METAL or PAPER STRAWS—and STOP USING PLASTIC STRAWS altogether.

Carry silverware or chopsticks with you to cut back on using plasticware at restaurants.

Use a **BAMBOO** toothbrush

instead of a plastic one.

BIRD FEEDER

Try to **REPURPOSE,** or **UPCYCLE,** plastic containers into toys, art, and other useful things instead of tossing them away.

kids
vs. PLASTIC

Do your part to help prevent single-use plastic items from reaching the ocean. Check out ideas here, and then grab an adult and go online for more.

natgeokids.com/KidsVsPlastic

CHOOSE THIS

NOT THAT

WHY?

You might use plastic bags for snacks, but for many animals, the plastic bag *is* the snack!

The glint of a plastic goodie bag floating in the water can look like a fish. As the plastic fills the animal's stomach, it blocks food from traveling through its intestines, causing it to starve. In fact, one Cuvier's beaked whale was recently discovered with more than 88 pounds (40 kg) of plastic—including snack bags, grocery bags, and nylon ropes—in its stomach.

So instead, store your treats in reusable containers, and then toss them in your backpack for on-the-go grub.

Grab an adult and go online to pledge to reduce your single-use plastic trash!

TAKE THE PLASTIC PLEDGE! natgeokids.com/ KidsVsPlastic

Pick Your Perfect SNACK SACK.

Find a reusable food container by choosing the phrase that fits you best.

1 I don't want my sandwich to get squished. **Stash it in a sturdy container.**

2 I want a light and flexible wrap. **Use a cloth or beeswax wrap.**

3 I need a container for messy munchies. **Grab a glass jar.**

4 I want a pouch that's flexible yet sturdy. **Stuff it in a silicone sack.**

LAST BAG If you have a few plastic snack bags left at home, keep using them! After each use, wash the bags with soap and water, let them air-dry, and then keep reusing. Once they wear out, find a place to recycle them: Many grocery stores accept the bags for recycling.

YOUR **PLASTIC-FREE** GUIDE TO

SNACKS

Chew on these three ideas for plastic-free snacking.

1
TRAIL MIX

Just mix all your favorite treats from the bulk section of the grocery store together in a bowl, and then eat! You can even sprinkle your mixture with sea salt, cinnamon, or another of your favorite spices for more flavor. Check out these ideas for ingredient inspiration.

- ☐ Pretzels
- ☐ Nuts like almonds, pistachios, or peanuts
- ☐ Pumpkin or sunflower seeds
- ☐ Dried fruit like apricots, raisins, or banana chips
- ☐ Chocolate chips
- ☐ Whole-grain cereal
- ☐ Shredded coconut

2
STOVETOP POPCORN

You'll need a paper bag full of popcorn kernels from the bulk section of the grocery store, some cooking oil, and a big pot with a lid. Make sure to get a parent's help with this recipe.

- ☐ Pour a splash of oil into the pot, using just enough to cover the bottom.
- ☐ Grab a parent and heat the pot on the stovetop over medium heat.
- ☐ Pour in enough popcorn kernels to create one layer along the bottom of the pot.
- ☐ Cover the pot with the lid.
- ☐ After a few minutes, listen for popping sounds. When the popping slows, remove the pot from the burner, take off the lid, and put the popcorn in a bowl.
- ☐ Top off your treat with salt, melted butter, or other spices.

3
BAKED APPLES

Turn this packaging-free fruit into a special snack with brown sugar, butter, and cinnamon. Make sure to get a parent's help with this recipe.

- ☐ Grab a parent and preheat the oven to 350°F (175°C). (You can also use the microwave.)
- ☐ Cut the apple in half, then scoop out the core.
- ☐ Put the apples in an ovenproof baking dish, and then spread a tablespoon of brown sugar and a tablespoon of butter on the inside of each apple half. Then sprinkle the apples with cinnamon.
- ☐ Bake the apples in the oven for about half an hour, in the microwave for about three minutes or until the fruit softens.

DIY Ice Pops

Help keep Earth healthy by ditching single-use plastic items. Make your own ice pops so you can skip the plastic-wrapped store-bought version.

YOU'LL NEED

- 2 cups (350 g) fresh fruit like strawberries, blueberries, peaches, and bananas
- 2 tablespoons (30 mL) honey
- 1/4 cup (60 mL) juice or water
- Blender
- 8 small paper cups
- Baking tin (optional)
- Aluminum foil or 8 foil muffin cups
- 8 wooden craft sticks

Left in outdoor trash cans, plastic wrappers can easily be blown into the environment, where animals might mistake them for food.

STEP ONE

Grab a parent and put the fruit, honey, and juice (or water) into the blender.

STEP TWO

Put the lid on the blender, and then blend the mixture until it's smooth.

STEP THREE

Fill the paper cups 3/4 full with the blended mixture. (You can put the cups in a baking tin to keep them stable while you pour.)

STEP FOUR

Cover the top of each paper cup with a piece of aluminum foil or a foil muffin cup.

STEP FIVE

Carefully poke a craft stick through the center of the foil on each cup.

STEP SIX

Slide each craft stick about halfway down into the mixture.

STEP SEVEN

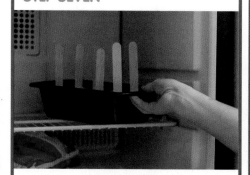

Place the cups on a flat surface in the freezer for about four hours, or until the mixture is fully frozen.

STEP EIGHT

Take the cups out of the freezer, remove the foil, peel away the paper cups, and enjoy!

QUIZ WHIZ

What's your eco-friendly IQ? Find out with this quiz!

Write your answers on a piece of paper. Then check them below.

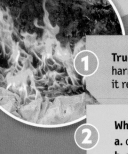

1 **True or false?** Burning plastic is harmful to the environment because it releases toxins into the air.

2 **What is a way to keep plastic out of the ocean?**
a. opt for package-free snacks
b. avoid using plastic baggies in your lunch box
c. shop with a reusable tote bag
d. all of the above

3 **About how many pieces of plastic can be found in the Great Pacific Garbage Patch?**
a. 180,000
b. 1.8 million
c. 1.8 billion
d. 1.8 trillion

4 **Sea turtles often mistake _____ for their favorite food, seagrass.**
a. seaweed
b. eels
c. floating trash
d. fish

5 **True or false?** Plastic and other trash get trapped in circulating ocean currents around the world called gyres.

Not **STUMPED** yet? Check out the *NATIONAL GEOGRAPHIC KIDS QUIZ WHIZ* collection for more crazy **ENVIRONMENT** questions!

ANSWERS: 1. True; 2. d; 3. d; 4. c; 5. True

HOMEWORK HELP

Write a Letter That Gets Results

Knowing how to write a good letter is a useful skill. It will come in handy when you want to persuade someone to understand your point of view. Whether you're emailing your congressperson or writing a letter for a school project or to your grandma, a great letter will help you get your message across. Most important, a well-written letter makes a good impression.

CHECK OUT THE EXAMPLE BELOW FOR THE ELEMENTS OF A GOOD LETTER.

Your address

Date

Salutation
Always use "Dear" followed by the person's name; use Mr., Mrs., Ms., or Dr. as appropriate.

Introductory paragraph
Give the reason you're writing the letter.

Body
The longest part of the letter, which provides evidence that supports your position. Be persuasive!

Closing paragraph
Sum up your argument.

Complimentary closing
Sign off with "Sincerely" or "Thank you."

Your signature

Maddie Smith
1234 Main Street
Peoria, Illinois 61525

April 22, 2022

Dear Owner of the Happy Hamburger,

I am writing to ask you to stop using single-use plastic at the Happy Hamburger.

This is my favorite restaurant. My family and I eat there almost every Saturday night. I always order the bacon cheeseburger with mac and cheese on the side. It's my favorite meal, ever!

The other day, my Dad brought home a to-go order from your restaurant. The order contained a plastic fork, knife, and spoon, all wrapped in plastic. It also came in a plastic bag. Now that's a lot of plastic!

I am concerned because plastic is a huge problem for the planet. Did you know that nine million tons of plastic waste end up in the ocean every year? Even worse, scientists think that the amount of plastic might triple by 2050.

Some other restaurants in town have cut back on their single-use plastic. The Hotdog Hangout uses paper bags instead of plastic bags for takeout. And servers at the Weeping Onion ask customers if they'd like plastic cutlery, instead of automatically including it in to-go orders.

These are simple changes that I hope you can make at the Happy Hamburger. That way, not only would you be serving the best burgers around, but you'd also be helping to protect the planet.

Thank you very much for your time.

Sincerely,

Maddie Smith

Maddie Smith

COMPLIMENTARY CLOSINGS

Sincerely, Sincerely yours, Thank you, Regards, Best wishes, Respectfully

AMAZING
ANIMALS

A great horned owl takes flight.

WHAT IS Taxonomy?

Because there are billions and billions of living things, called organisms, on the planet, people need a way of classifying them. Scientists created a system called taxonomy, which helps to classify all living things into ordered groups. By putting organisms into categories, we are better able to understand how they are the same and how they are different. There are eight levels of taxonomic classification, beginning with the broadest group, called a domain, followed by kingdom, down to the most specific group, called a species.

Biologists divide life based on evolutionary history, and they place organisms into three domains depending on their genetic structure: Archaea, Bacteria, and Eukarya. (See page 101 for "The Three Domains of Life.")

Where do animals come in?

Animals are a part of the Eukarya domain, which means they are organisms made of cells with nuclei. More than one million species of animals, including humans, have been named. Like all living things, animals can be divided into smaller groups, called phyla. Most scientists believe there are more than 30 phyla into which animals can be grouped based on certain scientific criteria, such as body type or whether or not the animal has a backbone. It can be pretty complicated, so there is another, less complicated system that groups animals into two categories: vertebrates and invertebrates.

HEDGEHOG

SAMPLE CLASSIFICATION
PHILIPPINE TARSIER

Domain:	Eukarya
Kingdom:	Animalia
Phylum:	Chordata
Class:	Mammalia
Order:	Primates
Family:	Tarsiidae
Genus:	*Carlito*
Species:	*syrichta*

TIP: Here's a sentence to help you remember the classification order: D̲id K̲ing P̲hillip C̲ome O̲ver F̲or G̲ood S̲oup?

BY THE NUMBERS

There are 14,735 vulnerable or endangered animal species in the world. The list includes:

• **1,299 mammals,** such as the snow leopard, the polar bear, and the fishing cat

• **1,486 birds,** including the Steller's sea eagle and the black-banded plover

• **2,849 fish,** such as the Mekong giant catfish

• **1,406 reptiles,** including the Round Island day gecko

• **1,819 insects,** such as the Macedonian grayling

• **2,276 amphibians,** such as the emperor newt

• **And more,** including 197 arachnids, 734 crustaceans, 234 sea anemones and corals, 201 bivalves, and 2,069 snails and slugs

ROUND ISLAND DAY GECKO

Vertebrates
Animals WITH Backbones

Fish are cold-blooded and live in water. They breathe with gills, lay eggs, and usually have scales.

Amphibians are cold-blooded. Their young live in water and breathe with gills. Adults live on land and breathe with lungs.

Reptiles are cold-blooded and breathe with lungs. They live both on land and in water.

Birds are warm-blooded and have feathers and wings. They lay eggs, breathe with lungs, and are usually able to fly. Some birds live on land, some in water, and some on both.

Mammals are warm-blooded and feed on their mothers' milk. They also have skin that is usually covered with hair. Mammals live both on land and in water.

BIRD: MANDARIN DUCK

AMPHIBIAN: POISON DART FROG

Invertebrates
Animals WITHOUT Backbones

Sponges are a very basic form of animal life. They live in water and do not move on their own.

Echinoderms have external skeletons and live in seawater.

Mollusks have soft bodies and can live either in or out of shells, on land or in water.

Arthropods are the largest group of animals. They have external skeletons, called exoskeletons, and segmented bodies with appendages. Arthropods live in water and on land.

Worms are soft-bodied animals with no true legs. Worms live in soil.

Cnidaria live in water and have mouths surrounded by tentacles.

MOLLUSK: MAGNIFICENT CHROMODORID NUDIBRANCH

SPONGE: SEA SPONGE

ARTHROPOD: PRAYING MANTIS

Cold-Blooded
versus
Warm-Blooded

Cold-blooded animals, also called ectotherms, get their heat from outside their bodies.

Warm-blooded animals, also called endotherms, keep their body temperatures level regardless of the temperature of their environment.

10 ADORABLE FACTS ABOUT ANIMAL BABIES

BABY HEDGEHOGS— also known as **HOGLETS—** are BORN with **TINY, SMOOTH SPIKES,** which eventually turn into **PRICKLY QUILLS.**

BABY RABBITS are called **KITTENS.**

Cotton-top tamarin monkeys have **TWINS MORE OFTEN** than they have **SINGLE BABIES.**

PUPPIES SLEEP as many as **20 hours** a day.

BABY RHINOS aren't born with a **HORN**—it takes a **FEW MONTHS** to start to **GROW IN.**

40

A **BABY GIRAFFE** can **STAND SOON AFTER** its **BIRTH** and learns to **WALK WITHIN AN HOUR.**

A newborn **DOLPHIN** is born with a **TINY PATCH** of **HAIR** on its chin.

Baby deer— called **fawns—** are born with **white spots** that look like **spots of sunlight** to help them **hide from predators.**

FEMALE RED SQUIRRELS are known to "ADOPT" ABANDONED SQUIRREL BABIES—CALLED PUPS—and RAISE THEM as THEIR OWN.

A **PANDA CUB** is about the **SIZE** of a **STICK OF BUTTER** AT BIRTH— about 1/900th the size of its mother.

EXTRAORDINARY ANIMALS

Aah, that's the spot!

THE CUB, ON THE RIGHT AND BELOW, IS LIKELY ABOUT TWO AND A HALF YEARS OLD.

Bears Get Backs Scratched

Yukon Territory, Canada

When a momma grizzly bear and her nearly full-grown cub spotted a metal road sign, the pair could *bearly* contain their excitement. The two stood up on their hind legs and rubbed their backs and faces against the pole like they were scratching bear-size itches!

But the two probably weren't itchy, says Tom Smith, a bear biologist at Brigham Young University in Utah, U.S.A. "Bears use these scratching behaviors to lay down their scent," he says. "It tells other bears that live there that these two are nearby, which can help bears avoid fights or find mates."

Bears living in forested areas often leave their scent on tree trunks. But in the treeless Canadian tundra, grizzlies spread their odor on boulders, muddy areas, and human-made objects like buildings and signposts. Sort of like a smelly text message!

THE METAL POLES HELP MARK THE ROAD WHEN SNOW FALLS.

Clean Sea = Happy Birds!

BOB THE FLAMINGO SWIMS IN THE CARIBBEAN SEA.

Flamingo Says "Save the Earth!"

Willemstad, Curaçao
Bob the flamingo likes taking dips in his own saltwater pool and getting foot massages on the beach. This hardworking bird deserves all the pampering: He's teaching kids about conservation.

Veterinarian and wildlife sanctuary founder Odette Doest rescued Bob after he flew into a hotel window. After rehabilitating him, she realized he wouldn't be able to survive in the wild. So Doest decided to keep Bob at her sanctuary and use the friendly bird to help educate people.

She often brings Bob to schools to teach kids about plastic pollution, which can harm wildlife when the animals become entangled in fishing gear or mistake discarded balloons for food. Bob helps people understand how a small change in their habits can have a big impact on his life, Doest says. Best bird ever!

BOB AND DOEST VISIT A LOCAL CLASSROOM.

Dog Flies Away

Rochester Hills, Michigan, U.S.A.
Tinkerbell the Chihuahua was relaxing with her owners at an outdoor market when a 70-mile (113-km)-an-hour blast of wind tore through the area. Tables and chairs flew into the air—and so did the six-pound (2.7-kg) pup. Her frantic owners chased after her, but the wind carried Tinkerbell away like a furry paper airplane.

For two days, owners LaVern and Dorothy Utley searched the area. But the only sign of Tinkerbell was her leash, found about a quarter of a mile (0.4 km) away. Desperate, the Utleys wandered along an old trail and called the dog one final time. She came running!

No one is sure how Tinkerbell survived her journey—or her landing. "She was probably only six or eight feet off the ground," meteorologist Dave Rexroth said. "I suspect she was tossed around like a tumbleweed until she got caught in small trees." Her owners, however, didn't care how she managed to survive. "We were just totally tickled to have her back," LaVern Utley said.

I must be part bird!

Hen Sails the World!

Sailing is so much easier than flying.

Brittany, France

Why did the chicken cross the sea? To keep the sailor company!

Guirec Soudée and Monique have been sailing buddies for years, visiting places such as Antarctica, the Caribbean islands, and South Africa. The hen stands beside Soudée while he hoists the sails, and she catches fish that have flopped onto the deck. "I knew that this little chicken was as adventurous as I am," says Soudée, author of *The Hen Who Sailed Around the World: A True Story.*

Monique lives in her own cabin filled with straw, and she's been known to lay an egg on board. Chicken behavior expert K-lynn Smith says Monique probably has a better life than most chickens, with more space and sunshine. This chicken definitely isn't cooped up!

SOUDÉE SAYS THAT MONIQUE OFTEN "SINGS" FOR HIM AS THEY SAIL.

Let me steer the boat.

MONIQUE USUALLY STAYS CLOSE TO HER OWNER, GUIREC SOUDÉE.

ANIMAL MYTHS BUSTED

Some people mistakenly think adult opossums hang by their tails or that porcupines shoot their quills. What other misconceptions are out there? Here are some common animal myths.

MYTH Elephants are afraid of mice.

HOW IT MAY HAVE STARTED People used to think that mice liked to crawl into an elephant's trunk, which could cause damage and terrible sneezing. So it makes sense that elephants would be afraid of the rodents.

WHY IT'S NOT TRUE Although elephants do get anxious when they hear sounds they can't identify, their eyesight is so poor that they could barely even see a mouse. Plus, if an elephant isn't afraid to live among predators such as tigers, rhinos, and crocodiles, a mouse would be the least of its worries!

Who are you again?

MYTH Goldfish only have a three-second memory.

HOW IT MAY HAVE STARTED While an adult human's brain weighs about three pounds (1.4 kg), an average goldfish's brain weighs only a tiny fraction of that. So how could there be any room for memory in there?

WHY IT'S NOT TRUE Research has shown that goldfish are quite smart. Phil Gee of the University of Plymouth in the United Kingdom trained goldfish to push a lever that dropped food into their tank. "They remembered the time of day that the lever worked and waited until feeding time to press it," Gee says. One scientist even trained goldfish to tell the difference between classical and blues music!

MYTH Touching a frog or toad will give you warts.

HOW IT MAY HAVE STARTED Many frogs and toads have bumps on their skin that look like warts. Some people think the bumps are contagious.

WHY IT'S NOT TRUE "Warts are caused by a human virus, not frogs or toads," says dermatologist Jerry Litt. But the wart-like bumps behind a toad's ears *can* be dangerous. These parotoid glands contain a nasty poison that irritates the mouths of some predators and often the skin of humans. So toads may not cause warts, but they can cause other nasties. It's best not to handle these critters—warty or not!

Cute Animal
SUPERLATIVES

Funky features. Super senses. Sensational speed. No doubt, all animals are cool. But whether they've got goofy grins, funky hair, or endless energy, some species are extra adorable. Here are 15 of the cutest creatures on Earth.

FURRIEST

Thick, white fur helps polar bears blend in with the ice and snow of their Arctic habitat. This fur even grows on the bottom of their paws! It gives them a better grip on the ice and protection from frozen surfaces.

BEST SNUGGLER

The smallest raptor in Africa, African pygmy falcons only grow to be about the length of a pencil. To stay warm in winter, these pint-size predators spend up to 15 hours a day snuggling together in their nests.

BEST CAMO

Is that a leaf—or a sea dragon? Thanks to leaf-shaped appendages that cover their bodies, these fish easily blend into the seaweed and kelp that grow in their underwater habitats.

BEST AT HANGING OUT

Spending more than 90 percent of their waking time in trees, orangutans—who have much longer arms than legs—are well suited for life in the forest canopy.

BEST HOPPER

Leaping lambs! All sheep are playful, but the young ones are especially energetic. They spend their days jumping, running around, and head-butting their pals for fun.

BEST HAIR DAY

Polish chickens sometimes go by the nickname of "top hat" because of the funky feathers at the top of their head, or crest. Their unique appearance made them prized birds among the rich and royalty in the 1700s. Despite their name, the breed known today comes from the Netherlands.

BEST DRESSED

Native to Madagascar, panther chameleons can be identified by their brightly colored skin, which ranges from blue and green to pink and yellow. It only takes a few minutes for a panther chameleon to change its coloring.

47

BEST SENSE OF SMELL

Elephants are super smellers. They use the nostrils at the edge of their trunks to sniff out sources of water and food from several miles away.

SMALLEST HOOVES

About the size of a rabbit, the Vietnamese mouse-deer—also known as a chevrotain—is the world's smallest hoofed animal. After not being seen in the wild in nearly 30 years, it was photographed in Vietnam in 2017.

BEST STRETCH

What's the benefit of having an extra-long neck? It's better to catch prey with! Snake-necked turtles use their stretchy necks—which can grow to be more than half the length of their shells—to strike at shrimp, worms, or fish.

FASTEST

Cheetahs are the swiftest species on land. When hunting prey, the big cats can accelerate to speeds of more than 60 miles an hour (97 km/h) in just three seconds.

BEST ACROBAT

Inchworms have a funny way of walking: With legs at both ends of their bodies but none in the middle, they shift from the front end to go forward, creating an awesome arch with their bodies as they move.

SLEEPIEST

Koalas sure catch a lot of z's! In fact, the marsupials sleep up to 22 hours a day, allowing their body to conserve plenty of energy, which is required to digest their food.

BEST WARNING

If you spot a poison dart frog in the wild, watch out! These teeny amphibians are among the world's most toxic animals. Their brightly colored skin—which can be yellow, gold, copper, red, green, blue, or black—sends a message to predators to stay away.

SLOWEST

Never expect a sloth to make it anywhere on time! The sluggish species travels at a top speed of some six to eight feet (1.8 to 2.4 m) a minute. Otherwise, it sleeps in treetops for about 20 hours a day.

49

Bet You Didn't Know!

6 facts that will BUG you!

1 **Dragonflies** appeared on Earth **140 million years before** the **first birds.**

2 **Mosquitoes** prefer to **bite people** who have **smelly feet.**

3 **Raw termites** taste like **pineapple.**

4 A housefly can **turn somersaults** in the **air.**

5 **Tiny bugs** called **mites** live in your **eyebrows.**

6 Most **female fireflies can't fly.**

SPIDERWEB STATS

A single spider can eat up to 2,000 insects every year. How do spiders catch all of those tasty treats? Using silk from special glands called spinnerets, spiders weave sticky webs to trap their delicious prey. But this silk can do much more than simply catch dinner. Stick around and learn more about the incredible spiderweb.

.00004–.00016
INCH (.001–.004 mm)
Thickness of silk a spider uses to build webs

-76°F TO 302°F
(-60°C to 150°C)
The extreme range of temperatures that a spider's silk can withstand

82
FEET (25 m)
Diameter of webs woven by Darwin's bark spider—the largest spiderwebs in the world!

ORB WEAVER SPIDER

5
Number of times stronger a spider's silk is compared to steel of the same diameter

2–8
Pairs of spinnerets, the glands a spider uses to make silk

Age of oldest spiderweb ever found embedded in amber:

140 MILLION YEARS OLD

SUN BEAR RESCUE

How kind caretakers helped an orphaned cub return to the wild

These bears are named for the golden or white "rising sun" patch on their chest, which experts think might help the bears seem bigger than they are.

A three-month-old sun bear huddles alone in a metal cage. A few days ago, poachers snatched the cub from the wild and brought her to a town in Malaysia, an island country in Southeast Asia, where she was sold as a pet, which is illegal. Now the orphan is stressed and hungry. If she stays in the cage, she may not survive.

BEAR AID

That's when caretakers from the Bornean Sun Bear Conservation Centre step in. They give the cub a name—Natalie—and take her in, giving her a special milk with extra protein, plus plenty of comfort and care. Within a few weeks, Natalie grows strong enough to head outside with a caretaker. She even climbs a tree! Soon, she joins three other bears in an outdoor enclosure. Together, the bears lounge, play, and learn to forage for their favorite treats of termites, earthworms, and honey.

WILD AGAIN

After five years at the rescue center, Natalie is ready to be released in the wild. A team of veterinarians gives the hundred-pound (45-kg) bear one last checkup before fitting her with a tracking collar so that they can watch where she goes for the first few months. They fly her on a helicopter in a crate to a protected wildlife reserve where people don't live. The rescuers use a long rope to open Natalie's crate from afar. She bursts out into the woods—finally a free bear again.

Scientists have spotted mother sun bears cradling cubs in their arms while walking on their hind legs.

WONG SIEW TE FEEDS NATALIE A SPECIAL MILK TO HELP HER GAIN WEIGHT.

WONG WATCHES OVER NATALIE LIKE HER MOTHER WOULD HAVE DONE IN THE WILD.

ASIA

BANGLADESH
INDIA
MYANMAR (BURMA)
LAOS
THAILAND
VIETNAM
CAMBODIA
South China Sea
INDIAN OCEAN
BRUNEI
MALAYSIA
INDONESIA

ASIA

AREA ENLARGED
PACIFIC OCEAN
INDIAN OCEAN
AUSTRALIA

Where sun bears live

53

PREPARE TO BE
AMAZED BY THIS
ACROBAT
OF THE FOREST ...

THE INCREDIBLE
RED PANDA

A red panda totters along the branch of an evergreen tree, placing one paw in front of the other like a gymnast on a balance beam. But then ... whoops! The panda loses its footing. A fall from this height— about 100 feet (30 m)—could be deadly. But the panda quickly grips the branch with all four paws and some seriously sharp claws, steadies itself, and keeps moving.

Red pandas spend about 90 percent of their time in the trees, says Mariel Lally, a red panda keeper at the Smithsonian's National Zoo in Washington, D.C., U.S.A. In fact, red pandas have adapted so well to life in the trees that they're famous for their incredible acrobatic skills. Check out three ways that red pandas land a perfect score with their amazing aerial act.

ASIA

Bay of
Bengal

South
China
Sea

INDIAN OCEAN

Where red pandas live

1. BUILT-IN BALANCE

A tightrope walker is all about balance. But red pandas can't exactly extend their arms like an acrobat. Instead, they hold their tails straight behind them. "If they start to swing in one direction, they can move their tails the opposite way," Lally says. "It's sort of like a tightrope walker's pole."

2. UNDER FUR COVER

What's the best way to avoid a hungry snow leopard? Never let it see you in the first place! The small red panda's fiery coat sticks out at the zoo, but in the fir trees of the Himalayan mountains, the fur hides the panda in the reddish moss and white lichen (a plant-like organism) that often hang on the trees. Red pandas are so hard to spot that even scientists have trouble locating these creatures.

3. FAKE THUMB

A trapeze artist needs her thumbs to wrap her whole hand around the trapeze as she swings. Otherwise she might fly off! Same idea with red pandas. They have a special thumb-like wrist bone that gives them an extra grip when climbing down trees headfirst.

RED PANDA ON THE RUN

Smithsonian's National Zoo, Washington, D.C., U.S.A.

Ashley Wagner was out with her family when she spotted an animal crossing the street. At first Wagner's mom thought they'd seen a raccoon, but as soon as the creature turned its face toward them, Wagner knew it was a red panda.

Rusty the runaway red panda had arrived at the zoo just a few weeks before. As he scampered under a fence, Wagner snapped photos, shared them on social media, and called the zoo. Soon a team came to the rescue, eventually nabbing him from a tree.

Today, Rusty has retired from his life on the run and settled down. The father of three red panda cubs, he lives at the Smithsonian Conservation Biology Institute.

SAVING THE RED PANDA

With their kitten-like faces, fluffy fur, and waddling walk, red pandas are adorable. But these endangered animals are also ideal targets for the illegal pet trade.

Luckily, people are trying to help them. There's the Red Panda Network, which hires local people to keep watch over the red pandas in Nepal, replant bamboo, and help paying tourists observe them without disturbing the creatures. Other organizations track poachers by using DNA samples from red pandas rescued from the black market to learn where the animals are being taken from.

You can help by asking your parents and older siblings not to "like" photos and videos of red pandas on social media unless you know that the group or person posting them is trustworthy (like a wildlife photographer or a conservation group).

BIG CATS

A young male jaguar

The National Geographic Big Cats Initiative's goal is to stop the decline of lions and other big cats in the wild through research, conservation, education, and global awareness. Visit natgeo.org/bigcats to learn more.

Not all wild cats are big cats, so what are big cats? To wildlife experts, they are: tigers, lions, leopards, snow leopards, jaguars, cougars, and cheetahs. The first five are members of the genus *Panthera*. They can all unleash a mighty roar, and, as carnivores, they survive solely on the flesh of other animals. Thanks to powerful jaws; long, sharp claws; and daggerlike teeth, big cats are excellent hunters.

WHO'S WHO?

BIG CATS IN THE *PANTHERA* GENUS MAY HAVE a lot of features in common, but if you know what to look for, you'll be able to tell who's who in no time.

FUR

SNOW LEOPARD

A snow leopard's thick, spotted fur helps the cat hide in its mountain habitat, no matter the season. In the winter its fur is off-white to blend in with the snow, and in the summer it's yellowish gray to blend in with plants and the mountains.

A jaguar's coat pattern looks similar to that of a leopard, as both have dark spots called rosettes. The difference? The rosettes on a jaguar's torso have irregularly shaped borders and at least one black dot in the center.

JAGUAR

Most tigers are orange-colored with vertical black stripes on their bodies. This coloring helps the cats blend in with tall grasses as they sneak up on prey. These markings are like fingerprints: No two stripe patterns are alike.

TIGER

Lions have a light brown, or tawny, coat and a tuft of black hair at the end of their tails. When they reach their prime, most male lions have shaggy manes that help them look larger and more intimidating.

LION

LEOPARD

A leopard's yellow coat has dark spots called rosettes on its back and sides. In leopards, the rosettes' edges are smooth and circular. This color combo helps leopards blend into their surroundings.

JAGUAR
100 to 250 pounds
(45 TO 113 KG)
5 to 6 feet long
(1.5 TO 1.8 M)

BENGAL TIGER
240 to 500 pounds
(109 TO 227 KG)
5 to 6 feet long
(1.5 TO 1.8 M)

LEOPARD
66 to 176 pounds
(30 TO 80 KG)
4.25 to 6.25 feet long
(1.3 TO 1.9 M)

AFRICAN LION
265 to 420 pounds
(120 TO 191 KG)
4.5 to 6.5 feet long
(1.4 TO 2 M)

SNOW LEOPARD
60 to 120 pounds (27 TO 54 KG)
4 to 5 feet long (1.2 TO 1.5 M)

Weirdest. Cat. Ever.

THE SERVAL MIGHT LOOK STRANGE, BUT THAT'S A GOOD THING WHEN IT COMES TO HUNTING.

SERVAL KITTENS STAY WITH MOM UP TO TWO YEARS BEFORE LIVING ON THEIR OWN.

SERVALS CAN CATCH UP TO 30 FROGS IN THREE HOURS WHILE HUNTING IN WATER.

Servals can chirp, purr, hiss, snarl, and growl.

ALL EARS

The serval's big ears are key to the animals' hunting success. Servals rely on sound more than any other sense when they're on the prowl. Thanks to their jumbo ears—the biggest of any wild cat's relative to body size—a serval can hear just about any peep on the savanna. (If a person had ears like a serval's, they'd be as big as dinner plates!) To make the most of their super hearing, servals avoid creating noise while hunting. So instead of stalking prey like some cats do, servals squat in clearings and sit still—sometimes for several hours—as they listen for food.

A serval sits patiently in a grassy field, swiveling its head back and forth like a watchful owl. The predator is scanning the savanna for a meal not with its eyes, but with its oversize ears. An unseen rodent stirs under the thick brush, and the wild cat tenses. It crouches on its legs and feet before launching itself up and over the tall grass. Guided only by sound, the serval lands directly on the once invisible rat.

Thanks to its extra-long legs, stretched-out neck, and huge ears, the serval is sometimes called the "cat of spare parts." The wild cat might look weird to some people. "But put together, their bizarre-looking body parts make them really successful hunters," says Christine Thiel-Bender, a biologist who studies servals in their African home.

In fact, servals catch their prey in more than half of their attempts, making them one of the best hunters in the wild cat kingdom. That's about 20 percent better than lions hunting together in a pride.

THE
MYSTERY OF THE
BLACK PANTHER

Are you superstitious?
Do you think it's bad luck if
a black cat crosses your path?

Many people once believed that black cats partnered with the devil. They show up regularly in comic books, posters, and movies. But in real life these big cats are as rare as parents who allow kids to eat dessert before dinner. What are these mysterious black cats, and where do they live?

"Black panthers are simply leopards with dark coats," says scientist John Seidensticker. "If you look closely, you can see the faint outline of spots in the dark fur," he adds.

Biologists used to think that black panthers were a separate species of leopard. The fierce black cats had a reputation for being more aggressive than spotted leopards, the way dark-maned lions are more aggressive than those with lighter manes. But zookeepers noticed that spotted leopards and black leopards can sometimes be born in the same litter (see below)—just as kids in the same family can have blue eyes or brown eyes.

BLENDING IN

Overall, black leopards are extremely rare in the wild. They are almost never seen in the leopard's range in Africa, and only occasionally in India. But surprisingly, these black cats are the only leopards known in the forests of Malaysia, in Southeast Asia. Black leopards are so much more common there that the people living in the country's forests don't even have a word in their vocabulary for *spotted* leopards.

Scientists don't really know why black leopards are the norm in Malaysia. One theory is that animals living in dark, humid forests like those in Malaysia tend to have darker fur for camouflage. African leopards spend most of their lives in grasslands and forests, where spots may be the best disguise.

The black cats are not evil creatures of witches and devils. They are cats at their best— evolving to blend with their habitat.

59

TIGERS in the Snow

These wild cats survive the cold of eastern Russia.

Many Amur tigers have beachfront access—they live in Russian forests on the edge of the Sea of Japan.

ilently moving through the trees, a tigress stalks her prey. Deep snow covers the ground, and with each step the big cat sinks to her belly. She knows the snow will muffle any sounds, so she can sneak up on a wild boar that is rooting around for pine nuts. A few yards away, the tiger pauses, crouches, and then launches her 280-pound (127-kg) body toward her prey. Snow sprays up with each leap as she prepares to pounce on the boar with her plate-size paws. A powdery cloud fills the air. Then the snow settles, revealing the three-foot (0.9-m)-long tail and orange, black, and white body. Now stained red, the tigress grasps the boar in her mouth.

She carries her catch behind some larch trees, and her two cubs join her from a nearby hill. Camouflaged in the trees, they were watching their mother hunt. Soon, they'll start hunting for themselves. But for now, they are content with the meal their mother has provided, followed by a nap.

These Siberian, or Amur, tigers live in the eastern reaches of Russia—farther north than any other tiger subspecies. Thick coats of fur insulate their bodies from the freezing winter temps. In the summer, their coats blend in with the forest, making them nearly impossible to see.

HUNGER GAMES

The tiger trio is among the some 600 Amur tigers that researchers think are left in the wild. As recently as 50 years ago, there were plenty of deer and wild boar, staples of a tiger's diet. Today, those prey animals are harder to find. People hunt

A TIGER CUB STICKS WITH MOM FOR AT LEAST 18 MONTHS.

them, and logging companies and fires destroy the forest where they live. Some tiger habitat is protected, but the cats wander beyond these safe zones in search of prey. Half of all tiger cubs die young because they are sick, killed by hunters, or orphaned. Cubs that survive leave Mom at about 18 months old, relying on the hunting skills they learned growing up. Sometimes a young male must travel far to find unclaimed land that has enough food. But the odds are that his journey will take him through areas where people live.

TROUBLESHOOTING

It is late winter when the male tiger leaves his mother's care. When he scratches against a tree, he catches his paw on something. He's walked into a wire snare, and the more he moves, the tighter it gets. A little while later, he hears voices. People. They stay behind the trees, and one of them raises a gun. The tiger roars at the sharp pain in his backside, then lies down and falls asleep. He's been shot by a researcher's tranquilizer gun, not a hunter. Unable to find enough food in the snowy forest, this tiger started taking livestock and dogs in a nearby town. Dale Miquelle and his team are called in to fix the problem. "Relocating them gives them a second chance," Miquelle says. Otherwise, the farmer would track down the tiger and shoot him.

The researchers quickly weigh and measure the tranquilized tiger. Then they fit a collar with a radio transmitter around his neck. This will let Miquelle's team keep track of the tiger's whereabouts for at least three years.

NEW TERRITORY

Two hours later, the tiger wakes up in the back of a truck about 150 miles (241 km) from the town. The cage gate opens, and the wild cat leaps out. Unfamiliar with the territory, he searches for signs of other tigers. He comes across a birch tree with a strong odor. Another male sprayed the tree and left scrape marks and urine on the ground to tell others, "Occupied. Keep moving."

The young tiger walks on. Miquelle's team monitors his movements using signals from the radio collar. They hope he can find food, avoid other males, find his own territory, and eventually mate with a local female. The tiger spots a deer ahead. Melting snow drips from the trees, masking his footsteps as he ambushes his prey. His odds just got a little better.

THIS TIGER'S SCRATCHES ON TREES ARE MESSAGES FOR OTHER TIGERS.

In the 1930s, only about 30 Amur tigers were left in the wild.

ICE-COLD WATER QUENCHES THIS TIGER'S THIRST.

A HIPPOPOTAMUS HELPS BABY ANIMALS CROSS A RAGING RIVER.

It's rush hour in Africa. Every October, thousands of wildebeests and zebras gather along the banks of the Mara River. They wait to cross the deep, rushing waters as part of their seasonal journey from the Masai Mara National Reserve in Kenya to the Serengeti National Park in Tanzania. The river flows so fast that full-grown animals struggle to swim to the other side. "When the river is full, lots of animals drown trying to cross," says Tom Yule, who ran the nearby Lemala Mara safari camp. Watching from the river's edge, Yule sees a wildebeest calf and later a zebra foal jump into the water. But he doesn't expect what happens next.

wild CROSSING GUARD

1

The little wildebeest tries to paddle across the river but is swept away by the strong current. The calf tries to keep its head above water while floating downstream. Suddenly something rises out of the water: a large, dark head followed by the hulking body of a hippopotamus. "The hippo was lying in the water near where the animals jump in, and it immediately goes after the calf," Yule says. Hippos can be very aggressive and even deadly when defending territory, so he wonders whether the hippo will attack the baby wildebeest.

The strong hippo defies the current and uses its body to stop the wildebeest calf's scary ride downstream. Like a tugboat guiding a ship filled with precious cargo, the hippo shepherds the youngster to the other side of the river. Yule and other bystanders watch in disbelief. "I have never witnessed anything like this," he says. The wildebeest reaches the opposite bank and runs back upstream to rejoin its herd.

WILDEBEEST CALF

ZEBRA IN TROUBLE

2

Yule thinks the drama is over when suddenly the river grabs hold of a small zebra foal. He watches as the tiny striped head dips underwater and then resurfaces. Just when it looks like the zebra won't make it, the hippo suddenly appears. Again, the huge hippo helps the baby across to the shallow water on the other side. But the exhausted foal can barely stand. Gently, the hippo nudges the zebra into a safe nook between two large rocks. "The hippo gets out of the water and starts to nuzzle the foal with its great jaws," Yule says. "And then the hippo coaxes the zebra to cross a small channel and climb up the slope of the opposite bank to its mom."

SAFE ON LAND

3

Yule thinks the hippo would be too exhausted for any more superhero moments. But instead, it settles back into the river to keep a watchful eye. "Animals are unpredictable, and each one has its own unique personality," Yule says. "This hippo's instincts are to help those that need assistance. It's just like protective people who say, 'Not on my watch!' as they help others."

UNIC○RNS

OF THE SEA

SCIENTISTS TRY TO **SOLVE THE MYSTERY** OF THE NARWHAL'S **GIANT TUSK.**

Chilly water laps against an iceberg in the Arctic Ocean. Suddenly a pod of narwhals—a species of whale that sports a unicorn-like horn on its head—emerges from the sea near the iceberg's edge.

Narwhals live in the Arctic Ocean. Like most whales, they're jumbo-size—up to 3,500 pounds (1,588 kg)—and surface to breathe. And like some whale species such as orcas, they live in pods. (Narwhals usually have 15 to 20 in their group.) But there's one thing a narwhal has that no other whale does: a giant tusk growing out of its noggin.

For centuries people have been trying to figure out what this tusk—actually an enlarged tooth—is used for. Luckily scientists have come up with some theories that may help solve this gnawing puzzle.

TUSK, TUSK

A narwhal's swordlike tusk first pokes from their jaw through the animal's upper lip when it's about three months old. This is the only tooth the whale develops. Over time, the tusk can grow to be half the length of the whale's body. New research shows that narwhals may use these long appendages to snag prey like arctic cod, using quick jabs to stun the fish before they eat them.

TOOTH SLEUTHS

Another theory is that male narwhals use the tooth to attract females. Similar to a peacock's flashy feathers, the tusk makes them stand out to potential mates. The animals have been observed scraping their tusks together, as though they are in a fencing match. This may be a way for male members of the pod to identify each other.

Although there's still plenty scientists don't know about narwhals, they will continue to look for answers. In the meantime, it appears that these mysterious whales still have a few secrets up their tusks.

SURFACING ABOVE WATER, A GROUP OF NARWHALS TAKES A BREATH OF AIR.

THIS POD OF MALES SWIMS THROUGH ARCTIC WATERS.

A NARWHAL MOM TRAVELS WITH HER BABY.

ROCK 'EM SOCK 'EM SHRIMP

SEA SNAIL

PUNCH!

THESE TINY CRUSTACEANS WILL KNOCK YOU OUT.

Burrowing under the sand near coral reefs lives a pint-size punk. Sure, this crustacean has a colorful shell and adorable eyes—but don't let that fool you. Although the peacock mantis shrimp is only between one to seven inches long (2.5 to 17.8 cm), it's a fearsome ocean predator. Dig deeper to discover some stunning facts about this tiny toughie.

PERFECT PUNCH

Many of the peacock mantis shrimps' favorite snacks—like crabs, clams, and sea snails—are protected by superhard shells. Good thing the shrimps have **two hinged, hammer-like limbs** that can thwap their targets with a force that's more than 2,500 times stronger than their body weight. (That'd be like you punching through a steel wall!) These animals also use their powerful punchers to defend their territory against other peacock mantis shrimps. In fact, they're so brawny that they've been known to **shatter aquarium tanks' glass.**

SPEED DEMON

Don't blink around peacock mantis shrimps: They strike so quickly that they could knock out 50 punches in the time it takes you to bat your eye. This swift motion forms a bubble of vapor around the prey's shell, which collapses less than a nanosecond later. If the prey hasn't escaped yet, watch out. The water briefly heats up to **8500°F (4704°C),** and a wave of energy thumps the victim like a tiny implosion.

BRAINIAC ATTACK

One reason peacock mantis shrimps are so tough is their braininess: They have to be smart about how—and when—they wield their weapons. "They can remember another mantis shrimp they've fought before, and whether they **won or lost,"** says Roy Caldwell, a biologist and professor at the University of California, Berkeley in California, U.S.A. And when they're going after a tricky meal, peacock mantis shrimps go in with a game plan. "If they're dealing with a crab, they'll first knock off the deadly claws, then the legs, then use their own limbs to hold the crab in just the right place for a shell-shattering punch," Caldwell says.

A male's shell is more colorful than a female's.

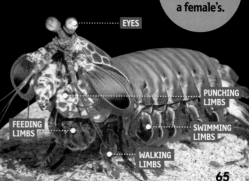

EYES

PUNCHING LIMBS

FEEDING LIMBS

SWIMMING LIMBS

WALKING LIMBS

THE SECRET LIVES OF

Orcas don't often dive very deep—their food is usually near the surface, so they are as well.

You'd need more than 650 cans of tuna to keep an orca full!

Orcas

"FRIENDING" OTHER DOLPHINS. **"LIKING"** FUN ACTIVITIES. **"CHATTING."** ORCAS MIGHT HAVE THE BEST **SOCIAL NETWORK** EVER.

A bottlenose dolphin flips its tail as it swims with its dolphin friends. A baby chimpanzee watches closely as its mom shows it how to crack a nut. A male wolf howls to gather the pack for a hunt.

Playing, teaching, and working together are known as social skills. Humans, of course, are social animals. So are bottlenose dolphins, chimps, and wolves. And according to scientists, it's time to move one animal higher up the list: orcas!

Orcas are dolphins, so scientists already knew about some of their social behaviors. "We knew orcas travel in pods," says biologist Janice Waite of the National Oceanic and Atmospheric Administration (NOAA), in the United States. But new research shows that the school-bus–size swimmers have more complex social behaviors than previously understood.

Could orcas be among the most social animals of all? Here are five stories to help you decide.

Orcas "adopt" orphans.

Springer watched curiously as a boat approached her. The young orca had been orphaned as a calf, so no one had taught her that boat propellers could injure her. Wanting to take a closer look, Springer swam closer until ... *whoosh!* An older female orca called Nodales forcefully shoved her away from danger.

"Nodales took Springer under her wing, even though they weren't related," says Paul Spong, co-director of OrcaLab, a research station in Canada. "It didn't take long for the young orca to understand she should keep away from boats." Today, Springer is a mother herself—and she stays out of water traffic.

Orcas "babysit" other orcas.

One day a female named Sharky moved close to a group of newborn orcas and their mothers. Sharky swam near a calf, and then led it away to play with her—giving the moms a break. Waite observed Sharky behave like that with other calves as well. "She's not the only young female we've seen 'babysit' other orcas," Waite says. "We think they do it as practice for when they have calves of their own."

ORCAS APPROACH A WEDDELL SEAL, HOPING TO MAKE IT THEIR MEAL.

Orcas are team players.

A Weddell seal lies on a sheet of floating ice in Antarctica. Suddenly five orcas begin nudging the ice. Then, a large female orca begins to make whistling and clicking noises. It's like a signal: The other orcas line up, swim toward the ice, and create a wave that knocks the seal into the water. Oddly, the orcas let the seal escape.

Some experts believe that the female orca was teaching hunting and teamwork to her calves. And as with any new skill, practice makes perfect!

Orcas put family first.

Researchers rarely spotted Plumper and Kaikash apart. But when older bro Plumper got sick, the researchers worried that he wouldn't be able to keep up with his younger sibling. But the brothers were inseparable. Kaikash would swim a short distance, and then wait for Plumper to catch up. "This went on for hours," Spong says. "Kaikash didn't seem to mind. Like human brothers, these two had each other's backs."

Researchers now know that orca families spend most of their days together. Although adults—especially males—sometimes split from the group to hunt, they stay close enough to hear family members. Says Waite, "They're probably as close with their families as we are with ours."

Orcas play together.

Orcas are known for breaching— or leaping out of the water—to show their playful side. "They get most excited when they meet up in groups," says biologist Candice Emmons of NOAA. She's seen orcas from different pods brush against each other to say hello. She's also watched orcas smacking their tails against the water (called lobbing) to show excitement. But Emmons's favorite thing to observe is "pec slapping."

"That's when they touch each other with their pectoral fins, which are like their arms," Emmons says. Sort of like orca high fives!

An orca's diet consists of whales, sea lions, penguins, seals, walruses, and a variety of fish and squid. *Chomp!*

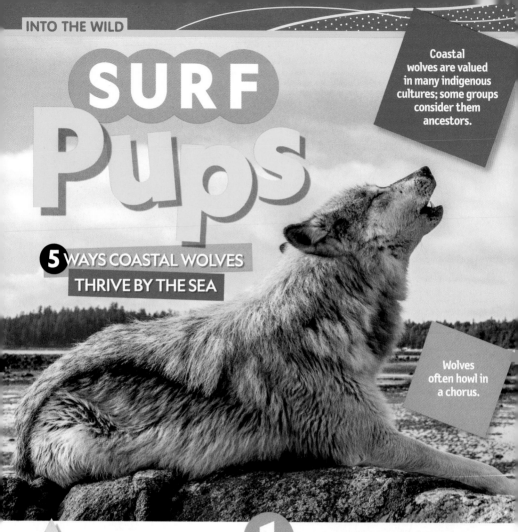

SURF Pups

5 WAYS COASTAL WOLVES THRIVE BY THE SEA

Coastal wolves are valued in many indigenous cultures; some groups consider them ancestors.

Wolves often howl in a chorus.

A wolf steps out onto a sandy beach. Catching a scent, it paws at the wet sand in search of a buried clam. *Crunch!* The wolf crushes the clam in its jaws and swallows. Still hungry, it splashes into the ocean waves and swims to a nearby island to find more food. Wolves on the beach might sound strange, but these special gray wolves have been living seaside for thousands of years. Known as coastal wolves, about 2,000 of these individuals make their homes among the islands and coastal rainforest of western British Columbia in Canada. (Another population lives in southeast Alaska, U.S.A.) "Their environment is so different from that of any other wolf," wildlife researcher Chris Darimont says. "So they've had to adapt to this unique place." Check out five ways these howlers are living their best life on the beach.

BEACH HAIR, DON'T CARE

Unlike most gray wolves, coastal wolves' fur is often streaked with reddish orange highlights. The color matches seaweed found on the shore, likely helping to camouflage these predators as they hunt on the beach.

Coastal wolves also have less underfur than other gray wolves. The cottony fluff helps wolves living in snowy places like Montana, U.S.A., keep warm, but coastal wolves' habitat is so mild that they don't need the extra layer.

> A wolf's sense of smell is about a hundred times more sensitive than a human's.

SEA SIZE

About the size of a German shepherd, coastal wolves are about 20 percent smaller than gray wolves living in North American forests. Scientists think it could be because these seafood eaters don't need the extra strength. After all, coastal wolves are wrestling otters, not gigantic moose like their gray wolf cousins. "They aren't chasing massive prey, so they don't need the large body size to take them down," Darimont says.

SWIM TEAM CHAMPS

One small island usually isn't big enough for coastal wolves to find and eat the seven pounds (3 kg) of food they need each day. So the canines dog-paddle from island to island in search of more food. "They swim between islands like we walk on sidewalks," conservationist Ian McAllister says. And these wolves really are super swimmers. Scientists have spotted them on nearly every one of the thousand islands and rocky outcrops in the area, McAllister says, sometimes swimming up to 7.5 miles (12 km) in between each strip of land.

> Some coastal wolves can get 90 percent of their diet from the sea.

SPLASHY SURPRISE

Gray wolves that live in open habitats like the tundra often hunt by chasing big, hoofed animals across a wide plain, Darimont says. But that style of hunting doesn't work on a coast that's full of thick rainforest or tiny islands too small to run across. Instead, they often sneak up on prey—then pounce. "The seals haul out of the ocean to get away from killer whales," McAllister says. "But on land, they're not safe from ambushing wolves."

SEAFOOD, PLEASE!

What's to eat? Coastal wolves use their powerful sense of smell to find whatever snacks the ocean served up that day. They might dig in the sand for crabs and clams, feast on fish eggs stuck to kelp, or sneak up on larger animals like sunbathing seals or otters.

Others get their fill of fish just from salmon. "They wait in the shallows where the salmons' backsides are poking out, then snap up the tastiest-looking fish they can find," Darimont says. A coastal wolf might scarf down 10 salmon in one morning. Talk about fish breath!

DO GORILLAS TALK?

A YOUNG MOUNTAIN GORILLA IN THE DEMOCRATIC REPUBLIC OF THE CONGO REACHES FOR A CAMERA.

Discover five surprising ways these apes communicate.

Keepers entering the gorilla enclosure at the Columbus Zoo and Aquarium in Ohio, U.S.A., often hear a noise that sounds like a babbling human. But it's just Mac, a western lowland gorilla. The ape greets his caregivers by making long, low grumbling sounds, gorilla-speak for "Hi, there!" When keepers exit the area in the evening, he makes a similar sound as if to say "Good night."

Mac isn't just making noise. Gorillas like him have things to say. And if you pick up a little gorilla language, you just might understand them.

"Apes are excellent communicators," Columbus Zoo curator Audra Meinelt says. And sound isn't the only way gorillas "talk." They use movements and even body odor to get their point across. It's no wonder experts think gorillas are among the most advanced animal communicators after humans. Check out these five amazing stories.

1 "What's in it for me?"

Nia, a western lowland gorilla, was excited when she discovered a new "toy"—a plastic cup—had been added to her habitat at the Columbus Zoo. When zookeepers came to replace the cup with another toy, Nia wouldn't give it up. So Nia's keepers offered her a treat as a reward. Nia gave up the cup—and realized that things she finds in her habitat can be valuable. The next time Nia found a cup in her space, the gorilla broke it into several pieces and only gave the keepers one piece at a time ... in exchange for a treat after every piece!

Other gorillas at the zoo caught on to Nia's trick. "They'll hold out an item they think we might want, but not all the way," zookeeper Heather Carpenter says. "If we try to get it, they'll pull it back like, 'Not so fast!' Their actions are telling us that they'll give us what we want—but only when we offer something *they* want."

A WESTERN LOWLAND GORILLA GOOFS OFF IN ITS ZOO ENCLOSURE.

③ "Follow me."

Kighoma the eastern lowland gorilla is the leader of his troop in the Democratic Republic of the Congo, a country in Africa. It's easy to spot the gorilla in charge, according to Sonya Kahlenberg, formerly of the Gorilla Rehabilitation and Conservation Education Center. Adult male leaders are identified by the silver fur on their back. (They're called, well, silverbacks.) And they're often belching!

"It sounds like *na-oom*, kind of like a throat clearing. It means, 'I'm over here,'" Kahlenberg says. "And whenever Kighoma is ready to move, he'll make that grumbling sound and the other gorillas know to follow him."

② "Help!"

Anthropologist Kelly Stewart wanted to see how the wild mountain gorillas she was observing would react to her new gorilla T-shirt. But when she opened her jacket to reveal the shirt to a young female, Simba, the gorilla screamed—a sound that means "I'm scared!" in young gorillas. And *that* told the older troop members that Simba needed help. The group's leader, Uncle Bert, barreled toward Stewart with a deep roar. Stewart quickly covered her shirt and stepped away from Simba, who stopped screaming. Uncle Bert backed off once Simba was quiet—the little gorilla was okay now that the unfamiliar "gorilla" was gone. "I never wore that T-shirt again!" Stewart says.

A SILVERBACK MOUNTAIN GORILLA IN RWANDA LEADS HIS TROOP.

④ "I'm not happy."

When zookeepers at the Dallas Zoo in Texas, U.S.A., smell a gym sock–like odor, they know it's time to do an extra check on the gorillas. The smell comes from the male apes' armpits, and it may mean that a squirrel has entered their exhibit, or that the males aren't getting along. Either way, the stink signifies that something's not quite right.

A GORILLA GETS A WHIFF OF SOMETHING GROSS.

⑤ "You've got this!"

Fasha the wild mountain gorilla had gotten her foot caught in a poacher's trap in the forests of Rwanda, Africa. She escaped, but couldn't keep up with her troop. But Icyororo the gorilla wasn't leaving her friend behind. Arms linked, they made their way through the forest. Every few minutes Icyororo turned and patted Fasha as if to say, "We're almost there."

When the pals crossed a river together, Icyororo gave Fasha a hug, demonstrating gorillas' amazing ability to encourage their loved ones.

You can do this!

SUPER SNAKES

Snakes are masters of disguise, skilled hunters, and champion eaters. More than 3,000 species of these reptiles slither around the world. Check out these surprising facts about snakes.

AMAZON TREE BOA

AFRICAN SAW-SCALED VIPER

SNAKES SMELL WITH THEIR TONGUES.

Smell that mouse? A snake uses its tongue to help it smell. It flicks its long, forked tongue to pick up chemical molecules from the air, ground, or water. The tongue carries the smelly molecules back to two small openings—called the Jacobson's organ—in the roof of the snake's mouth. Cells in the Jacobson's organ analyze the scent. Mmm, lunch!

SNAKE VENOM CAN KILL.

By sinking two hollow, pointy fangs into their prey, many snakes inject venom to paralyze or kill victims before devouring them. Africa's puff adder is thought to be one of the world's deadliest snakes. Up to six feet (1.8 m) long and weighing as much as 13 pounds (6 kg), the puff adder strikes fast. Its venom can cause severe pain, tissue damage, and even death in humans. It's a snake to be respected ... from a distance.

PUFF ADDER

GOLDEN TREE SNAKE

SNAKES CHANGE THEIR SKIN.

Snakes literally grow out of their skin. Every few months, most start rubbing against the ground or tree branches. Starting at the mouth, a snake slithers out of its too-tight skin. Like a sock, the skin comes off inside out. Voilà—the snake has a fresh, shiny look. Nice makeover.

CONSTRICTORS GIVE WICKED HUGS.

Boas, anacondas, pythons, and other snakes called constrictors are amazing squeezers. This kind of snake wraps its muscular body around a victim and squeezes until the animal suffocates. The twisted talent comes from muscles attached to 200 or more vertebrae in a snake's backbone. (Humans are born with only 33 vertebrae.)

DIONE RAT SNAKE

5 COOL REASONS TO LOVE BATS

1 FLIP, FLAP, AND FLY
Bats are the only mammals that can truly fly. A bat's wings are basically folds of skin stretched between extra-long finger and hand bones.

2 VALUABLE DROPPINGS
Bat droppings, called guano, are super rich in nitrogen, a main ingredient in plant food. The ancient Inca of South America protected bats as a valuable source of fertilizer for their crops. Guano is still used in farming today.

3 MARVELOUS MOSQUITO MUNCHERS
Many bats are born bug-eaters, filling their bellies with moths, mosquitoes, and other winged insects. The brown bat gulps down as many as a thousand mosquito-size insects in an hour. Each night the bats from one Texas, U.S.A., cave consume about 200 tons (181 t) of bugs, many of them crop-eating pests. That's about the weight of six fully loaded cement trucks.

4 EXTREME FLIGHT
Hoary bats migrate up to 1,000 miles (1,609 km) south from Canada each fall. Mexican free-tailed bats often fly up to 3 miles (5 km) high, where tailwinds help speed them along at more than 60 miles an hour (97 km/h).

5 SUPERMOM STRENGTH
A newborn bat may weigh as much as one-third of its mother's weight, yet the mom can hold her baby while clinging by her toes to a crack in a cave's ceiling.

Going Batty

LITTLE BROWN BAT
"Little" is right—a brown bat weighs about as much as two small coins!

SHORT-TAILED FRUIT BAT
After just one night of dining, this bat can scatter up to 60,000 undigested seeds—crucial to rainforest plant growth.

COMMON VAMPIRE BAT
Vampires' main diet is the blood of cows and horses. Rarely do they take a bite out of humans.

WHITE TENT BATS
These fruit-eaters often create "tents" to roost in. They make bites in a large leaf so it folds over itself. Then the bats snuggle under.

FLYING FOX
There are about 60 species of bats called flying foxes (above). This kind sometimes roosts in a "camp" of up to a million individuals.

VELVETY FREE-TAILED BAT
This bat fills its cheek pouches with insects in midair, and then chews and swallows them later.

PALLID BAT
Using big ears to listen for rustlings, a pallid bat locates and grabs its prey from the ground.

DESERT LONG-EARED BAT
Sonar emitted by this kind of bat echoes off prey, signaling where its meal lies.

OLD WORLD LEAF-NOSED BAT
Complex nose structures for hunting gave this bat its name.

Bet You Didn't Know!

Bat Spit May Save Lives
A substance in the saliva of vampire bats could help victims of strokes survive, according to researchers at Monash University in Melbourne, Australia. Strokes happen when a blood clot blocks blood flow to the brain. An anticlotting substance in bat spit makes blood flow freely, so a bat can continue to feed. The researchers think the same substance may be able to dissolve blood clots in stroke patients. Fortunately, the substance would be contained in medicine, and bats would not be required to bite patients!

6 Tips Every Polar

L ife in the frozen wilds of the Arctic Circle isn't exactly easy, even if you're a polar bear, the world's largest land-dwelling predator. To withstand the subzero temperatures, snow-covered landscapes, and day after day without sun, they need to put all 1,500 pounds (680 kg) of their muscle, bone, and body fat to good use. If you were a polar bear, here's what you'd need to know to survive on the Arctic ice.

1 Walk, Don't Run ... or Better Yet, Sit Still.

When walking or running, a polar bear expends more than twice the energy used by most other mammals. Want to save energy? Don't move at all. If you do run, make it a short trip. After a five-mile (8-km) run, even young bears in good shape can become overheated.

2 Barefoot ... *hmm* ... *Bear*foot Is Best.

Ever wonder why your paws are so big? On an adult, they're huge—up to 12 inches (30 cm) across. Working like snowshoes, they spread weight across the snow and ice, keeping you from sinking. That way your paws don't make any crunching noises, which could warn prey that "Bigfoot" is on the way.

3 Don't Let Cubs Become Polar Bear Snacks.

It's a harsh fact of Arctic life that adult males sometimes kill and eat polar bear cubs, so mother bears are very protective. Most will chase away male polar bears much bigger than they are. Male bears are not the only threats from which moms defend their cubs. Some brave mothers will rear up on their hind legs to leap at hovering helicopters!

Bear Should Know

4 Fat's Where It's At.

Because you live in the cold Arctic climate, having a layer of fat is a good thing. That fat, called blubber, works like a fleece vest—it insulates your body from the frosty air and near-freezing water. When food is scarce, your four-inch (10-cm)-thick blubber gives you energy and helps keep you afloat when you swim because fat weighs less than water.

5 Neatness Counts. So Does Drying Off.

A clean bear is a warm bear. That's because dirty, matted fur doesn't hold body heat like clean fur does. After eating, spend up to 15 minutes cleaning yourself—licking your chest, paws, and muzzle with your long tongue. In summertime, take baths right after you eat. Then dry yourself by shaking off excess moisture or using snow like a thick, fluffy towel to rub away the water.

6 Always Wear White.

You may have noticed that the hairs in your thick fur coat aren't really white. Each is transparent with a hollow core that reflects light. This helps you to blend in with your surroundings—a neat trick, especially while you're hunting wary seals. Good thing wearing white is always stylish for polar bears.

HOW TO
SPEAK
DOG

C'MON! CATCH ME IF YOU CAN!

Watch a group of dogs playing at a park. These pups don't know each other, yet within a few minutes of meeting, they'll start playing a doggie game. As they wrestle and chase, it's obvious they're "talking." But instead of words, they're using body language. Learning to "listen" to your pup's body language will help you get closer to your pet. Check out what your dog may be trying to tell you through these five behaviors.

THE PLAY-BOW

The play-bow means your pup is ready for fun with another dog. She'll crouch down with her "elbows" almost touching the ground, her tail waving madly, and her rump in the air. After holding this pose for a few seconds, she'll take off running, checking over her shoulder to make sure the other dog is following. When her new playmate comes bounding after her, the two dogs will race and chase. If one dog bangs into the other too hard, it'll do a quick play-bow to say, "Oops!" So the next time your dog play-bows, let the games begin!

A dog's tail should never be pulled. Pulling it could dislocate the bones and cause nerve damage. Then the tail won't move anymore.

THE SHOWY TAIL

A dog strutting around with his tail held high is showing he's in charge. This works even better if the dog has a tail that's easy to see. Maybe that's why wolves have big bushy tails, and why many dogs have tails with lighter-colored hair on the underside. The light color shows when their tails go up, a perfect signal flag.

NEW TO
**SPEAk
DOG**
A GUIDE TO DECODING
DOG LANGUAGE

**Check out
this book!**

THE BEGGING STARE

That sweet little beggar staring directly at you while you eat isn't starving. He's controlling you. A staring dog is communicating with you. Outside, he might be telling you that he's the boss so you'd better not come too close. But at the dinner table, he's probably begging for a scrap. And if you sneak him a bite, he might think he's got you well trained—and taking orders from *him!* So ignore a staring, begging dog. Make sure that nobody else feeds him from the table, either. Eventually the pooch will realize *you're* in charge and that begging doesn't work. Next time you tell him to go lie down, he might just do it.

Scientists say dogs are four times more likely to steal food when they think you're not looking.

A dog can make about 100 different facial expressions.

THE BUTT-SNIFF

Dogs sure have a weird way of saying hello. Instead of shaking paws, they sniff each other's rear ends! One dog lets the other sniff him. Then they switch positions. Why? Dogs identify friends by the way they smell, not by looks. It's the anal glands—located in a pooch's bottom—that give each pup a signature scent. To a dog, another pup's personal smell carries as much data as an ID card. This information tells if a dog is healthy or sick, young or old, and even what he ate for dinner.

THE BELLY-UP

Time for a belly rub! That's what it looks like a dog is saying when she rolls onto her back with her front legs bent and her belly exposed. When you start rubbing, sometimes one hind leg will kick, and she'll look super content. The kicking leg is just a reflex—kind of like what happens when the doctor taps your knee with a rubber hammer. But the real meaning of this dog's position is submission and trust. She's saying that you're in charge, and she's okay with that.

5 Silly Pet Tricks

JUST CALL ME STEPH FURRY.

Rabbit Plays Basketball
Los Angeles, California, U.S.A.

1

Before he goes to bed at night, Bini the Holland lop tries to make a slam dunk. If the rabbit misses, he grabs the rebound and tries again. "He won't go to sleep until he makes a basket," owner Shai Lighter says. Bini started shooting hoops on his own—sort of. One night, Lighter saw the rabbit dropping the same ball inside a box over and over again. So he bought Bini a miniature basketball hoop and rewarded the slam dunks with the animal's preferred treat: oat seeds. In addition to playing basketball, Bini also loves helping Lighter with chores. "He knows how to use a mini vacuum cleaner."

> Most Holland lops enjoy playing with cat toys.

THIS IS JUST HOW I ROLL.

Pug Coasts on Skateboard
Washington, D.C., U.S.A.

2

Jumping on his skateboard, Mr. Butts pushes off with a paw, and then zips past his favorite bakery. "Mr. Butts has about a 20 percent chance of being distracted by a pastry," owner Justin Siemaszko says. If he's not, the pup is usually rewarded with bread after he shows off some sweet boarding moves. And he'll sneeze to let his owners know if he hasn't gotten his baked goods fast enough after hopping off the board. "The bigger the sneeze, the bigger his disapproval," Siemaszko says. To train for the trick, Siemaszko and his wife, Beth, first taught Mr. Butts to sit and stay on the board while it wasn't moving. Later, they upped the difficulty by practicing while the board was rolling, starting with only two of the pug's feet on the board. "Once he could push off successfully, he started boarding by himself," Siemaszko says. Mr. Butts's favorite spot to zoom past? The Washington Monument on D.C.'s National Mall!

> Some pugs in ancient China had their own mini palaces and bodyguards.

Pig Makes Art
Franschhoek, South Africa

Pigcasso, the 1,000 (454-kg)-pound rescue pig, doesn't take her art too seriously—she prefers to dance while she paints. "She tosses her head and flaps her ears," says Joanne Lefson, the founder of Farm Sanctuary SA, where Pigcasso lives. The pig first learned to paint after she picked up a stray paintbrush with her mouth. Noticing the pig's fascination, Lefson set up a canvas and prepped a brush with paint to see what Pigcasso would do. "She started painting on it almost right away," Lefson says. When art time is over, Pigcasso dramatically tosses the brush into the air. That's not the only unusual thing this artist does. Says Lefson, "When the painting is completely done, she dips her nose in beetroot ink and 'signs' the artwork for a finishing touch."

I BET THIS WILL BE WORTH A MILLION DOLLARS ONE DAY.

I'M BASICALLY FLYING. NBD.

Pigs prefer to sleep nose-to-nose.

A guinea pig's teeth never stop growing.

BOW BEFORE YOUR ONE TRUE RULER.

4 Guinea Pig Clears Hurdles
Austin, Texas, U.S.A.

Rolly the guinea pig jumps like a champion show pony. But unlike a pony, Rolly jumps over little bars stuck into toilet-paper-roll tubes—and she sometimes squeaks while soaring. Owner Malia Canann taught her pet the trick by encouraging Rolly to follow bits of lettuce over small hurdles she placed close to the ground. As Rolly learned, Canann increased the height of the hurdles. Now her jumps are as high as a toilet-paper-roll tube!

5 Cat Strikes Pose
Dana Point, California, U.S.A.

Touchdown! Why does this cat throw her paws up in the air like a referee? Because she's super pumped about lapping up a bit of coconut oil. Keys the cat stood on her hind legs and placed her paws in the air for the first time a few years ago while trying to get her owner out of bed. Peter Mares thought the move was cute and rewarded Keys with a little coconut oil. The cat's been doing the move ever since. But what if Mares doesn't have any coconut oil? "She'll work for a little bit of ice cream," he says.

Prehistoric TIMELINE

HUMANS HAVE WALKED on Earth for some 200,000 years, a mere blip in the planet's 4.5-billion-year history. A lot has happened during that time. Earth formed, and oxygen levels rose in the millions of years of the Precambrian time. The productive Paleozoic era gave rise to hard-shelled organisms, vertebrates, amphibians, and reptiles.

Dinosaurs ruled Earth in the mighty Mesozoic. And 66 million years after dinosaurs became extinct, modern humans emerged in the Cenozoic era. From the first tiny mollusks to the dinosaur giants of the Jurassic and beyond, Earth has seen a lot of transformation.

THE PRECAMBRIAN TIME

4.5 billion to 541 million years ago

- Earth (and other planets) formed from gas and dust left over from a giant cloud that collapsed to form the sun. The giant cloud's collapse was triggered when nearby stars exploded.
- Low levels of oxygen made Earth a suffocating place.
- Early life-forms appeared.

THE PALEOZOIC ERA

541 million to 252 million years ago

- The first insects and other animals appeared on land.
- 450 million years ago (mya), the ancestors of sharks began to swim in the oceans.
- 430 mya, plants began to take root on land.
- More than 360 mya, amphibians emerged from the water.
- Slowly, the major landmasses began to come together, creating Pangaea, a single supercontinent.
- By 300 mya, reptiles had begun to dominate the land.

What Killed the Dinosaurs?

It's a mystery that's boggled the minds of scientists for centuries: What happened to the dinosaurs? Although various theories have bounced around, a recent study confirms that the most likely culprit is an asteroid or comet that created a giant crater. Researchers say that the impact set off a series of natural disasters like tsunamis, earthquakes, and temperature swings that plagued the dinosaurs' ecosystem and disrupted their food chain. This, paired with intense volcanic eruptions that caused drastic climate changes, is thought to be why half of the world's species—including the dinosaurs—died in a mass extinction.

DINO TIMES

THE MESOZOIC ERA

252 million to 66 million years ago

The Mesozoic era, or the age of the reptiles, consisted of three consecutive time periods (shown below). This is when the first dinosaurs began to appear. They would reign supreme for more than 150 million years.

TRIASSIC PERIOD

252 million to 201 million years ago

- The first mammals appeared. They were rodent-size.
- The first dinosaur appeared.
- Ferns were the dominant plants on land.
- The giant supercontinent of Pangaea began breaking up toward the end of the Triassic.

JURASSIC PERIOD

201 million to 145 million years ago

- Giant dinosaurs dominated the land.
- Pangaea continued its breakup, and oceans formed in the spaces between the drifting landmasses, allowing sea life, including sharks and marine crocodiles, to thrive.
- Conifer trees spread across the land.

CRETACEOUS PERIOD

145 million to 66 million years ago

- The modern continents developed.
- The largest dinosaurs developed.
- Flowering plants spread across the landscape.
- Mammals flourished, and giant pterosaurs ruled the skies over small birds.
- Temperatures grew more extreme. Dinosaurs lived in deserts, swamps, and forests from the Antarctic to the Arctic.

THE CENOZOIC ERA—TERTIARY PERIOD

66 million to 2.6 million years ago

- Following the dinosaur extinction, mammals rose as the dominant species.
- Birds continued to flourish.
- Volcanic activity was widespread.
- Temperatures began to cool, eventually ending in an ice age.
- The period ended with land bridges forming, which allowed plants and animals to spread to new areas.

DINO Classification

Classifying dinosaurs and all other living things can be a complicated matter, so scientists have devised a system to help with the process. Dinosaurs are put into groups based on a very large range of characteristics.

Scientists put dinosaurs into two major groups: the bird-hipped ornithischians and the lizard-hipped saurischians.

Ornithischian

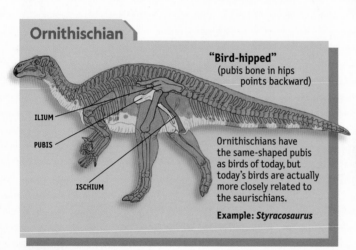

"Bird-hipped"
(pubis bone in hips points backward)

ILIUM
PUBIS
ISCHIUM

Ornithischians have the same-shaped pubis as birds of today, but today's birds are actually more closely related to the saurischians.

Example: *Styracosaurus*

Saurischian

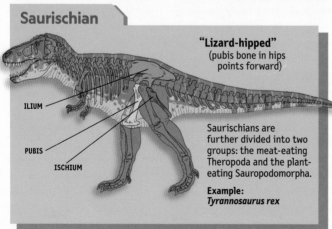

"Lizard-hipped"
(pubis bone in hips points forward)

ILIUM
PUBIS
ISCHIUM

Saurischians are further divided into two groups: the meat-eating Theropoda and the plant-eating Sauropodomorpha.

**Example:
*Tyrannosaurus rex***

Within these two main divisions, dinosaurs are then separated into orders and then families, such as Stegosauria. Like other members of the Stegosauria, *Stegosaurus* had spines and plates along the back, neck, and tail.

NO ONE KNOWS WHAT COLORS DINOSAURS WERE.

ALL DINOSAURS LAID EGGS AND SOME HAD FEATHERS.

DINOSAUR BONES WERE ONCE MISTAKEN FOR DRAGON BONES.

A *T. REX* FOSSIL ONCE SOLD FOR MORE THAN EIGHT MILLION DOLLARS.

③ NEWLY DISCOVERED DINOS

Humans have been searching for—and discovering—dinosaur remains for hundreds of years. In that time, at least 1,000 species of dinos have been found all over the world, and thousands more may still be out there waiting to be unearthed. Recent discoveries include *Dineobellator notohesperus*, a feathered meat-eating raptor with razor-sharp teeth and claws.

1

Dineobellator notohesperus
(Saurischian)

Name Meaning: Navajo warrior from the Southwest

Length: 7 feet (2.0 m), not including tail

Time Range: Late Cretaceous

Where: New Mexico, U.S.A.

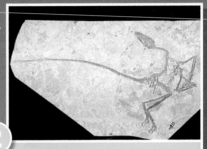

2

Wulong bohaiensis
(Saurischian)

Name Meaning: Dancing dragon

Length: About the size of a crow

Time Range: Early Cretaceous

Where: Liaoning Province, China

3

Allosaurus jimmadseni (Saurischian)

Name Meaning: Jim Madsen's different reptile

Length: 26–29 feet (8–9 m)

Time Range: Late Jurassic

Where: Utah, U.S.A.

DINO DEFENSES

Scientists don't know for sure whether plant-eating dinos used their amazing attributes to battle their carnivorous cousins, but these herbivores were armed with some pretty wicked ways they could have used to defend themselves.

ARMOR: *GASTONIA*
(GAS-TONE-EE-AH)

Prickly *Gastonia* was covered in heavy defensive armor. To protect itself from the strong jaws of meat-eaters, it had four horns on its head, thick layers of bone shielding its brain, rows of spikes sticking out from its back, and a tail with triangular blades running along each side.

SPIKES: *KENTROSAURUS*
(KEN-TROH-SORE-US)

Stand back! This cousin of *Stegosaurus* had paired spikes along its tail, which it could swing at attackers with great speed. One paleontologist estimated that *Kentrosaurus* could have swung its treacherous tail fast enough to shatter bones!

CLUB TAIL:
ANKYLOSAURUS
(AN-KYE-LOH-SORE-US)

Steer clear! *Ankylosaurus* possessed a heavy, knobby tail that it could have used to whack attackers. It may not have totally protected the tanklike late Cretaceous dino from a determined *T. rex*, but a serious swing could have generated enough force to do some real damage to its rival reptile.

WHIP TAIL:
DIPLODOCUS
(DIH-PLOD-UH-KUS)

Some scientists think this late Jurassic giant's tail—about half the length of its 90-foot (27-m) body—could have been used like a whip and swished at high speeds, creating a loud noise that would send potential predators running.

HORNS:
TRICERATOPS
(TRI-SERR-UH-TOPS)

There's no evidence *Triceratops* ever used its horns to combat late Cretaceous snack-craving carnivores. But scientists do believe the famous three-horned creature used its frills and horns in battle with other members of its species.

QUIZ WHIZ

Explore just
how much you know
about animals
with this quiz!

Write your answers
on a piece of paper.
Then check them below.

1 How did a hippo in Masai Mara National Reserve in Kenya help other animals?

a. by taking in their babies
b. by giving them extra food
c. by providing them with shelter
d. by helping them cross the river

2 After eating, a polar bear will spend up to 15 minutes doing what?

a. cleaning its fur
b. taking a nap
c. flossing
d. looking for its next meal

3 True or false? Apes are excellent communicators.

4 When hunting for food, peacock mantis shrimp _____.

a. form a bubble of vapor
b. unleash a powerful punch
c. use their limbs to hold down prey
d. all of the above

5 What does it mean if a dog does a play-bow?

a. he's in charge
b. he wants to play
c. he's hungry
d. he's scared

Not **STUMPED** yet? Check out the *NATIONAL GEOGRAPHIC KIDS QUIZ WHIZ* collection for more crazy **ANIMAL** questions!

ANSWERS: 1. d; 2. a; 3. True; 4. d; 5. b

Seahorse

Wildly Good Animal Reports

Your teacher wants a written report on the seahorse. Not to worry. Use these organizational tools so you can stay afloat while writing a report.

STEPS TO SUCCESS: Your report will follow the format of a descriptive or expository essay (see page 197 for "How to Write a Perfect Essay") and should consist of a main idea, followed by supporting details and a conclusion. Use this basic structure for each paragraph, as well as the whole report, and you'll be on the right track.

1. Introduction
State your **main idea.**
Seahorses are fascinating fishes with many unique characteristics.

2. Body
Provide **supporting points** for your main idea.
Seahorses are very small fishes.
Seahorses are named for their head shape.
Seahorses display behavior that is rare among almost all other animals on Earth.

Then **expand** on those points with further description, explanation, or discussion.
Seahorses are very small fishes.
Seahorses are about the size of an M&M at birth, and most adult seahorses would fit in a teacup.
Seahorses are named for their head shape.
With long, tubelike snouts, seahorses are named for their resemblance to horses.
A group of seahorses is called a herd.
Seahorses display behavior that is rare among almost all other animals on Earth.
Unlike most other fish, seahorses stay with one mate their entire lives. They are also among the only species in which dads, not moms, give birth to the babies.

3. Conclusion
Wrap it up with a **summary** of your whole paper.
Because of their unique shape and unusual behavior, seahorses are among the most fascinating and easily distinguishable animals in the ocean.

KEY INFORMATION

Here are some things you should consider including in your report:
What does your animal look like?
To what other species is it related?
How does it move?
Where does it live?
What does it eat?
What are its predators?
How long does it live?
Is it endangered?
Why do you find it interesting?

SEPARATE FACT FROM FICTION: Your animal may have been featured in a movie or in myths and legends. Compare and contrast how the animal has been portrayed with how it behaves in reality. For example, penguins can't dance the way they do in *Happy Feet*.

PROOFREAD AND REVISE: As you would do with any essay, when you're finished, check for misspellings, grammatical mistakes, and punctuation errors. It often helps to have someone else proofread your work, too, as he or she may catch things you have missed. Also, look for ways to make your sentences and paragraphs even better. Add more descriptive language, choosing just the right verbs, adverbs, and adjectives to make your writing come alive.

BE CREATIVE: Use visual aids to make your report come to life. Include an animal photo file with interesting images found in magazines or printed from websites. Or draw your own! You can also build a miniature animal habitat diorama. Use creativity to help communicate your passion for the subject.

THE FINAL RESULT: Put it all together in one final, polished draft. Make it neat and clean, and remember to cite your references.

SCIENCE and TECHNOLOGY

An illustrator imagines a futuristic green city that includes gardens on rooftops and along buildings.

10 FASCINATING FACTS ABOUT PHONES AND OTHER DEVICES

In the **Mobile Phone Throwing World Championships,** held in Finland, **contestants hurled** old phones for sport.

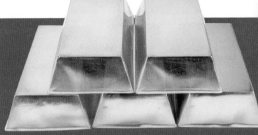

The average **CELL PHONE** contains more than **$1.00** worth of **GOLD.**

A HOME in Somerville, Massachusetts, U.S.A., was the **FIRST** to have a telephone line some **145 YEARS AGO.**

Some **five billion people**—or more than 64 percent of the world's population—**own a mobile device.**

After receiving the patent for the first **TELEPHONE** in 1876, Alexander Graham Bell recommended answering by saying **"AHOY."**

INVENTED IN 1992, THE **FIRST SMARTPHONE** WAS NAMED **"SIMON"** AND WEIGHED ABOUT AS MUCH AS A **CAN OF SOUP.**

Emojis were first introduced on an early version of a smartphone in the late 1990s in Japan.

One of the world's **FIRST HANDHELD COMPUTERS,** introduced in 1989, **RAN FOR 50 HOURS** on a pair of **AA batteries.**

To keep new products secret, **APPLE** gives them code names such as **"PURPLE"** for the iPhone and **"GIZMO"** for the Apple Watch.

There are **NO PHONES** on the International Space Station.

5 COOL INVENTIONS

SUPERSMART GADGETS, ACCESSORIES, AND VEHICLES THAT COULD CHANGE YOUR LIFE.

① BIKE TAKES FLIGHT

The Speeder has a seat and handlebars just like a motorcycle, but this contraption travels to a place you could never reach on a regular bike—**the sky!** Just press a button to take off. Four **turbojet engines** on the bike's front and back launch it off the ground. Steer the handlebars to move the craft **through the air.** Weighing about 230 pounds (104 kg), the bike won't require a pilot's license to fly. Although still being tested, the Speeder is expected to reach speeds of **60 miles an hour** (96.6 km/h) and climb up to **15,000 feet** (4,572 m). Talk about getting a lift!

② SOLAR-POWERED TENT

Normally you'd be out of luck if your smartphone battery drained while you were camping—but this time you're sleeping in a **Bang Bang solar-powered tent.** The brightly colored four-person tent comes with a **solar panel** that soaks up sunlight all day. This creates enough energy to charge a lithium battery bank inside the tent. All you have to do is **connect your gadget** to the battery bank and charge away. Now you'll always have plenty of juice in your phone to have that **dance party under the stars.**

4

BIRD PHOTO BOOTH

Snap pictures of hungry swallows or chickadees with the Bird Photo Booth. Simply pop your phone in the enclosure in this bird feeder, then sneak into your house and watch the birds chow down in real time from a live feed on your computer tablet. See the perfect shot? Click away as you get the ultimate up-close pics of your backyard birds. But these aren't ordinary snaps: The Bird Photo Booth's high-quality lens lets your phone take images that'll rival those of a real-life wildlife photographer. Say "tweet!"

WESTERN SCRUB-JAY

3 # DOG WATER FOUNTAIN

Your dog can sit, fetch, and play dead, but can it drink from a water fountain? That trick is simple for your pet with the Pawcet, which lets thirsty dogs get a fresh drink whenever they want with the touch of a paw. Just hook up the Pawcet to your garden hose, and all your pup has to do is step on the platform to drink. Now that's something that'll really get your dog's tail wagging.

5 # JET-POWERED SURFBOARD

Surf's up! But the big waves are crashing so far away from the shore. No need to exhaust yourself paddling to them—just hop on a WaveJet, a jet-propelled surfboard, to reach the swells without breaking a sweat. Powered by a pair of battery-operated engines at the base of the board, simply hit a switch on a wristband to pick up your speed to 10 miles an hour (16 km/h), about five times the average person's paddling speed. Not a surfer? The removable engine pod can be attached to stand-up paddleboards, boogie boards, and kayaks, so you'll get a boost however you hit the water.

History's Greatest Hits

GEORGE WASHINGTON CARVER'S quest for knowledge made him a world-famous scientist and inventor. Find out about the groundbreaking life of this American hero.

START

Around 1864

George Washington Carver is born into slavery on a farm in Missouri, U.S.A. When slavery is abolished in 1865, his former owners, Moses and Susan Carver, decide to raise the orphaned George as their son.

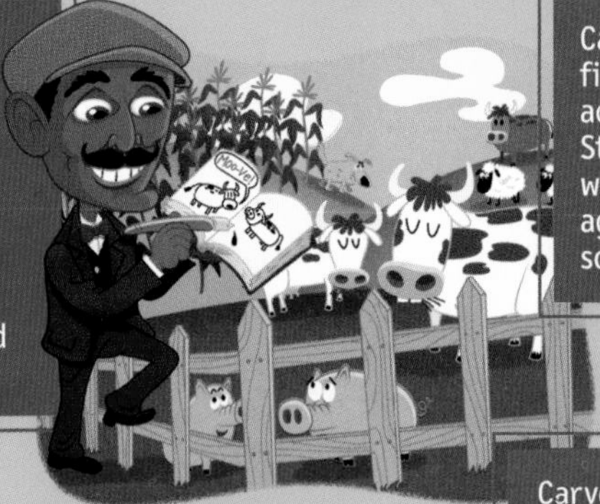

1891 to 1896

Carver becomes the first Black student accepted at Iowa State University, where he studies agriculture, the science of farming.

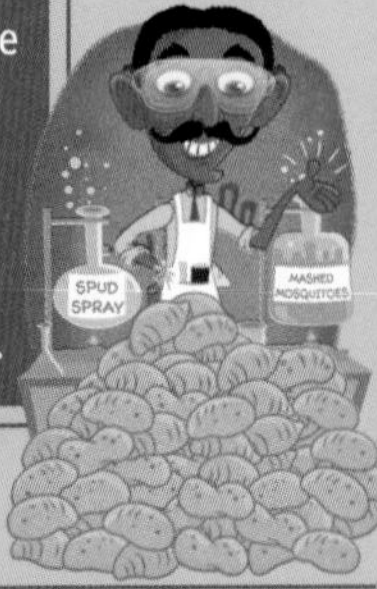

1896

Carver becomes a teacher at Tuskegee University in Alabama, U.S.A. He invents hundreds of products, including new kinds of paints and insecticides (chemicals used to kill insects).

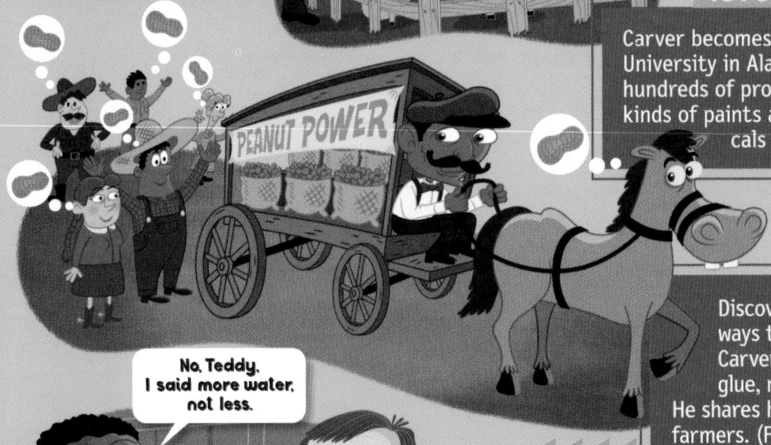

1906

Discovering more than 300 ways to use peanut plants, Carver turns the nuts into glue, medicine, and paper. He shares his knowledge with farmers. (Fun fact: Carver did not invent peanut butter.)

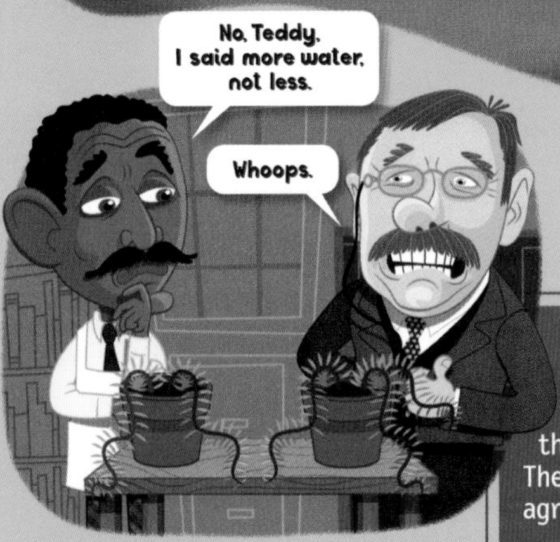

1915

Carver becomes famous for his farming smarts, and even advises the former U.S. president Theodore Roosevelt on agricultural matters.

1943

By the end of his career, Carver is a symbol of the important contributions of African Americans and inspires people all over, no matter what their skin color is.

No, Teddy. I said more water, not less.

Whoops.

PEANUT POWER

ACCIDENTS Happen

BUT SOMETIMES THEY RESULT IN AMAZING DISCOVERIES.

THE INVENTION: THE POPSICLE

THE MOMENT OF "OOPS": Overnight freezing

THE DETAILS: When 11-year-old Frank Epperson left a glass of powdered soda mix overnight on his porch in Oakland, California, U.S.A., in 1905, he made snack history. The next morning, he discovered that his drink had frozen after an unusually cold night, the mixing stick still propped up in the glass. Hoping to salvage his soda after failing to pull it out of the glass, Epperson ran the cup under warm water. Pop! The primitive Popsicle slid out, complete with the stirrer stick as a handle. Twenty years later, Epperson patented his idea, calling it the Popsicle.

THE INVENTION: THE SLINKY

THE MOMENT OF "OOPS": Falling objects

THE DETAILS: In 1943, engineer Richard James was at his desk in Pittsburgh, Pennsylvania, U.S.A., when a box of shipbuilding supplies in a nearby shelf suddenly tipped over. Startled, James looked up from his work. In the middle of everything falling, he noticed a metal spring slink to the ground. As he watched it walk over itself down some books stacked on the ground, he was struck with an idea: It might make a great toy! The Slinky—named by James's wife, Betty—was an instant hit, with the first 400 selling out in 90 minutes.

HOW TO FACE FAILURE

Some people might hate hearing the word "failure." But we say it's not so bad. Follow these tips to make failure fantastic.

FAILURE IS THE BEST TEACHER.

Embrace the teaching power of screwing up. Fill in your teammates on your embarrassment on the soccer field. They'll learn how to avoid making the same mistake themselves.

SUCCESS IS NOTHING WITHOUT FAILURE.

When you fell off your bike, you weren't a failure unless you stayed on the ground. But you hopped back on the seat and kept trying. Failing first makes success feel extra sweet!

FAILURE STINGS—AND THAT'S OKAY!

Don't ignore a flunked test or a missed pop fly because they're painful. Do better next time by studying harder and practicing more. But most important, just move on.

FUTURE WORLD:

What will restaurants be like decades from now? "You can expect a lot of changes in terms of using technology to grow and order our meals," says Paul Takhistov, a food scientist at Rutgers University in New Brunswick, New Jersey, U.S.A. "We'll also be able to personalize our food more." Check out what's cooking at this restaurant of the future.

HUNGRY? PRESS PRINT

A quick finger scan at your table shows that you're low on certain nutrients. Just press a button, and a 3D printer uses pureed food cartridges to "print" lasagna that's packed with specific vitamins that your body needs. "Healthy food isn't one size fits all," Takhistov says. "We have different bodies, so we need different nutrients." These printers will also increase efficiency, allowing chefs to quickly print personalized food for large crowds.

FOOD-IN-A-BOX

Some of the lettuce in this kitchen is sad. Or rather, one of the lettuce emojis on the giant computer screens is frowning. That's because the chef didn't use the right recipe of sunlight, water, and nutrients to get the real-life leafy plant inside a box behind the screen to grow. So she taps the touch screen to make the temperature cooler, and the lettuce's frown turns upside down on the fridge-shaped "box farm." Without planting seeds in soil, this restaurant can grow all the fruits and vegetables it needs. "Anybody can be a farmer," says Hildreth England, a senior strategist at the Massachusetts Institute of Technology. "If you live in Iceland, you can grow strawberries that taste as if they're from Mexico."

WASTE NOT

Researchers are currently working on ways to convert human waste into nutrients. Whether you're eating on Earth or during a space vacation, in the future some of your food will likely have recycled ingredients.

Food

GROW UP

What will happen to farms in the future? Some will be *much* taller. Cities will continue to expand as the human population climbs to nine billion people, leaving less land to farm. Agriculture will likely be housed in towering vertical skyscrapers situated in these cities. Luckily, indoor farms typically use less water, and plants seem to grow faster in these environments.

HUNTING FOR HOLOGRAMS

Let's go fishing ... in the kitchen? The catch of the day is a 3D hologram that the chef hooks in midair. One day people will stock their kitchens by gathering ingredients in a virtual world. Simply pick a berry from a digital bush or choose a cut of beef from a cow on a virtual farm. After you're done foraging, the hologram setup sends details to a local market that delivers your order. Scientists working on this program hope to connect people to their food sources and make shopping more fun.

GET SMART

To order with ease and keep germs from spreading at your favorite restaurant, you tap the table to open a digital menu and choose from freshly grown salads and 3D-printed creations. An alarm lets you know when your food is waiting in the cubby at one side of the table—just lift the door and take your meal. Forgot something? A robot server will stop by to see if you need anything else.

FUTURE WORLD:

A buzzer goes off, marking the start of a race. Your heart is pounding— not that you can hear it over the sound of revving engines. Your car weaves through the other vehicles, making its way to the front of the pack. Peering through the windshield, you see the finish line ahead. Your car crosses first! The crowd roars.

You aren't actually in the car. But thanks to a pair of smartglasses you're wearing in the stands, you experienced exactly what the real driver did on the course.

"In the future, advanced technology will enable us to feel as if we're part of the event," says Aymeric Castaing, founder of Umanimation, a future-tech media company. Take a peek at more ways we'll be entertained by 2060 and beyond—but first, check out two terms to know.

1. Augmented reality (AR): Technology that layers computer-generated images onto things in the real world (like in Pokémon GO)

2. Virtual reality (VR): A computer-generated experience that makes you feel as if you're inside a totally different world

SUPER STADIUMS

Didn't see that catch? No worries: In the future, 3D holograms could appear in midair above the field to show replays of sports moments. For some events, you'll even get a seat in a flying pod that can put you close to the action. (The pod even flies you home afterward!) Meanwhile, say goodbye to long lines for food or team jerseys. Through an app, flying drones will deliver anything you order right to your seat.

GAME ON

A colorful alien zooms directly toward you, attempting to knock you aside with its spaceship. You put your hands in front of you, blocking the alien with a powerful force field. A crowd cheers your dramatic victory.

To the group assembled in front of you in the park, it looks like you just took down an alien spaceship—thanks to VR goggles and a suit with motion sensors. Everything you saw through your goggles was projected onto a video screen at a virtual gaming playground. There, the audience can watch and cheer as you go up against the aliens. They can also wear headsets and feel as if they're in outer space, too!

Entertainment

Barton Canyon
Lydia Girard, Canadian
Painter and Author

Sunrise on Lake MaKinaw
Jeffrey Ross
Part 1 of a

allery

CINEMA 3D

MUSEUMS TO GO

Museums of the future will blend real life with AR and VR. For example, you can check out a sculpture at an art museum with AR glasses, getting details about the artist and style. Then, using your VR headset, you can draw your own masterpiece inspired by what you saw. Not feeling creative? "Using your in-home VR headset and a 3D printer, you can create what you saw in the museum in your bedroom," Castaing says. It's like taking the museum home with you—sort of.

THE BIG SCREEN

There won't be a bad seat in the house at movie theaters in the future. Films will surround the audience with 3D screens in every direction ... including the floor and ceiling. You'll feel like you're underwater at the latest ocean adventure blockbuster. Plus, robots will deliver the snacks you've ordered from your seat's tablet directly to your rotating chair.

DROID BEATS

Ready to rock out to your favorite band? Whether it's pop-star robots or a robot orchestra conductor, future music may be in nonhuman hands. And audiences won't just hear music played by robots—they'll be able to see it. AR glasses will allow audiences to see which notes are coming out of the instruments in front of them. "AR glasses could even enable beginning musicians to take their lessons on the go," Castaing says. "The glasses could essentially become their teacher."

WHAT IS LIFE?

This seems like such an easy question to answer. Everybody knows that singing birds are alive and rocks are not. But when we start studying bacteria and other microscopic creatures, things get more complicated.

SO WHAT EXACTLY IS LIFE?

Most scientists agree that something is alive if it can reproduce, grow in size to become more complex in structure, take in nutrients to survive, give off waste products, and respond to external stimuli, such as increased sunlight or changes in temperature.

KINDS OF LIFE

Biologists classify living organisms by how they get their energy. Organisms such as algae, green plants, and some bacteria use sunlight as an energy source. Animals (like humans), fungi, and some single-celled microscopic organisms called Archaea use chemicals to provide energy. When we eat food, chemical reactions within our digestive system turn our food into fuel.

Living things inhabit land, sea, and air. In fact, life also thrives deep beneath the oceans, embedded in rocks miles below Earth's crust, in ice, and in other extreme environments. The life-forms that thrive in these challenging environments are called extremophiles. Some of these draw directly upon the chemicals surrounding them for energy. Because these are very different forms of life than what we're used to, we may not think of them as alive, but they are.

HOW IT ALL WORKS

To understand how a living organism works, it helps to look at one example of its simplest form—the single-celled bacterium called *Streptococcus*. There are many kinds of these tiny organisms, and some are responsible for human illnesses. What makes us sick or uncomfortable are the toxins the bacteria give off in our bodies.

A single *Streptococcus* bacterium is so small that at least 500 of them could fit on the dot above this letter *i*. These bacteria are some of the simplest forms of life we know. They have no moving parts, no lungs, no brain, no heart, no liver, and no leaves or fruit. Yet this life-form reproduces. It grows in size by producing long-chain structures, takes in nutrients, and gives off waste products. This tiny life-form is alive, just as you are alive.

What makes something alive is a question scientists grapple with when they study viruses, such as the ones that cause the common cold and COVID-19. They can grow and reproduce within host cells, such as those that make up your body. Because viruses lack cells and cannot metabolize nutrients for energy or reproduce without a host, scientists ask if they are indeed alive. And don't go looking for them without a strong microscope—viruses are a hundred times smaller than bacteria.

Scientists think life began on Earth some 4.1 to 3.9 billion years ago, but no fossils exist from that time. The earliest fossils ever found are from the primitive life that existed 3.5 billion years ago. Other life-forms, some of which are shown below, soon followed. Scientists continue to study how life evolved on Earth and whether it is possible that life exists on other planets.

MICROSCOPIC ORGANISMS

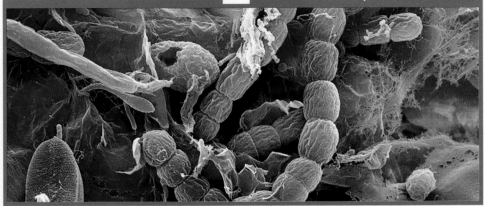

The Three Domains of Life

Biologists divide all living organisms into three domains, or groups: Bacteria, Archaea, and Eukarya. Archaea and Bacteria cells do not have nuclei—cellular parts that are essential to reproduction and other cell functions—but they are different from each other in many ways. Because human cells have a nucleus, we belong to the Eukarya domain.

1 **BACTERIA**

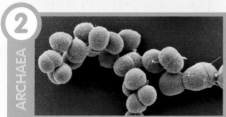

DOMAIN BACTERIA: These single-celled microorganisms are found almost everywhere in the world. Bacteria are small and do not have nuclei. They can be shaped like rods, spirals, or spheres. Some of them are helpful to humans, and some are harmful.

2 **ARCHAEA**

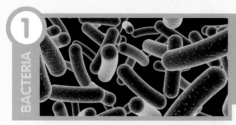

DOMAIN ARCHAEA: These single-celled micro-organisms are often found in extremely hostile environments. Like Bacteria, Archaea do not have nuclei, but they have some genes in common with Eukarya. For this reason, scientists think the Archaea living today most closely resemble the earliest forms of life on Earth.

3 **EUKARYA**

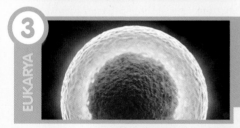

DOMAIN EUKARYA: This diverse group of life-forms is more complicated than Bacteria and Archaea, as Eukarya have one or more cells with nuclei. These are the tiny cells that make up your whole body. Eukarya are divided into four groups: fungi, protists, plants, and animals.

FYI

WHAT IS A DOMAIN? Scientifically speaking, a domain is a major taxonomic division into which natural objects are classified (see page 38 for "What Is Taxonomy?").

FUNGI

KINGDOM FUNGI Mainly multicellular organisms, fungi cannot make their own food. Mushrooms and yeast are fungi.

PROTISTS

PROTISTS Once considered a kingdom, this group is a "grab bag" that includes unicellular and multicellular organisms of great variety.

PLANTS

KINGDOM PLANTAE Plants are multi-cellular, and many can make their own food using photosynthesis (see page 102 for "Photosynthesis").

ANIMALS

KINGDOM ANIMALIA Most animals, which are multicellular, have their own organ systems. Animals do not make their own food.

HOW DOES YOUR GARDEN GR🌻W?

The plant kingdom is about 400,000 species strong, growing all over the world: on top of mountains, in the sea, in frigid temperatures—everywhere. Without plants, life on Earth would not be able to survive. Plants provide food and oxygen for animals, including humans.

Plants have three distinct characteristics:

1. Most have chlorophyll (a green pigment that makes photosynthesis work and turns sunlight into energy), while some are parasitic. Parasitic plants don't make their own food—they take it from other plants.
2. Plants cannot change their location on their own.
3. Their cell walls are made from a stiff material called cellulose.

Photosynthesis

Plants are lucky—most don't have to hunt or shop for food. Most use the sun to produce their own food. In a process called photosynthesis, a plant's chloroplast (the part of the plant where the chemical chlorophyll is located) captures the sun's energy and combines it with carbon dioxide from the air and nutrient-rich water from the ground to produce a sugar called glucose.

Plants burn the glucose for energy to help them grow. As a waste product, plants emit oxygen, which humans and other animals need to breathe. When we breathe, we exhale carbon dioxide, which the plants then use for more photosynthesis—it's all a big, finely tuned system. So the next time you pass a lonely houseplant, give it thanks for helping you live.

SOIL STATS

Look around your garden and you'll see lots of living things: pretty flowers, chirping birds, and more.

Dig around in the dirt and you'll find up to

30 EARTHWORMS

per square foot (.09 sq m). They break down organic matter in the soil.

But did you know there's a whole living world hidden in the soil beneath your feet? Next time you dig in the dirt, think about these fascinating facts!

1 TEASPOON (4 g) OF SOIL CONTAINS:

9 FEET (3 m) OF FUNGI STRANDS

100 TINY SOIL INSECTS

HUNDREDS OF CILIATES AND NEMATODES

There can be as much as

4,000 POUNDS

(1,814 kg) of plant roots in every acre (4,047 sq m) of soil.

UP TO 1 BILLION BACTERIA

SEVERAL THOUSAND FLAGELLATES AND AMOEBAS

Your Amazing Body!

The human body is a complicated mass of systems—nine systems, to be exact. Each system has a unique and critical purpose in the body, and we wouldn't be able to survive without all of them.

The **NERVOUS** system controls the body.

The **MUSCULAR** system makes movement possible.

The **SKELETAL** system supports the body.

The **CIRCULATORY** system moves blood throughout the body.

The **RESPIRATORY** system provides the body with oxygen.

The **DIGESTIVE** system breaks down food into nutrients and gets rid of waste.

The **IMMUNE** system protects the body against disease and infection.

The **ENDOCRINE** system regulates the body's functions.

The **REPRODUCTIVE** system enables people to produce offspring.

Weird but true!

YOUR **BRAIN** CAN HOLD **100 TIMES** MORE INFORMATION THAN AN AVERAGE **COMPUTER.**

A speck of **blood** contains about **5 million red blood** cells.

Your hands and wrists contain 26 percent of the bones in your body.

LOOK OUT!

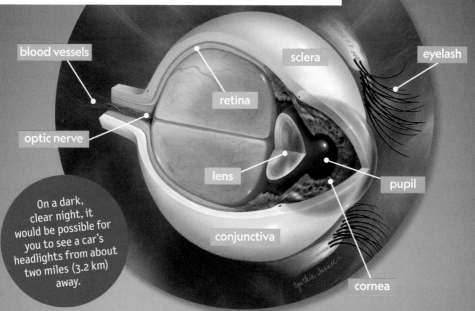

blood vessels

sclera

eyelash

retina

optic nerve

lens

pupil

conjunctiva

cornea

On a dark, clear night, it would be possible for you to see a car's headlights from about two miles (3.2 km) away.

Your eyes are two of the most amazing organs in your body.

These small, squishy, fluid-filled balls have almost three-quarters of your body's sensory receptors. They're like two supersmart cameras, but more complex.

So how do you see the world around you? It begins when you open the protective cover of your eyelid and let in the light. Light enters your eye through the window of your cornea and passes through the aqueous humor, a watery fluid that nourishes the eye tissue. It enters the black circle in the iris (the colored part of your eye), called the pupil. Because people need to be able to see in both bright and low light, muscles in the iris automatically make the pupil smaller when the light is strong and wider when the light is dim. Light then travels to the lens, whose muscles adjust it to be able to see objects both near and far. Then the light goes through the vitreous humor (a clear jellylike substance) to the retina. The retina, a layer of about 126 million light-sensitive cells, lines the back of your eyeball. When these cells absorb the light, they transform it into electrical signals that are sent along the optic nerve to the brain. The brain then makes sense of what you are seeing.

A TOPSY-TURVY WORLD

Turn this over in your mind: You're looking at the world topsy-turvy, and you don't even know it. Like a camera lens, your lens focuses light, creates an image, and turns it upside down. Yep, when your lens focuses light inside your eye, it flips the image so it lands on your retina upside down. But your brain knows to flip the image automatically to match your reality. But what if your reality suddenly changed? A well-known experiment in the mid-20th century in which a person wore special light-inverting goggles showed that his brain actually adjusted to the new, inverted world by eventually seeing the reversed view as normal! It is thought that newborns see the world upside down for a short while, until their brains learn how to turn things right side up.

CAMERA LENS

WHY can't
I eat peanuts or pet a fluffy dog without
FEELING ICKY?

Sounds like you have an allergy, and you're not alone! As many as 30 percent of grown-ups and 40 percent of kids suffer from allergies. Allergic reactions include itching, sneezing, coughing, a runny nose, vomiting, rashes, and shortness of breath. They happen when your body's immune system—which normally fights germs—treats something harmless, like food or a particular medicine, like it's a dangerous invader. Once it detects one of these intruders, called an allergen, your immune system goes into high alert. It creates antibodies to repel the intruder, causing the tissues around the allergen to become inflamed or swollen, which can make it hard for you to breathe. Extreme reactions can even result in a potentially deadly full-body response known as anaphylactic shock.

AWFUL allergens

PEANUTS
One of the most common food allergens, along with shellfish.

PET DANDER
Tiny flakes of shed fur and feathers can make your eyes water and your nose go *ahchoo!*

DUST MITES
Millions of these microscopic arachnids live in your house, feasting on your dead skin cells. Cleaning stirs up clouds of mite shells and their micro-poop.

PENICILLIN
Antibiotics like penicillin kill bacteria that make us sick, but they can do more harm than good for patients allergic to them.

POLLEN
Plants project this fine powdery substance into the breeze to fertilize other plants. It can irritate the nasal passages of allergy sufferers, causing sneezing and watery eyes—a condition commonly called hay fever.

Why do we have allergies?

Stories of allergies go back to ancient Egypt, yet their causes largely remain a mystery. Not everyone has allergies. Some form in childhood. Some happen later in life. And sometimes they go away as you get older. You may inherit a likelihood of having allergies from your parents but usually not their particular allergies.

Scientists suspect humans evolved with these extreme and mysterious immune reactions to combat genuinely deadly threats, such as parasitic worms or other toxins. And though doctors are doubtful they can ever cure allergies, they've come up with many ways to test for them and provide medications that treat the symptoms.

A majority of food allergies are caused by "the Big 8"— milk, eggs, fish, shellfish, tree nuts, peanuts, wheat, and soy.

WHY can't I USE
my left hand as well as my right one
(or the other way around)?

About nine out of ten of you reading this book will turn its pages with your right hand—

the same hand you use to write a note or chuck a fastball. About 90 percent of humans are right-handed, meaning their right hand is their dominant hand. The other 10 percent are left-handed. Activities that feel natural with the dominant hand are awkward or difficult with the other one. Ever try to sign your name with your nondominant hand? Not so easy!

Cave paintings going back more than 5,000 years show humans favoring their right or left hands according to the same nine-to-one ratio we see today. And the same goes for the stone tools our evolutionary ancestors used 1.5 million years ago: Studies show a similar dominance of the right hand long before the human species, *Homo sapiens,* appeared on the fossil record.

So **why** is one hand dominant?

Scientists have discovered a sequence of genes linked to hand dominance, making it a trait that's passed along to children just like hair color or dimples. These traits determine how our brains are wired. How? The brain is split into two symmetrical halves known as hemispheres. In about 90 percent of people, the left side of the brain processes language skills. These people are typically right-handed. People born with genes for left-handedness—about 10 percent of the population—typically have brains that process speech on the right side.

So whichever side of the brain controls speech usually corresponds with a dominant hand on the opposite side. Because the left side of the brain controls the right side of the body and vice versa, scientists suspect that the evolution of our dominant hand is somehow connected to the development of our language capabilities. Humans can have a dominant eye, foot, and ear, too—but scientists aren't quite sure why. That's just one of many reasons the human brain is considered the most complex object in the universe.

ARE YOU A "mixed-hander"?

What about people who can use their nondominant hand almost as well as their dominant? They're called mixed-handers. (Scientists don't like using the term "ambidextrous," which implies neither hand is dominant.) About one percent of people are elite lefties/righties. Are you? Grab a piece of scratch paper and find out!

MICROORGANISMS AND YOU

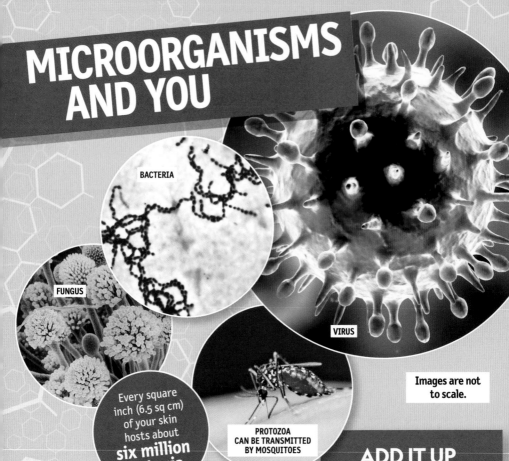

BACTERIA

FUNGUS

VIRUS

Images are not to scale.

Every square inch (6.5 sq cm) of your skin hosts about **six million bacteria.**

PROTOZOA CAN BE TRANSMITTED BY MOSQUITOES

Some microorganisms (tiny living things) can make your body sick. They are too small to see with the naked eye. These creatures—bacteria, viruses, fungi, and protozoa—are what you may know as germs.

Bacteria are microscopic organisms that live nearly everywhere on Earth, including on and in the human body. Good bacteria help our digestive systems work properly. Harmful bacteria can cause ailments, including ear infections and strep throat.

A virus, like a cold or the flu, needs to live inside another living thing (a host) to survive; then it can grow and multiply throughout the host's body.

Fungi get their food from the plants, animals, or people they live on. Some fungi can get on your body and cause skin diseases such as ringworm.

Protozoa are single-celled organisms that can spread disease to humans through contaminated water and dirty living conditions. Protozoa can cause infections such as malaria, which occurs when a person is bitten by an infected mosquito.

ADD IT UP

So you know that you have bacteria on your skin and in your body. But do you know how many? Trillions. That's more than 1,000,000,000,000! Most are harmless and some are pretty friendly, keeping more dangerous bacteria at bay, protecting you from some skin infections, and helping your cuts heal.

GERM **SHOWDOWN**

Scientists in Wales studied three greeting styles to determine which was the cleanest. Find out which one has the upper hand.

HANDSHAKE

AN AVERAGE HANDSHAKE TRANSFERRED **MORE THAN 5 TIMES AS MUCH BACTERIA** AS A FIST BUMP. (A STRONG HANDSHAKE TRANSFERRED **10 TIMES** AS MUCH.)

HIGH FIVE

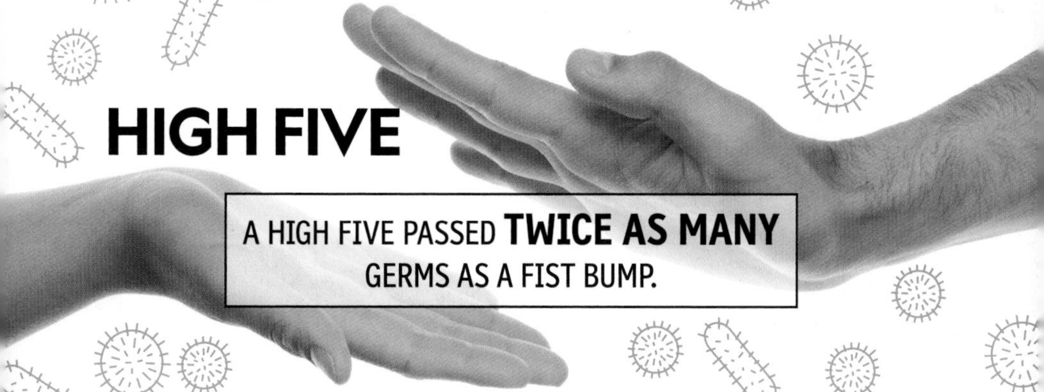

A HIGH FIVE PASSED **TWICE AS MANY** GERMS AS A FIST BUMP.

FIST BUMP

WINNER:

FIST BUMPS HAVE THE **LEAST SKIN-TO-SKIN CONTACT** OF THE GREETINGS, WHICH MAKES IT LESS LIKELY FOR MICROBES TO JUMP **FROM ONE HAND TO ANOTHER.**

THE SCIENCE OF
SPOOKY

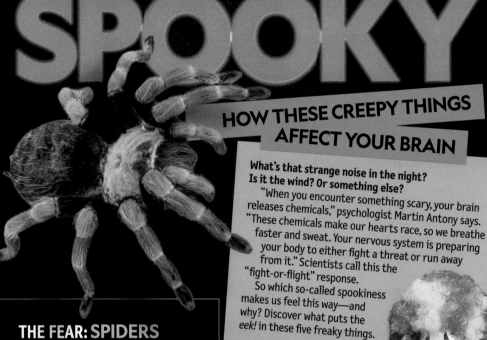

HOW THESE CREEPY THINGS AFFECT YOUR BRAIN

What's that strange noise in the night? Is it the wind? Or something else?

"When you encounter something scary, your brain releases chemicals," psychologist Martin Antony says. "These chemicals make our hearts race, so we breathe faster and sweat. Your nervous system is preparing your body to either fight a threat or run away from it." Scientists call this the "fight-or-flight" response.

So which so-called spookiness makes us feel this way—and why? Discover what puts the *eek!* in these five freaky things.

THE FEAR: SPIDERS

SCIENTIFIC NAME: Arachnophobia
SPOOKY SCIENCE: Humans have been afraid of spiders since our ancient human ancestors thought they carried deadly diseases. "Today, we know that's not true," psychology professor Kyle Rexer says. "But a lot of people still have incorrect ideas about how dangerous spiders are." Although some spiders *can* be deadly, most are not. In fact, humans actually benefit from the existence of spiders. By eating disease-carrying critters such as mosquitoes and cockroaches, these arachnids act as a form of pest control. Plus, scientists are currently studying spider venom in the hope that it can one day be used in medicines to manage pain or cure illnesses.

THE FEAR: CLOWNS

SCIENTIFIC NAME: Coulrophobia
SPOOKY SCIENCE: One way we decide if a person is friend or foe is by evaluating their facial expressions. Clowns—with their makeup, wigs, and fake noses—are hard to read, which is what makes them scary to some people. "It's hard to tell how a clown is feeling," psychology professor Frank McAndrew says. "So we think, If clowns can hide their emotions, what else might they be hiding?"

FIGHT THE FRIGHT

It's natural to avoid things that scare us. "But to get over your fears—whether you're afraid of spiders, clowns, the dark, or, well, anything—you have to *focus* on them instead of avoid them," Rexer says. He shares some useful tips to help you manage your fears.

THE FEAR: HEIGHTS

SCIENTIFIC NAME: Acrophobia

SPOOKY SCIENCE: When you're standing on solid ground, your eyes work with your inner ears to help you stay balanced. But if you're standing, say, at the edge of a cliff, your sense of balance can get out of whack. "Your inner ear is saying you're surrounded by solid ground, but your eyes are saying, 'Nope,'" inner-ear specialist Dennis Fitzgerald says. Your brain is getting mixed signals, which can cause vertigo, or dizziness that makes heights feel scary.

THE FEAR: DARKNESS

SCIENTIFIC NAME: Nyctophobia

SPOOKY SCIENCE: As with other phobias, humans developed a fear of the dark to avoid danger. Our ancestors had to be extra cautious at night to protect themselves against things like animal predators and human invaders. (This was before electric lighting!) "Many people still have that fear of the dark today," Antony says. "It's a fear of the unknown."

THE FEAR: SMALL SPACES

SCIENTIFIC NAME: Claustrophobia

SPOOKY SCIENCE: Maybe you've been stuck in an elevator before and thought it was no big deal. For some people, though, just the fear of being stuck can cause them to take the stairs. "Small spaces might cause some people to worry about running out of oxygen, or never being able to get out—no matter how unlikely that is," Antony says. "To increase our chances of survival, people have evolved to avoid being trapped. For some, that could be anywhere."

● Expose yourself to things that you're afraid of in a way that you feel safe. For example, if you fear public speaking, try practicing in front of a mirror first, and then give the speech to a small group of trusted friends.

● If you feel anxious, place one or both of your hands on your stomach and focus on breathing slowly and deeply. Regulating your breathing will help you feel calmer and can lessen your sense of panic.

● Don't be too hard on yourself! Everyone's afraid of *something*. Just make sure it doesn't stop you from living your life. Talk to an adult if it feels like too much to handle on your own.

QUIZ WHIZ

Test your science and technology smarts by taking this quiz!

Write your answers on a piece of paper. Then check them below.

1 In the future, customized 3D-printed food may include which special ingredient?

a. vitamins specific to our bodies' needs

b. extra sugar

c. invisible broccoli

d. freeze-dried ice cream

2 **True or false?** About 90 percent of humans are left-handed.

3 One teaspoon of _____ contains 9 feet (3 m) of fungi strands.

a. pasta sauce

b. pond water

c. sand

d. soil

4 What is the scientific name for the fear of the dark?

a. coulrophobia

b. claustrophobia

c. nyctophobia

d. arachnophobia

5 **True or false?** Scientists study microscopic organisms on Earth to see if it's possible that life exists on other planets.

Not **STUMPED** yet? Check out the *NATIONAL GEOGRAPHIC KIDS QUIZ WHIZ* collection for more crazy **SCIENCE AND TECHNOLOGY** questions!

This Is How It's Done!

Sometimes, the most complicated problems are solved with step-by-step directions. These "how-to" instructions are also known as a process analysis essay. Although scientists and engineers use this tool to program robots and write computer code, you also use process analysis every day, from following a recipe to putting together a new toy or gadget. Here's how to write a basic process analysis essay.

Step 1: Choose Your Topic Sentence

Pick a clear and concise topic sentence that describes what you're writing about. Be sure to explain to the readers why the task is important—and how many steps there are to complete it.

Step 2: List Materials

Do you need specific ingredients or equipment to complete your process? Mention these right away so the readers will have all they need to do this activity.

Step 3: Write Your Directions

Your directions should be clear and easy to follow. Assume that you are explaining the process for the first time, and define any unfamiliar terms. List your steps in the exact order the readers will need to follow to complete the activity. Try to keep your essay limited to no more than six steps.

Step 4: Restate Your Main Idea

Your closing idea should revisit your topic sentence, drawing a conclusion relating to the importance of the subject.

EXAMPLE OF A PROCESS ANALYSIS ESSAY

Downloading an app is a simple way to enhance your tablet. Today, I'd like to show you how to search for and add an app to your tablet. First, you will need a tablet with the ability to access the internet. You'll also want to ask a parent for permission before you download anything onto your tablet. Next, select the specific app you're seeking by going to the app store on your tablet and entering the app's name into the search bar. Once you find the app you're seeking, select "download" and wait for the app to load. When you see that the app has fully loaded, tap on the icon and you will be able to access it. Now you can enjoy your app and have more fun with your tablet.

A woman in Venice, Italy, poses in a traditional mask and costume during Carnival—an annual festival celebrated before the Christian season of Lent.

CULTURE
CONNECTION

CELEBRATIONS

UP HELLY AA
January 25

This annual daylong festival celebrating the history of Shetland, Scotland, involves costume-clad participants marching through town with torches and the burning of a full-scale replica of a Viking longship.

LUNAR NEW YEAR
February 1

Also called Chinese New Year, this holiday marks the new year according to the lunar calendar. Families celebrate with parades, feasts, and fireworks. Young people may receive gifts of money in red envelopes.

QINGMING FESTIVAL
April 5

Also known as Grave Sweeping Day, this Chinese celebration calls on people to return to the graves of their loved ones. There, they tidy up the graves, as well as light firecrackers, burn fake money, and leave food as an offering to the spirits.

RAMADAN AND EID AL-FITR
April 2*–May 1**

A Muslim holiday, Ramadan is a month long, ending in the Eid al-Fitr celebration. Observers fast during this month—eating only after sunset. People pray for forgiveness and hope to purify themselves through observance.

EASTER
April 17 †

A Christian holiday that honors the resurrection of Jesus Christ, Easter is celebrated by giving baskets filled with gifts, decorated eggs, or candy to children.

LEI DAY
May 1

Celebrating the "aloha spirit" in Hawaii, this day is all about the leis, or the traditional flower garland worn as a necklace or a crown. Events include hula shows, lei making, and craft shows.

Around the World

ROSH HASHANAH
September 25*-27

A Jewish holiday marking the beginning of a new year on the Hebrew calendar. Celebrations include prayer, ritual foods, and a day of rest.

DIWALI
October 24-28

To symbolize the inner light that protects against spiritual darkness, people light their homes with clay lamps for India's largest and most important holiday.

HANUKKAH
December 18*-26

This Jewish holiday is eight days long. It commemorates the rededication of the Temple in Jerusalem. Hanukkah celebrations include the lighting of menorah candles for eight days and the exchange of gifts.

CHRISTMAS DAY
December 25

A Christian holiday marking the birth of Jesus Christ, Christmas is usually celebrated by decorating trees, exchanging presents, and having festive gatherings.

*Begins at sundown.
**Dates may vary slightly by location.
† Orthodox Easter is April 24.

2022 CALENDAR

JANUARY
S	M	T	W	T	F	S
						1
2	3	4	5	6	7	8
9	10	11	12	13	14	15
16	17	18	19	20	21	22
23	24	25	26	27	28	29
30	31					

FEBRUARY
S	M	T	W	T	F	S
		1	2	3	4	5
6	7	8	9	10	11	12
13	14	15	16	17	18	19
20	21	22	23	24	25	26
27	28					

MARCH
S	M	T	W	T	F	S
		1	2	3	4	5
6	7	8	9	10	11	12
13	14	15	16	17	18	19
20	21	22	23	24	25	26
27	28	29	30	31		

APRIL
S	M	T	W	T	F	S
					1	2
3	4	5	6	7	8	9
10	11	12	13	14	15	16
17	18	19	20	21	22	23
24	25	26	27	28	29	30

MAY
S	M	T	W	T	F	S
1	2	3	4	5	6	
7	8	9	10	11	12	13
14	15	16	17	18	19	20
21	22	23	24	25	26	27
28	29	30	31			

JUNE
S	M	T	W	T	F	S
			1	2	3	4
5	6	7	8	9	10	11
12	13	14	15	16	17	18
19	20	21	22	23	24	25
26	27	28	29	30		

JULY
S	M	T	W	T	F	S
					1	2
3	4	5	6	7	8	9
10	11	12	13	14	15	16
17	18	19	20	21	22	23
24	25	26	27	28	29	30
31						

AUGUST
S	M	T	W	T	F	S
	1	2	3	4	5	6
7	8	9	10	11	12	13
14	15	16	17	18	19	20
21	22	23	24	25	26	27
28	29	30	31			

SEPTEMBER
S	M	T	W	T	F	S
				1	2	3
4	5	6	7	8	9	10
11	12	13	14	15	16	17
18	19	20	21	22	23	24
25	26	27	28	29	30	

OCTOBER
S	M	T	W	T	F	S
						1
2	3	4	5	6	7	8
9	10	11	12	13	14	15
16	17	18	19	20	21	22
23	24	25	26	27	28	29
30	31					

NOVEMBER
S	M	T	W	T	F	S
		1	2	3	4	5
6	7	8	9	10	11	12
13	14	15	16	17	18	19
20	21	22	23	24	25	26
27	28	29	30			

DECEMBER
S	M	T	W	T	F	S
				1	2	3
4	5	6	7	8	9	10
11	12	13	14	15	16	17
18	19	20	21	22	23	24
25	26	27	28	29	30	31

Bet You Didn't Know!

8 New Year's Celebrations Across the Globe

1 **Giant water fights IN THAILAND** ring in the new year in early spring.

2 **IN IRAN**, festivities kick off with the **arrival of spring** and last 13 days.

3 Kids in **BELGIUM** **write letters** to their parents and godparents and read them aloud on New Year's Day.

4 **IN LONDON**, New Year's revelers have been showered with **edible banana confetti** and **peach-flavored snow** at midnight.

5 Residents in **SCOTLAND** **open** their front doors before midnight on New Year's Eve to let the **old year out** and the **new year in.**

6 New Year's **IN ETHIOPIA** happens in **September**, which is the end of the rainy season.

7 More than 2,000 **CANADIANS** **take an icy plunge** at Vancouver's Polar Bear Swim each New Year's Day.

8 **IN THE UNITED STATES**, the Creek tribe's new year starts **in midsummer**, after the **corn ripens.**

What's Your Chinese Horoscope?
Locate your birth year to find out.

In Chinese astrology, the zodiac runs on a 12-year cycle, based on the lunar calendar. Each year corresponds to one of 12 animals, each representing one of 12 personality types. Read on to find out which animal year you were born in and what that might say about you.

RAT
1972, '84, '96, 2008, '20
Say cheese! You're attractive, charming, and creative. When you get mad, you can have really sharp teeth!

HORSE
1966, '78, '90, 2002, '14
Being happy is your *mane* goal. And though you're smart and hardworking, your teacher may ride you for talking too much.

OX
1973, '85, '97, 2009, '21
You're smart, patient, and as strong as an ... well, you know what. Though you're a leader, you never brag.

SHEEP
1967, '79, '91, 2003, '15
Gentle as a lamb, you're also artistic, compassionate, and wise. You're often shy.

TIGER
1974, '86, '98, 2010, '22
You may be a nice person, but no one should ever enter your room without asking—you might attack!

MONKEY
1968, '80, '92, 2004, '16
No "monkey see, monkey do" for you. You're a clever problem-solver with an excellent memory.

RABBIT
1975, '87, '99, 2011, '23
Your ambition and talent make you jump at opportunity. You also keep your ears open for gossip.

ROOSTER
1969, '81, '93, 2005, '17
You crow about your adventures, but inside you're really shy. You're thoughtful, capable, brave, and talented.

DRAGON
1976, '88, 2000, '12
You're on fire! Health, energy, honesty, and bravery make you a living legend.

DOG
1970, '82, '94, 2006, '18
Often the leader of the pack, you're loyal and honest. You can also keep a secret.

SNAKE
1977, '89, 2001, '13
You may not speak often, but you're very smart. You always seem to have a stash of cash.

PIG
1971, '83, '95, 2007, '19
Even though you're courageous, honest, and kind, you never hog all the attention.

Try This! GINGERBREAD HOUSES

YOU WILL NEED

- 1 CAN READY-MADE VANILLA FROSTING
- 1/4 TEASPOON CREAM OF TARTAR
- CARDBOARD
- GRAHAM CRACKERS (OR GINGERBREAD)
- SERRATED KNIFE (ASK FOR AN ADULT'S HELP)
- ASSORTED CANDY, PRETZELS, AND COOKIES, INCLUDING SQUARE CARAMELS (NOT SHOWN)
- SHREDDED COCONUT

WHAT TO DO

MIX THE "GLUE": Frosting will hold each graham cracker building together. Combine the vanilla frosting with the cream of tartar. To apply the frosting, squeeze it out of a sealed freezer bag with a hole cut in one corner.

BUILD THE HOUSE:

BASE Cut a piece of cardboard that's big enough to hold the scene.

WALLS The front and back walls are each made of a whole graham cracker turned horizontally. Ask an adult to create the two remaining sides. For each, use a serrated knife to gently saw the top of a whole graham cracker into a peak (inset, above). Run a thin line of icing along the bottom edge and sides of the crackers. "Glue" them together in a rectangle on top of the cardboard. Prop up the walls while you work.

PEAKED ROOF Run icing along the tops of the walls. Place two whole graham crackers—turned horizontally—on top of the sides, using icing to hold them in place. Let the icing set overnight.

WAGON USE QUARTER CRACKERS FOR THE BOTTOM AND SIDES. USE HALF OF A QUARTER CRACKER FOR THE BACK. "GLUE" THE PIECES IN PLACE. ADD PRETZEL WHEELS AND A CARAMEL UNDER THE WAGON FOR SUPPORT.

SILO CUT OFF THE TOPS OF TWO CAKE ICE-CREAM CONES, THEN FROST THE OPEN ENDS TOGETHER. STICK ON COLORFUL LICORICE AND TOP WITH A FOIL BAKING CUP.

SNOWMAN SKEWER TWO MARSHMALLOWS ONTO A PRETZEL STICK. USE GUMDROPS FOR THE HAT, EYES, AND NOSE; PRETZELS FOR THE ARMS; AND STRING LICORICE FOR A SCARF.

Fun Winter Gift Idea

Snow Globes

YOU WILL NEED
- SMALL JAR WITH A LID (A BABY FOOD JAR WORKS WELL.)
- SANDPAPER
- INSTANT-BONDING GLUE (FOLLOW DIRECTIONS ON THE TUBE AND USE WITH ADULT SUPERVISION.)
- PLASTIC ANIMAL OR FIGURINE THAT FITS IN THE JAR
- NAIL POLISH REMOVER
- BABY OIL
- 1/2 TEASPOON WHITE GLITTER

WHAT TO DO
Turn the jar's lid upside down. Use sandpaper to scuff the inside of the lid. Glue the bottom of the figurine to the center of the lid. (Nail polish remover cleans glue off skin and surfaces.) Let dry for four hours. Fill the jar with baby oil. Add glitter. To seal, put glue around the rim of the jar. Close the lid tightly and let dry for four hours. Turn the jar over, and let it snow!

DOGHOUSE Follow the steps at left for the gingerbread house, but use quarter crackers for all sides and the roof.

BARN Use graham cracker halves for the barn's roof and sides. For the front and back, cut a peak in a whole graham cracker (inset, above left).

DECORATIONS "Glue" on your favorite treats to create doors, rooftops, trees, and anything else you can imagine. Let everything set overnight. Cover the cardboard base with shredded coconut to finish your snowy scene.

DOG "GLUE" TWO GUMDROPS TOGETHER TO FORM THE BODY. STICK ON PIECES OF GUMDROPS FOR THE EARS, NOSE, AND TAIL.

10 WOW-WORTHY WAYS TO GET AROUND

In Madeira, Portugal, you can take a 10-minute toboggan ride down a curvy road in the capital city.

Consisting of just two stations, **continental Europe's oldest subway** line in Istanbul, Turkey, transports passengers **UP or DOWN** a steep hill.

A **HABEL-HABEL** IS A MOTORCYCLE USED IN THE PHILIPPINES WITH AN **EXTRA-LONG SEAT** THAT CAN CARRY **FOUR TO FIVE PEOPLE.**

IN THAILAND, TAXIS COME IN THE FORM OF **TUK-TUKS**— THREE-WHEELED CARS WITH OPEN SIDES AND A COVERED TOP.

Stretching **5,772 miles** (9,289 km) and passing through **seven time zones,** the TRANS-SIBERIAN RAILWAY is the **longest train route** in the world.

Residents in Lapland, Finland—which has about the same number of reindeer as people—take sled rides to get from here to there.

TO GET FROM PLACE TO PLACE IN PAKISTAN, YOU CAN **RIDE A TANGAH,** a chauffeured wagon pulled by one or two horses.

Roosevelt Island in New York City is accessible by a tramway that travels 250 feet (76 m) above the East River.

VISITORS TO THE COLUMBIA ICEFIELD IN JASPER, ALBERTA, CANADA, CLIMB ONTO A GIANT VEHICLE THAT'S **PART SCHOOL BUS, PART MONSTER TRUCK.**

To go between Greek islands, visitors can take a **hydrofoil,** a high-speed ferry that skims the water.

123

MONEY AROUND THE WORLD!

The Southern Cross constellation appears on **Brazilian coins.**

ACCORDING to some **PEOPLE, CANADA'S $100 BANKNOTE** gives off the scent of **MAPLE SYRUP.**

A British businessman created his own currency —named the **PUFFIN**— for an island he owned off of England.

IN FEBRUARY 2015, SCUBA DIVERS **OFF ISRAEL FOUND MORE THAN** 2,600 GOLD **COINS DATING BACK AS FAR AS THE NINTH CENTURY.**

Bank of **BOTSWANA**

D 85 400141

This note is legal tender for

F 400141 **Ten Pula** 10

A **JANITOR** at a **GERMAN LIBRARY** found and turned in a **BOX OF RARE COINS** thought to be worth **HUNDREDS OF THOUSANDS OF DOLLARS.**

Botswana's currency is named **PULA,** meaning **"RAIN,"** which is **VALUABLE** in this **ARID NATION.**

ANCIENT GREEKS believed that **PLACING A COIN IN A DEAD PERSON'S MOUTH** would pay for the ferry ride to the afterlife.

COINS CREATED IN 1616 FOR WHAT IS NOW **BERMUDA** WERE NICKNAMED **"HOGGIES"** BECAUSE THEY HAD IMAGES OF **HOGS** ON THEM.

More than **$5 TRILLION** in **MONOPOLY MONEY** has been printed since 1935.

IN INDIA, the **SLANG TERM** for **100,000 RUPEES IS** *PETI*, **OR SUITCASE.** You might need one to carry that much money!

KING TUT APPEARS ON THE EGYPTIAN 1-POUND COIN.

A BRITISH ARTIST MADE A DRESS OUT OF USED **BANKNOTES** FROM AROUND THE **WORLD.**

MONEY TIP! CLIP COUPONS FOR YOUR PARENTS. Ask if they'll put the money they save into your piggy bank.

CHEW ON THIS

QUESADILLAS!

The quesadilla you order at a restaurant can be filled with lots of things, but the traditional treat from Mexico is almost sure to have one ingredient: cheese. Think of a quesadilla—or, roughly translated, "little cheesy thing" in Spanish—as a twist on a grilled cheese sandwich that you can add other ingredients to.

Astronauts take **TORTILLAS** into space because they produce fewer crumbs than bread.

ZUCCHINI gets its name from the Italian word for squash.

Eating **MONTEREY JACK CHEESE** may help prevent cavities.

The spicy flavor of a **JALAPEÑO** is concentrated near its seeds.

One ear of **CORN** produces about 600 kernels.

MAKE YOUR OWN QUESADILLAS

Get a parent's help to heat up this cheesy dish.

1 Preheat the oven to 400°F (200°C). In a skillet, heat 3 tablespoons (45 mL) of olive oil over medium heat.

2 Cut 1 zucchini in half lengthwise and thinly slice the halves crosswise.

3 Add zucchini and 1 cup (128 g) of frozen corn kernels to the skillet. Cook, stirring occasionally, for 6 minutes.

4 Brush one side of 4 tortillas with olive oil. Lay 2 of the tortillas, oiled side down, on a baking sheet.

5 Place half of the vegetable filling on each tortilla, and sprinkle each with 1 cup (100 g) of grated Monterey Jack cheese.

6 Place the remaining 2 tortillas on top, with their oiled side up.

7 Bake for 5 minutes, and then flip. Continue baking until cheese has melted, for about 5 more minutes.

8 Cut each quesadilla into wedges and top with a handful of sliced jalapeños.

CANDY APPLES!

Legend has it that a store owner just wanted to sell more cinnamon-flavored candies. Instead, he sparked a candy apple craze! After dipping some apples into the melted red sweets, the man displayed the fruit in his window. He then discovered that customers didn't want just the cinnamon candy—they wanted the whole treat, apple and all. Soon he was selling thousands of candy apples a year.

COCONUTS were once so valued that their shells were sometimes mounted and painted in gold.

One **PISTACHIO** tree can produce about 50,000 nuts every two years.

CARAMEL, butterscotch, and toffee share most of the same ingredients but are cooked at different temperatures.

CANDY CORN was sold as a summertime treat in the 1950s.

Pilgrims on the *Mayflower* brought **APPLE** seeds from England to the United States.

MAKE YOUR OWN CARAMEL APPLES

Get a parent's help to create some fun fruit.

1 Wash and dry 6 apples and remove the stems. Stick a wooden skewer in the stem end of each apple. (You can also use ice pop sticks.)

2 Unwrap and place 40 individual caramels in a microwave-safe bowl with 2 tablespoons (30 mL) of milk.

3 Microwave the mixture for 2 minutes, stirring once. Allow the caramel to cool.

4 Roll each apple in the caramel, twirling to make sure the apple is completely coated.

5 Place the apples on a baking sheet covered with parchment paper. Sprinkle the apples with your favorite topping—such as pistachios or candy corn—and allow them to set.

SAVING
Languages At Risk

Today, there are more than 7,000 languages spoken on Earth. But by 2100, more than half of those may disappear. In fact, experts say one language dies every two weeks, due to the increasing dominance of larger languages such as English, Spanish, and Mandarin.

So what can be done to keep dialects from disappearing altogether? To start, several National Geographic explorers have embarked on various projects around the planet. Together, they are part of the race to save some of the world's most threatened languages, as well as to protect and preserve the cultures they belong to. Here are some of the explorers' stories.

The Explorer: Tam Thi Ton
The Language: Bahnar

TON IN A BAHNAR CLASSROOM

The Work: By gathering folklore like riddles and comics, Ton is creating bilingual learning materials for elementary students to teach them Bahnar, the language of an ethnic group living in Vietnam's Central Highlands.

NARAYANAN SHARES STORIES FROM THE FIELD AT NATIONAL GEOGRAPHIC'S HEADQUARTERS IN WASHINGTON, D.C., U.S.A.

The Explorer: Sandhya Narayanan
The Languages: Quechua and Aymara

The Work: By immersing herself in the indigenous languages of the Andean region along the Peru-Bolivia border, Narayanan aims to understand how interactions between indigenous groups affect language over time.

The Explorer: K. David Harrison
The Language: Koro-Aka

The Work: Harrison led an expedition to India which identified Koro-Aka, a language that was completely new to science. He is also vice president of the Living Tongues Institute for Endangered Languages, dedicated to raising awareness and revitalizing small languages.

HARRISON DOING AN INTERVIEW

The Explorer: Susan Barfield
The Language: Mapudungun

The Work: Barfield shines a light on the language of the Mapuche people of Southern Chile with her trilingual children's book, *El Copihue*. The book is based on a Mapuche folktale and is illustrated by Mapuche students.

BARFIELD PRESENTS AN OFFERING DURING A BOOK BLESSING CEREMONY.

PERLIN INTERVIEWS A VILLAGE LEADER.

The Explorer: Ross Perlin
The Language: Seke

The Work: In an effort to preserve the Seke language of northern Nepal, Perlin has been working closely with speakers both in their villages and in New York, where many now live, including young speakers determined to document their own language.

The Explorer: Lal Rapacha
The Language: Kiranti-Kõits

The Work: As the founder and director of the Research Institute for Kiratology in Kathmandu, Nepal, Rapacha carries out research on the lesser-known languages of indigenous Himalayan people, including Kiranti-Kõits, his endangered mother tongue.

RAPACHA WORKING IN THE FIELD IN NEPAL

MYTHOLOGY

GREEK

EGYPTIAN

The ancient Greeks believed that many gods and goddesses ruled the universe. According to this mythology, the Olympians lived high atop Greece's Mount Olympus. Each of these 12 principal gods and goddesses had a unique personality that corresponded to particular aspects of life, such as love or death.

Egyptian mythology is based on a creation myth that tells of an egg that appeared on the ocean. When the egg hatched, out came Ra, the sun god. As a result, ancient Egyptians became worshippers of the sun and of the nine original deities, most of whom were the children and grandchildren of Ra.

THE OLYMPIANS

Aphrodite was the goddess of love and beauty.

Apollo, Zeus's son, was the god of the sun, music, and healing. Artemis was his twin.

Ares, Zeus's son, was the god of war.

Artemis, Zeus's daughter and Apollo's twin, was the goddess of the hunt and of childbirth.

Athena, born from the forehead of Zeus, was the goddess of wisdom and crafts.

Demeter was the goddess of fertility and nature.

Hades, Zeus's brother, was the god of the underworld and the dead.

Hephaestus, the son of Hera, was the god of fire.

Hera, the wife and older sister of Zeus, was the goddess of women and marriage.

Hermes, Zeus's son, was the messenger of the gods.

Poseidon, the brother of Zeus, was the god of the seas and earthquakes.

Zeus was the most powerful of the gods and the top Olympian. He wielded a thunderbolt and was the god of the sky and thunder.

THE NINE DEITIES

Geb, son of Shu and Tefnut, was the god of the earth.

Isis (Ast), daughter of Geb and Nut, was the goddess of fertility and motherhood.

Nephthys (Nebet-Hut), daughter of Geb and Nut, was protector of the dead.

Nut, daughter of Shu and Tefnut, was the goddess of the sky.

Osiris (Usir), son of Geb and Nut, was the god of the afterlife.

Ra (Re), the sun god, is generally viewed as the creator. He represents life and health.

Seth (Set), son of Geb and Nut, was the god of the desert and chaos.

Shu, son of Ra, was the god of air.

Tefnut, daughter of Ra, was the goddess of rain.

All cultures around the world have unique legends and traditions that have been passed down over generations. Many myths refer to gods or supernatural heroes who are responsible for occurrences in the world. For example, Norse mythology tells of the red-bearded Thor, the god of thunder, who is responsible for creating lightning and thunderstorms. And many creation myths, especially those from some of North America's native cultures, tell of an earth-diver represented as an animal that brings a piece of sand or mud up from the deep sea. From this tiny piece of earth, the entire world takes shape.

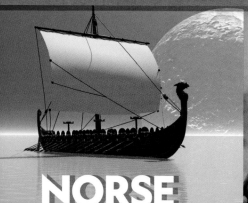

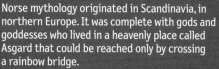

NORSE

ROMAN

Norse mythology originated in Scandinavia, in northern Europe. It was complete with gods and goddesses who lived in a heavenly place called Asgard that could be reached only by crossing a rainbow bridge.

Although Norse mythology is lesser known, we use it every day. Most days of the week are named after Norse gods, including some of these major deities.

NORSE GODS

Balder was the god of light and beauty.

Freya was the goddess of love, beauty, and fertility.

Frigg, for whom Friday was named, was the queen of Asgard. She was the goddess of marriage, motherhood, and the home.

Heimdall was the watchman of the rainbow bridge and the guardian of the gods.

Hel, the daughter of Loki, was the goddess of death.

Loki, a shape-shifter, was a trickster who helped the gods—and caused them problems.

Skadi was the goddess of winter and of the hunt. She is often represented as the "Snow Queen."

Thor, for whom Thursday was named, was the god of thunder and lightning.

Tyr, for whom Tuesday was named, was the god of the sky and war.

Wodan, for whom Wednesday was named, was the god of war, wisdom, death, and magic.

Much of Roman mythology was adopted from Greek mythology, but the Romans also developed a lot of original myths as well. The gods of Roman mythology lived everywhere, and each had a role to play. There were thousands of Roman gods, but here are a few of the stars of Roman myths.

ANCIENT ROMAN GODS

Ceres was the goddess of the harvest and motherly love.

Diana, daughter of Jupiter, was the goddess of hunting and the moon.

Juno, Jupiter's wife, was the goddess of women and fertility.

Jupiter, the patron of Rome and master of the gods, was the god of the sky.

Mars, the son of Jupiter and Juno, was the god of war.

Mercury, the son of Jupiter, was the messenger of the gods and the god of travelers.

Minerva was the goddess of wisdom, learning, and the arts and crafts.

Neptune, the brother of Jupiter, was the god of the sea.

Venus was the goddess of love and beauty.

Vesta was the goddess of fire and the hearth. She was one of the most important of the Roman deities.

GREEK MYTHS

POSEIDON: GOD OF THE SEAS

Poseidon—along with his brother Hades and his sisters, Hestia, Demeter, and Hera—was swallowed at birth by his father, Cronus. Then a sixth child, Zeus, who was never swallowed, and thus had never known humiliation, freed them. Poseidon sized things up: Zeus was a force to be reckoned with—he was the guy to follow.

For 10 long years, the six brothers and sisters fought their father and aunts and uncles—the mighty Titans. It was a nasty war, but what war isn't? Poseidon gritted his teeth and did his part. He was no coward, after all. But now and then there was a lull in the battle, perhaps because Zeus got distracted or because the Titans needed a rest. Who knew? Whatever the case, Poseidon was grateful, and in those moments he took refuge in visiting Pontus, the ancient god of all the waters, the partner to his grandmother Gaia, Mother Earth, and his grandfather Uranus, Father Heaven. He swam in Pontus's waters, and despite how badly his life had gone so far, despite all the long years of savage war, he was happy.

Best of all, Poseidon found a friend in Nereus. He loved the watery depths as much as Poseidon did. Together they plunged to the corals and sponges that lived along the seabed. They rode on the backs of turtles. They flapped their arms like the rays they followed and then let their arms hang in the water, moving at the whim of the currents.

But then it was back to war ... until the glorious moment when the hundred-handed sons of Gaia joined the battle on Zeus's side, and then the Cyclopes gave Zeus the thunderbolt and Hades the helmet that made him invisible and Poseidon the trident. It worked, that

POSEIDON,
GOD OF
THE SEAS,
WITH HIS
TRIDENT

With his hair flying out behind him, he swam the seas in search of those who might need help. And when he wasn't patrolling, he let himself be absorbed in the watery mysteries.

That's when he discovered the finest mystery ever. She was the daughter of the sea god Phorcys and the sea goddess Ceto. That heritage made her the perfect wife in Poseidon's eyes. She was one of three sisters, called the Gorgons. The other two sisters were immortal, like the gods. But Medusa, as she was called, was mortal.

Poseidon found her mortality that much more alluring. How amazing to know someone vulnerable. He put his arms out and let the serpents of her hair swarm around them. Good! Those serpents could bite and poison—good protection. He gingerly touched the wings that jutted from her shoulder blades. Good! Those wings could carry her far from an attacker. He stroked her scales. Very good! They were harder than armor. And most assuring of all, she had a special power: Anything mortal that looked directly at her face would turn instantly to stone.

And so Poseidon felt almost safe in loving Medusa. They reveled together comfortably in his sea kingdom. At least for a while ...

TREASURY OF
GREEK
MYTHOLOGY

**CHECK OUT
THIS BOOK!**

trident. Poseidon struck it on the ground and the entire Earth shook. The Olympian gods won.

Zeus appointed Poseidon ruler of the seas. Poseidon knew his brother felt the seas were an inferior realm. Ha! Nothing could've pleased Poseidon more.

THE MORTAL
MEDUSA
EMBRACES
HER HUSBAND,
POSEIDON.

133

World Religions

Around the world, religion takes many forms. Some belief systems, such as Christianity, Islam, and Judaism, are monotheistic, meaning that followers believe in just one supreme being. Others, like Hinduism, Shintoism, and most native belief systems, are polytheistic, meaning that many of their followers believe in multiple gods.

All of the major religions have their origins in Asia, but they have spread around the world. Christianity, with the largest number of followers, has three divisions—Roman Catholic, Eastern Orthodox, and Protestant. Islam, with about one-quarter of all believers, has two main divisions—Sunni and Shiite. Hinduism and Buddhism account for almost another one-fifth of believers. Judaism, dating back some 4,000 years, has more than 14 million followers, less than one percent of all believers.

CHRISTIANITY

Based on the teachings of Jesus Christ, a Jew born some 2,000 years ago in the area of modern-day Israel, Christianity has spread worldwide and actively seeks converts. Followers in Switzerland (above) participate in an Easter season procession with lanterns and crosses.

BUDDHISM

Founded about 2,400 years ago in northern India by the Hindu prince Gautama Buddha, Buddhism spread throughout East and Southeast Asia. Buddhist temples have statues, such as the Mihintale Buddha (above) in Sri Lanka.

HINDUISM

Dating back more than 4,000 years, Hinduism is practiced mainly in India. Hindus follow sacred texts known as the Vedas and believe in reincarnation. During the festival of Navratri, which honors the goddess Durga, the Garba dance is performed (above).

Novice Monks

Members of the Wild Boars youth soccer team were rescued from a flooded Thai cave in July 2018. A few weeks later, 11 of the boys were ordained as novice Buddhist monks and spent nine days in a monastery. This act honored Saman Gunan, a Thai Navy SEAL who died while rescuing them.

ISLAM

Muslims believe that the Quran, Islam's sacred book, records the words of Allah (God) as revealed to the Prophet Muhammad beginning around A.D. 610. Believers (above) circle the Kaaba in the Grand Mosque in Mecca, Saudi Arabia, the spiritual center of the faith.

JUDAISM

The traditions, laws, and beliefs of Judaism date back to Abraham (the patriarch) and the Torah (the first five books of the Old Testament). Followers pray before the Western Wall (above), which stands below Islam's Dome of the Rock in Jerusalem.

QUIZ WHIZ

How vast is your knowledge about the world around you? Quiz yourself!

Write your answers on a piece of paper. Then check them below.

1 Some people think that Canada's $100 banknote gives off the scent of _____.

a. roses
b. bubble gum
c. maple syrup
d. licorice

2 Lapland, Finland, has about the same number of _____ as people.

a. roosters
b. rats
c. rabbits
d. reindeer

3 Which animal is represented in Chinese astrology?

a. tiger
b. dragon
c. snake
d. all of the above

4 In Hawaii, _____ is a holiday celebrating the "aloha spirit."

5 True or false? The ancient Romans believed in thousands of gods.

Not **STUMPED** yet? Check out the *NATIONAL GEOGRAPHIC KIDS QUIZ WHIZ* collection for more crazy **CULTURE** questions!

HOMEWORK HELP

Explore a New Culture

YOU'RE A STUDENT, but you're also a citizen of the world. Writing a report on a foreign nation or your own country is a great way to better understand and appreciate how different people live. Pick the country of your ancestors, one that's been in the news, or one that you'd like to visit someday.

STAMPS OF BRAZIL

Brasil 93   CR$ 22,00

BRASIL-CORREIO

AMERICA

CURRENCY AND COINS OF BRAZIL

FLAG OF BRAZIL

Passport to Success

A country report follows the format of an expository essay because you're "exposing" information about the country you choose.

The following step-by-step tips will help you with this monumental task.

1 **RESEARCH.** Gathering information is the most important step in writing a good country report. Look to internet sources, encyclopedias, books, magazine and newspaper articles, and other sources to find important and interesting details about your subject.

2 **ORGANIZE YOUR NOTES.** Put the information you gathered into a rough outline. For example, sort everything you found about the country's system of government, climate, etc.

3 **WRITE IT UP.** Follow the basic structure of good writing: introduction, body, and conclusion. Remember that each paragraph should have a topic sentence that is then supported by facts and details. Incorporate the information from your notes, but make sure it's in your own words. And make your writing flow with good transitions and descriptive language.

4 **ADD VISUALS.** Include maps, diagrams, photos, and other visual aids.

5 **PROOFREAD AND REVISE.** Correct any mistakes, and polish your language. Do your best!

6 **CITE YOUR SOURCES.** Be sure to keep a record of your sources.

FUN and GAMES

Two brown bears play-fight in Alaska, U.S.A.

GREEN SCENE

You're the newly elected mayor of this busy city. The first order of business? Transform it into the greenest town in the world. Start by finding 15 pieces of litter from the list below. Then locate eight blue recycling bins and two green compost bins to clean up the city.

ANSWERS ON PAGE 338

1. cardboard box
2. crumpled-up paper
3. soda can
4. paper cup
5. phone book
6. cereal box
7. newspapers
8. half-eaten apple
9. egg carton
10. paper bag
11. banana peel
12. glass bottle
13. magazine
14. takeout box
15. milk carton

WHAT IN THE WORLD?

RING TOSS

These images show close-up and faraway views of items with ring shapes. On a separate sheet of paper, unscramble the letters to identify what's in each picture.

ANSWERS ON PAGE 338

SLAKLTBBAE TNE

LAUH-OPOH

LNPEIPEAP

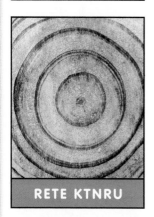

RETE KTNRU

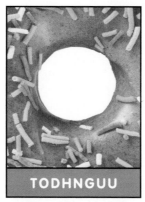

TODHNGUU

YKE IGNR

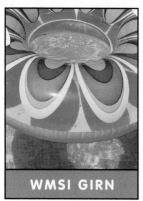

WMSI GIRN

ODDRRATBA

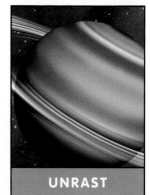

UNRAST

141

FIND THE HIDDEN ANIMALS

Animals often blend in with their environments for protection. Find each animal listed below in one of the pictures. On a separate sheet of paper, write the letter of the correct picture and the animal's name.

ANSWERS ON PAGE 338

1. American alligator
2. gray tree frog
3. eastern screech owl
4. black-tailed deer
5. black rhino
6. feather star shrimp

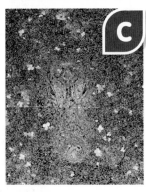

CRITTER CHAT

I'M A LEAN, GREEN, BUG-EATING MACHINE!

If animals used social media, what would they say? Follow this red-eyed tree frog's day as it updates its feed.

Red-Eyed Tree Frog

LIVES IN: Southern Mexico and Central America
SCREEN NAME FabFrog
FRIENDS

KEEL-BILLED TOUCAN	CENTRAL AMERICAN AGOUTI	KINKAJOU
BananaBeak	ForestFriend	KinkaWoo

START

7:20 p.m.

FabFrog: New profile pic alert! How do I look?

BananaBeak: Uh, like a snack. But I've found a different treat, so you can chill out ... for now.

FabFrog: Hey @BananaBeak, where's that tree you're tasting from? I'll munch up whatever fruit you drop.

ForestFriend

KinkaWoo: Now *I'm* in the mood for something sweet. Anybody seen a beehive? #AskingForMyTongue

10 p.m.

FabFrog: Thanks to my suction-cup toes, I'm totally an acrobat—er, acro-*frog!*

KinkaWoo: That looks like a lot of work when you could just *hang* out. Tails are for winners.

BananaBeak: You're all just bummed you're stuck to the trees. I'm a sky princess.

ForestFriend: The forest floor is good enough for me. I like my home so much I rub my butt all over it so it smells like me. #Normal

FabFrog: That's so gross, even for me—and I ooze smelly slime.

5 a.m.

FabFrog: Now you see me—now you don't. #PerfectCamouflage

ForestFriend: Are we playing hide-and-seek? I'm pretty great at disappearing in the brush.

KinkaWoo: Oh, that reminds me ... I've got to go find my hide-and-sleep tree hole. See y'all tomorrow!

FabFrog: PSYCH! I was only hiding to jump out and ambush a moth. #Crunchy

BananaBeak: Whoa—you've got some serious leaping skills. And I thought *I* was the only one that could fly!

FUNNY FILL-IN

Ask a friend to give you words to fill in the blanks in this story and write them on a separate sheet of paper. Then read the story out loud and fill in the words for a laugh.

My family went on safari in _____ to ride a raft down the _____ and check
                              country   body of water

out _____. I boarded first. Suddenly the raft began to _____. I was
      water animal, plural   verb

_____ down the _____ by myself! _____ miles later a bunch
verb ending in –ing   liquid   large number

of _____ surrounded me. They flapped their _____;
   something that flies, plural   animal body part, plural

then without warning they grabbed my _____ and lifted me high into the air.
                                       article of clothing

"_____!" I yelled. When I finally got the nerve to look down, I saw some _____
  exclamation   furry animal

cubs and a(n) _____ _____ that could run faster than _____.
              color   spotted animal   famous athlete

Then I spotted my parents. "Thanks!" I called to the fliers as they _____ me on
                                                                      past-tense verb

the ground. No one at home will believe this _____ tale.
                                              adjective

Play more Funny Fill-In!
natgeokids.com/ffi

144

WHAT IN THE WORLD?

OVER THE RAINBOW

These photographs show close-up views of rainbow-colored objects. On a separate sheet of paper, unscramble the letters to identify what's in each picture.

ANSWERS ON PAGE 338

APNTI EST

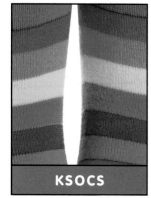

KSOCS

POLPLIOL

TRAORP

AKEC

YOCARSN

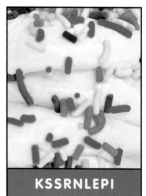

KSSRNLEPI

LABMRELU

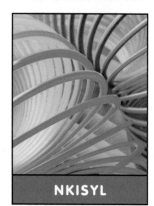

NKISYL

145

"YOUR MOM SENT ME UP SO YOU WON'T BE LATE FOR SCHOOL AGAIN!"

"DIDN'T I TELL YOU TO CLEAN OFF YOUR BELLY BEFORE SNACK TIME?"

"IT'S JUST UNTIL THE BRACES COME OFF."

"AW, MOM. DO I REALLY HAVE TO GO TO SCHOOL TODAY?"

The new neighbors must be door mice.

Just Joking

CROCODILE

KNOCK, KNOCK.
Who's there?
Dinosaur.
Dinosaur who?
Dinosaur because he fell down!

Q What happened when 500 hares got loose in the center of town?

A The police had to comb the area.

Q What do you call a very popular perfume?

A A best smeller.

TONGUE TWISTER Say this fast three times:
Six slick sightseers click.

FUNNY FILL-IN

Ask a friend to give you words to fill in the blanks in this story and write them on a separate sheet of paper. Then read the story out loud and fill in the words for a laugh.

My friends and I _____ a machine that can _____ stuff. But before we could show it off,
past-tense verb / verb

we had to _____ it. I put a(n) _____ on a table and _____ a button. Then there was
verb / noun / past-tense verb

a(n) _____ blast. Suddenly I saw green strips towering above me. It was grass—we
adjective

_____ _____ ourselves! We heard a noise. I turned and saw a(n) _____
adverb ending in -ly / past-tense verb / noun

with eight eyes. My friend quickly scaled a nearby _____ , while the rest of us tied our
something in nature

_____ together to make a rope. Our friend pulled us to safety, with the creature
article of clothing, plural

_____ toward us. A(n) _____ picked us up from there, dropping us on top of our machine.
verb ending in -ing / flying animal

We gathered together and _____ on the button. I opened my _____ . I was
past-tense verb / body part, plural

_____ enough to see into my house! Our big adventure had come to a close.
adjective

148

WHAT IN THE WORLD?

WILD STYLE

These images show close-up views of African animals. On a separate sheet of paper, unscramble the letters to identify what's in each picture.

ANSWERS ON PAGE 338

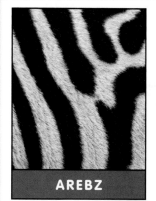

AREBZ

LIGAMNOF

FAEIRGF

AHLNEPET

ALMDILNR

NACHOMEEL

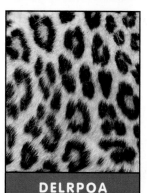

DELRPOA

TRSEITOO

RIFACNA IDLW OGD

149

FIND THE HIDDEN ANIMALS

Animals often blend in with their environments for protection. Find each animal listed below in one of the pictures. On a separate sheet of paper, write the letter of the correct picture and the animal's name.

ANSWERS ON PAGE 338

1. crabs
2. hare
3. alligator
4. praying mantis
5. seal
6. frogfish

FUNNY FILL-IN

Ask a friend to give you words to fill in the blanks in this story and write them on a separate sheet of paper. Then read the story out loud and fill in the words for a laugh.

This weekend, my mother, sister, and I _____ our _____ _____
                                        past-tense verb   adjective   type of transportation

to a car wash. As a(n) _____ waved us in, we heard a(n) _____. A huge
                          type of job   funny sound

_____ was _____ cars! "_____!" we yelled. Using its
   animal   verb ending in –ing   exclamation

_____, it wiped the back of the _____ in front of us. _____ dripped
   body part   noun   something gross

from a(n) _____ strapped to its hoof as it sprayed _____ with its trunk. Then the
             noun   noun

creature _____ the cars with its ears. Everyone was covered in _____.
            past-tense verb   type of liquid

Who knows where that _____ came from—but our car has never
                         same animal

been so _____!
           adjective

WHAT IN THE WORLD?

POSITIVELY PURPLE

These images show close-up views of purple objects. On a separate sheet of paper, unscramble the letters to identify what's in each picture.

ANSWERS ON PAGE 338

UMLSP

ANYR

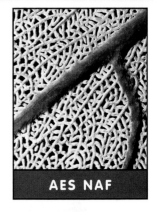

AES NAF

LCOHASEE

ESA RTAS

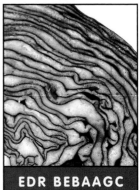

EDR BEBAAGC

ARYOSCN

DCRHOI

TMHESATY

SIGNS OF THE TIMES

Seeing isn't always believing. Two of these funny signs are not real. Can you figure out which two are fake?

ANSWERS ON PAGE 338

1

ON THIS SITE IN 1897 NOTHING HAPPENED.

2

ANT XING

3

ΠΡΟΣΟΧΗ ΚΙΝΔΥΝΟΣ
ΔΡΟΜΟΣ ΟΛΙΣΘΗΡΟΣ
ΕΚ ΣΤΑΦΥΛΟΧΥΜΟΥ
Caution Danger Road Slippery With Grape Juice

4

ATTRACTIONS·AHEAD

Myway Orda Highway

Visitor Center ?

5

COWGIRL PARKING ONLY
ALL OTHERS WILL BE LASSOED

6

PUSH

7

153

Just Joking

DACHSHUND

KNOCK, KNOCK.
Who's there?
Howl.
Howl who?
Howl you feeling today?

Q How did the flea get from one dog to the other?

A It itchhiked.

Q What did the dog bring on her camping trip?

A A pup-up tent.

Q What's the biggest problem with corgi jokes?

A They're too short.

Just Joking DOGS

Check out this book!

FUNNY FILL-IN

Ask a friend to give you words to fill in the blanks in this story and write them on a separate sheet of paper. Then read the story out loud and fill in the words for a laugh.

Play more Funny Fill-In!
natgeokids.com/ffi

_____ and I have a winter tradition. Every year we put on all the sweaters we can find,
_{friend's name}

pack sandwiches and a thermos of _____ , and go hiking in the mountains. All that changed when
_{liquid}

my family moved to _____ , where it's always _____°F! But we had to follow our
_{warm place} _{large number}

tradition. So this year we put on our _____ , packed _____ soup, and
_{type of warm clothing, plural} _{something gross}

rented a(n) _____ . We _____ up a tall _____ until we could see all
_{type of transportation} _{past-tense verb} _{noun}

the way to _____ . We _____ our _____ onto our
_{faraway city} _{past-tense verb} _{type of athletic equipment, plural}

_____ and, with a(n) _____ , pushed ourselves down. We were moving faster than
_{body part, plural} _{sound}

a(n) _____ , and _____ were _____ our faces. "_____!"
_{animal} _{something small, plural} _{verb ending in -ing} _{exclamation}

we yelled. It was a total blast until we realized our ride was right where we left it—way up at the top.

155

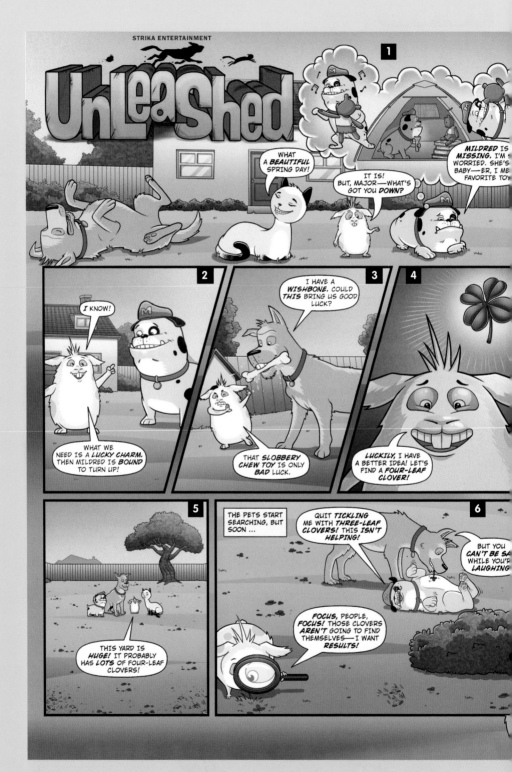

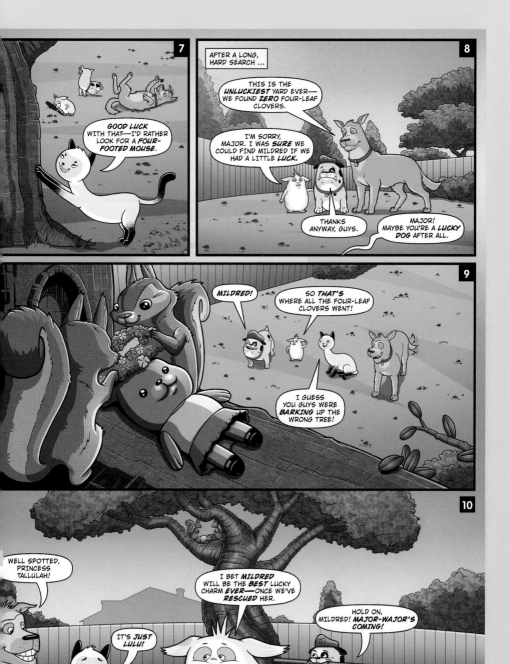

Macrophotography provides a
close-up look at bismuth crystals.

SPACE and EARTH

A LOOK INSIDE

The distance from Earth's surface to its center is some 4,000 miles (6,437 km) at the Equator. There are four layers: a thin, rigid crust; the rocky mantle; the outer core, which is a layer of molten iron; and finally the inner core, which is believed to be mostly solid iron.

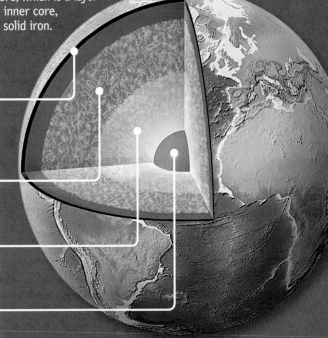

The **CRUST** includes tectonic plates, landmasses, and the ocean. Its average thickness varies from 5 to 25 miles (8 to 40 km).

The **MANTLE** is about 1,800 miles (2,900 km) of hot, thick, solid rock.

The **OUTER CORE** is liquid molten rock made mostly of iron and nickel.

The **INNER CORE** is a solid center made mostly of iron and nickel.

What if you could dig to the other side of Earth?

Got a magma-proof suit and a magical drill that can cut through any surface? Then you're ready to dig some 7,900 miles (12,714 km) to Earth's other side. But first you'd need to drill about 25 miles (40 km) through the planet's ultra-tough crust to its mantle. The heat and pressure at the mantle are intense enough to turn carbon into diamonds—and to, um, crush you. If you were able to survive, you'd still have to bore 1,800 more miles (2,897 km) to hit Earth's Mars-size core that can reach 11,000°F (6093°C). Now just keep drilling through the core and then the mantle and crust on the opposite side until you resurface on the planet's other side. But exit your tunnel fast. A hole dug through Earth would close quickly as surrounding rock filled in the empty space. The closing of the tunnel might cause small earthquakes, and your path home would definitely be blocked. Happy digging!

ROCK STARS

Rocks and minerals are everywhere on Earth! And it can be a challenge to tell one from the other. So what's the difference between a rock and a mineral? A rock is a naturally occurring solid object made mostly from minerals. Minerals are solid, nonliving substances that occur in nature—and the basic components of most rocks. Rocks can be made of just one mineral or, like granite, of many minerals. But not all rocks are made of minerals: Coal comes from plant material, while amber is formed from ancient tree resin.

Igneous

Named for the Greek word meaning "from fire," igneous rocks form when hot, molten liquid called magma cools. Pools of magma form deep underground and slowly work their way to Earth's surface. If they make it all the way, the liquid rock erupts and is called lava. As the layers of lava build up, they form a mountain called a volcano. Typical igneous rocks include obsidian, basalt, and pumice, which is so chock-full of gas bubbles that it actually floats in water.

ANDESITE

GRANITE PORPHYRY

Metamorphic

Metamorphic rocks are the masters of change! These rocks were once igneous or sedimentary, but thanks to intense heat and pressure deep within Earth, they have undergone a total transformation from their original form. These rocks never truly melt; instead, the heat twists and bends them until their shapes substantially change. Metamorphic rocks include slate as well as marble, which is used for buildings, monuments, and sculptures.

MICA SCHIST

BANDED GNEISS

Sedimentary

When wind, water, and ice constantly wear away and weather rocks, smaller pieces called sediment are left behind. These are sedimentary rocks, also known as gravel, sand, silt, and clay. As water flows downhill, it carries the sedimentary grains into lakes and oceans, where they are deposited. As the loose sediment piles up, the grains eventually get compacted or cemented back together again. The result is new sedimentary rock. Sandstone, gypsum, limestone, and shale are sedimentary rocks that have formed this way.

LIMESTONE

HALITE

Identifying Minerals

With so many different minerals in the world, it can be a challenge to tell one from another. Fortunately, each mineral has physical characteristics that geologists and amateur rock collectors use to tell them apart. Check out the physical characteristics below: color, luster, streak, cleavage, fracture, and hardness.

Color

When you look at a mineral, the first thing you see is its color. In some minerals, this is a key factor because their colors are almost always the same. For example, azurite, below, is always blue. But in other cases, impurities can change the natural color of a mineral. For instance, fluorite, above, can be green, red, violet, and other colors as well. The change makes it a challenge to identify by color alone.

FLUORITE

AZURITE

Luster

"Luster" refers to the way light reflects from the surface of a mineral. Does a mineral appear metallic, like gold or silver? Or is it pearly like orpiment, or brilliant like diamond? "Earthy," "glassy," "silky," and "dull" are a few other terms used to describe luster.

ORPIMENT

DIAMOND

Streak

The "streak" is the color of the mineral's powder. When minerals are ground into powder, they often have a different color than when they are in crystal form. For example, the mineral pyrite usually looks gold, but when it is rubbed against a ceramic tile called a "streak plate," the mark it leaves is black.

PYRITE

Cleavage

"Cleavage" describes the way a mineral breaks. Because the structure of a specific mineral is always the same, it tends to break in the same pattern. Not all minerals have cleavage, but the minerals that do, like this microcline, break evenly in one or more directions. These minerals are usually described as having "perfect cleavage." But if the break isn't smooth and clean, cleavage can be considered "good" or "poor."

MICROCLINE

GOLD

Fracture

Some minerals, such as gold, do not break with cleavage. Instead, geologists say that they "fracture." There are different types of fractures, and, depending on the mineral, the fracture may be described as jagged, splintery, even, or uneven.

Hardness

The level of ease or difficulty with which a mineral can be scratched refers to its "hardness." Hardness is measured using a special chart called the Mohs Hardness Scale. The Mohs scale goes from 1 to 10. Softer minerals, which appear on the lower end of the scale, can be scratched by the harder minerals on the upper end of the scale.

RATING	MINERAL NAME	EXAMPLES
1	TALC	BAR OF SOAP
2	GYPSUM	FINGERNAIL
3	CALCITE	COPPER PENNY
4	FLUORITE	SOFT IRON NAIL
5	APATITE	STEEL POCKETKNIFE BLADE
6	ORTHOCLASE	WINDOW GLASS
7	QUARTZ	HARDENED STEEL FILE
8	TOPAZ	TOPAZ
9	CORUNDUM	RUBY, SAPPHIRE
10	DIAMOND	DIAMOND

HOW TO MAKE A
DIAMOND

These sparkly gems have been treasured for thousands of years, but geologists still aren't exactly sure how diamonds formed on Earth. Here's how scientists think natural diamonds are made.

1 FIND CARBON BURIED

^{6}C

100 MILES
(161 km)
BELOW EARTH'S SURFACE.

2 HEAT TO ABOUT

2200°F
(1204°C)
IN EARTH'S MANTLE.

3 SQUEEZE UNDER HIGH PRESSURE OF

725,000
POUNDS PER SQUARE INCH
(50,973 kg per sq cm).

The largest rough diamond was discovered in **1905** and weighed **1.4 POUNDS** (635 g).

4 WAIT

1–3 BILLION YEARS
(THAT'S ALMOST 75 PERCENT OF THE AGE OF EARTH!)

5
CUT RAW STONE INTO THE CLASSIC DIAMOND SHAPE WITH

58 FACETS.

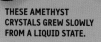

EVERY MINERAL HAS ITS OWN SPECIAL CRYSTAL SHAPE, CALLED ITS HABIT.

Mineral crystals usually begin as a liquid. As the liquid cools or evaporates, the atoms in the liquid begin to join together to form the crystal. Large well-formed crystals will only grow if the conditions are right.

Salt of the Earth

THESE AMETHYST CRYSTALS GREW SLOWLY FROM A LIQUID STATE.

In this experiment you can try your hand at growing two different types of crystals using some simple salt solutions.
Here's what you'll need:

| 2 small 8 oz (250 mL) disposable clear plastic cups | Container of table salt | Container of Epsom salts (available at most pharmacies) | Hot water | Permanent marker | Magnifying glass |

1 Use the marker to label one cup "plain salt" and the other "Epsom salts." Fill each cup about halfway with hot water.

2 Stir in 5 or 6 teaspoons (25–30 mL) of table salt into the cup labeled "plain salt" so that all the salt dissolves. Use a different teaspoon to do the same with the Epsom salts in the other cup.

3 Place both cups in a safe location, and allow the water to evaporate completely. It should take about a week or so.

4 After the water has completely evaporated from each cup, carefully observe the crystals that have formed on the bottom of each cup by using the magnifying glass.

You will see that the crystal habit of the table salt is little cubes, while the Epsom salt appears to be long needlelike prisms. You can experiment further by mixing different amounts of the two salts together to see what types of crystals they produce.

TABLE SALT

EPSOM SALT

A HOT TOPIC

WHAT GOES ON
INSIDE A STEAMING, BREWING VOLCANO?

If you could look inside a volcano, you'd see something that looks like a long pipe, called a conduit. It leads from inside the magma chamber under the crust up to a vent, or opening, at the top of the mountain. Some conduits have branches that shoot off to the side, called fissures.

When pressure builds from gases inside the volcano, the gases must find an escape, and they head up toward the surface! An eruption occurs when lava, gases, ash, and rocks explode out of the vent.

CRATER

VENT

CONDUIT

FISSURE

MAGMA CHAMBER

HARDENED LAVA AND ASH LAYER

TYPES OF VOLCANOES

CINDER CONE VOLCANO
Eve Cone, Canada

Cinder cone volcanoes look like an upside-down bowl. They spew cinder and hot ash. Some of these volcanoes smoke and erupt for years at a time.

COMPOSITE VOLCANO
Licancábur, Chile

Composite volcanoes, or stratovolcanoes, form as lava, ash, and cinder from previous eruptions harden and build up over time. These volcanoes spit out pyroclastic flows, or thick explosions of hot ash that travel at hundreds of miles an hour.

SHIELD VOLCANO
Mauna Loa, Hawaii, U.S.A.

The gentle, broad slopes of a shield volcano look like an ancient warrior's shield. Its eruptions are often slower. Lava splatters and bubbles rather than shooting forcefully into the air.

LAVA DOME VOLCANO
Mount St. Helens, Washington, U.S.A.

Dome volcanoes have steep sides. Hardened lava often plugs the vent at the top of a dome volcano. Pressure builds beneath the surface until the top blows.

RING OF FIRE

Although volcanoes are found on every continent, most are located along an arc known as the Ring of Fire. This area, which forms a horseshoe shape in the Pacific Ocean, stretches some 24,900 miles (40,000 km). Several of the large, rigid plates that make up Earth's surface are found here, and they are prone to shifting toward each other and colliding. The result? Volcanic eruptions and earthquakes—and plenty of them. In fact, the Ring of Fire hosts 90 percent of the world's recorded earthquakes and about 75 percent of active volcanoes. Turn the page for more hot facts about the Ring of Fire!

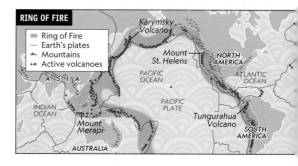

RING OF FIRE

- Ring of Fire
- Earth's plates
- Mountains
- Active volcanoes

Karymsky Volcano

Mount St. Helens

NORTH AMERICA

ASIA

PACIFIC OCEAN

ATLANTIC OCEAN

INDIAN OCEAN

PACIFIC PLATE

Tungurahua Volcano

SOUTH AMERICA

Mount Merapi

AUSTRALIA

10 HOT THINGS ABOUT THE RING OF FIRE

MOST OF THE 450-PLUS VOLCANOES FOUND ALONG THE RING OF FIRE ARE LOCATED **UNDERWATER.**

With **more than a dozen recorded eruptions** since 1519, Popocatépetl in Mexico is among the **most dangerous volcanoes** in the Ring of Fire.

Part of the **RING OF FIRE**, Russia's **KAMCHATKA PENINSULA** contains more than **150 VOLCANOES**, about 30 of which are active.

EXPERTS THINK THE RING OF FIRE STARTED TO FORM SOME **100 MILLION YEARS AGO—** DURING THE **CRETACEOUS PERIOD** WHEN DINOSAURS WERE WIDESPREAD.

The world's **strongest earthquake** to date— **Chile's Valdivia earthquake** in 1960—resulted from activity along the Ring of Fire.

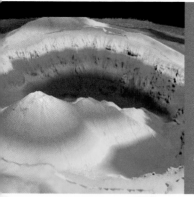

A DEEP-SEA ROBOT USED **SONAR** TO CREATE A COLORFUL PHOTO OF THE **UNDERWATER BROTHERS VOLCANO,** SUBMERGED ABOUT A MILE (1,600 M) DEEP IN THE PACIFIC OCEAN.

The Ring of Fire is home to the Mariana Trench. At **7 MILES** (11 km) deep, it's the **deepest part** of any of the world's oceans.

The **Ring of Fire** is **not an actual ring—** rather it is in the **shape of a horseshoe.**

LAVA GULLS that live on the Galápagos Islands, which are located on the Ring of Fire, have **DARK PLUMAGE** to blend in with the **DARK VOLCANIC ROCK.**

ABOUT **10 PERCENT** OF THE WORLD'S VOLCANIC ACTIVITY OCCURS IN **JAPAN,** WHICH LIES ALONG THE WESTERN **EDGE OF THE RING OF FIRE.**

A Universe of Galaxies

5 FAR-OUT FEATURES

When astronauts first journeyed beyond Earth's orbit in 1968, they looked back to their home planet. The big-picture view of our place in space changed the astronauts' lives—and perhaps humanity. If you could leave the universe and similarly look back, what would you see? Remarkably, scientists are mapping this massive area. They see ... bubbles. Not literal soap bubbles, of course, but a structure that looks like a pan full of them. Like bubble walls, thin surfaces curve around empty spaces in an elegantly simple structure. Zoom in to see that these surfaces are groups of galaxies. Zoom in farther to find one galaxy, with an ordinary star—our sun—orbited by an ordinary planet—Earth. How extraordinary.

2 DARK MATTER

The universe holds a mysterious source of gravity that cannot be properly explained. This unseen matter—the ghostly dark ring in this composite Hubble telescope photo—seems to pull on galaxy clusters, drawing galaxies toward it. But what is this strange stuff? It's not giant black holes, planets, stars, or anti-matter. These would show themselves indirectly. For now, astronomers call this source of gravity "dark matter."

1 GALAXY CLUSTERS AND SUPERCLUSTERS

Gravity pulls things together—gas in stars, stars in galaxies. Galaxies gather, too, sometimes by the thousands, forming galaxy clusters and superclusters with tremendously superheated gas. This gas can be as hot as 180 million degrees Fahrenheit (100 million degrees Celsius), filling space between them. These clusters hide a secret. The gravity among the galaxies isn't enough to bring them together. The source of the extra gravity is a dark secret.

DIGITAL TRAVELER!

Take a simulated flight through our universe, thanks to the data collected by the Sloan Digital Sky Survey. Ask an adult to help you search the internet for "APOD flight through universe sdss." Sit back and enjoy the ride!

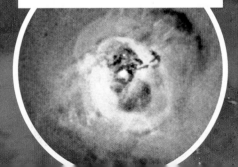

3 IT STARTED WHEN ...
The Big Bang

Long ago, the universe was compressed: It was hotter, smaller, denser than now, and completely uniform—almost. Extremely minor unevenness led to a powerful energy release that astronomers call the big bang. In a blip of time, the universe expanded tremendously. The first particles formed. Atoms, galaxies, forces, and light ... all developed from this. Today's great filaments (see fact 4) may be organized where those first uneven patches existed.

4 FILAMENTS AND SHEETS
Bubbles of Space

What is the universe like at its grandest scale? The biggest big-picture view is jaw-dropping. Clusters and superclusters of galaxies—red and yellow areas in this illustration—along with dark matter, string together to form structures that are millions and billions of light-years long. These so-called walls, sheets, or filaments surround vast voids, or "bubbles," of nearly empty space—the blue areas. The universe has a structure, nonrandom and unexpected.

5 COLLISION ZONE

Saying that galaxies form clusters and superclusters is like saying two soccer teams simply meet. During a game, there's a lot of action and energy. Similarly, as clusters and superclusters form, there's lots going on—as evidenced by the super-high-energy x-rays that are detected (pink in this colorized image).

PLANETS

CERES

MARS

EARTH

VENUS

MERCURY

JUPITER

SUN

MERCURY
Average distance from the sun:
 35,980,000 miles (57,900,000 km)
Position from the sun in orbit: 1st
Equatorial diameter: 3,030 miles (4,878 km)
Length of day: 59 Earth days
Length of year: 88 Earth days
Known moons: 0
Fun fact: On Mercury, the sun appears to rise and set twice a day.

VENUS
Average distance from the sun:
 67,230,000 miles (108,200,000 km)
Position from the sun in orbit: 2nd
Equatorial diameter: 7,520 miles (12,100 km)
Length of day: 243 Earth days
Length of year: 224.7 Earth days
Known moons: 0
Fun fact: The surface pressure on Venus is so strong that it could melt lead and crush a submarine.

EARTH
Average distance from the sun:
 93,000,000 miles (149,600,000 km)
Position from the sun in orbit: 3rd
Equatorial diameter: 7,900 miles (12,750 km)
Length of day: 24 hours
Length of year: 365 days
Known moons: 1
Fun fact: Scientists believe a "mini moon"—most likely a small asteroid— recently circled Earth.

MARS
Average distance from the sun:
 141,633,000 miles (227,936,000 km)
Position from the sun in orbit: 4th
Equatorial diameter: 4,221 miles (6,794 km)
Length of day: 25 Earth hours
Length of year: 1.9 Earth years
Known moons: 2
Fun fact: Some dust storms on Mars may last for several months.

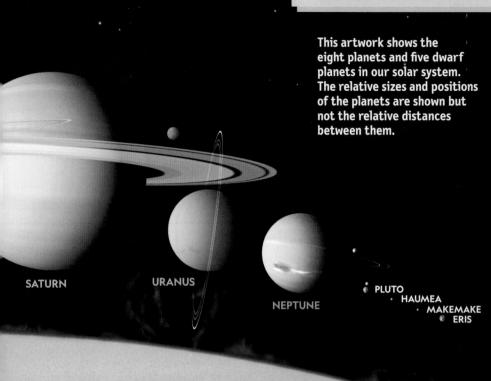

This artwork shows the eight planets and five dwarf planets in our solar system. The relative sizes and positions of the planets are shown but not the relative distances between them.

SATURN

URANUS

NEPTUNE

PLUTO
HAUMEA
MAKEMAKE
ERIS

JUPITER

Average distance from the sun:
   483,682,000 miles (778,412,000 km)
Position from the sun in orbit: 6th
Equatorial diameter: 88,840 miles (142,980 km)
Length of day: 9.9 Earth hours
Length of year: 11.9 Earth years
Known moons: 79*
Fun fact: A rover is expected to enter Jupiter's orbit in 2029.

SATURN

Average distance from the sun:
   890,800,000 miles (1,433,600,000 km)
Position from the sun in orbit: 7th
Equatorial diameter: 74,900 miles (120,540 km)
Length of day: 10.7 Earth hours
Length of year: 29.5 Earth years
Known moons: 82*
Fun fact: Some of the chunks of rock and ice that make up Saturn's rings are as big as a mountain.

URANUS

Average distance from the sun:
   1,784,000,000 miles (2,871,000,000 km)
Position from the sun in orbit: 8th
Equatorial diameter: 31,760 miles (51,120 km)
Length of day: 17.2 Earth hours
Length of year: 84 Earth years
Known moons: 27
Fun fact: Winds on Uranus can be 7.5 times stronger than hurricane winds on Earth.

NEPTUNE

Average distance from the sun:
   2,795,000,000 miles (4,498,000,000 km)
Position from the sun in orbit: 9th
Equatorial diameter: 30,775 miles (49,528 km)
Length of day: 16 Earth hours
Length of year: 164.8 Earth years
Known moons: 14
Fun fact: Neptune may have oceans of liquid diamond.

*Includes provisional moons, which await confirmation and naming from the International Astronomical Union.

For information about dwarf planets, see page 174.

DWARF PLANETS

Haumea

Eris

Pluto

Thanks to advanced technology, astronomers have been spotting many never-before-seen celestial bodies with their telescopes. One new discovery? A population of icy objects orbiting the sun beyond Pluto. The largest, like Pluto itself, are classified as dwarf planets. Smaller than the moon but still massive enough to pull themselves into a ball, dwarf planets nevertheless lack the gravitational "oomph" to clear their neighborhood of other sizable objects. So, although larger, more massive planets pretty much have their orbits to themselves, dwarf planets orbit the sun in swarms that include other dwarf planets as well as smaller chunks of rock or ice.

So far, astronomers have identified five dwarf planets: Ceres, Pluto, Haumea, Makemake, and Eris. There are many more newly discovered dwarf planets that will need additional study before they are named. Astronomers are observing hundreds of newly found objects in the frigid outer solar system. As time and technology advance, the family of known dwarf planets will surely continue to grow.

CERES
Position from the sun in orbit: 5th
Length of day: 9.1 Earth hours
Length of year: 4.6 Earth years
Known moons: 0

PLUTO
Position from the sun in orbit: 10th
Length of day: 6.4 Earth days
Length of year: 248 Earth years
Known moons: 5

HAUMEA
Position from the sun in orbit: 11th
Length of day: 3.9 Earth hours
Length of year: 282 Earth years
Known moons: 2

MAKEMAKE
Position from the sun in orbit: 12th
Length of day: 22.5 Earth hours
Length of year: 305 Earth years
Known moons: 1*

ERIS
Position from the sun in orbit: 13th
Length of day: 25.9 Earth hours
Length of year: 561 Earth years
Known moons: 1

*Includes provisional moons, which await confirmation and naming from the International Astronomical Union.

Bet You Didn't Know!

9 marvelous facts about Mars

1 MARS has 2 small MOONS.

2 A YEAR ON MARS lasts nearly twice as long as one on Earth.

3 The average TEMPERATURE on Mars is **-81°F** (-63°C).

4 You could JUMP 3 TIMES HIGHER on Mars than on Earth.

5 It takes 6 to 11 MONTHS for a spacecraft to TRAVEL from Earth to Mars.

6 By the 2040s, astronauts might VISIT MARS.

7 From Mars's surface, the SKY is the color of BUTTERSCOTCH.

8 One VOLCANO on MARS is about 3 TIMES TALLER than Mount Everest.

9 Mars is nicknamed THE RED PLANET because it's covered in RED DUST.

BLACK HOLES

A black hole really seems like a hole in space. Most black holes form when the core of a massive star collapses, falling into oblivion. A black hole has a stronger gravitational pull than anything else in the known universe. It's like a bottomless pit, swallowing anything that gets close enough to it to be pulled in. It's black because it pulls in light. Black holes come in different sizes. The smallest known black hole has a mass about three times that of the sun. The biggest one scientists have found so far has a mass about three billion times greater than the sun's. Really big black holes at the centers of galaxies probably form by swallowing enormous amounts of gas over time. In 2019, scientists released the first image of a black hole's silhouette (left). The image, previously thought impossible to record, was captured using a network of telescopes.

BLACK HOLE →

SKY DREAMS

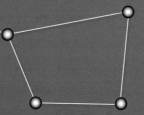

The Big Dipper, also called the Plough, is part of the constellation commonly known as the Great Bear.

LONG AGO, people looking at the sky noticed that some stars made shapes and patterns. By playing connect the dots, they imagined people and animals in the sky. Their legendary heroes and monsters were pictured in the stars.

Today, we call the star patterns identified by the ancient Greeks and Romans "constellations." There are 88 constellations in all. Some are only visible when you're north of the Equator, and some only when you're south of it.

In the 16th-century age of exploration, European ocean voyagers began visiting southern lands, and they named the constellations that are visible in the Southern Hemisphere, such as the Southern Cross. Astronomers used the star observations of these navigators to fill in the blank spots on their celestial maps.

Constellations aren't fixed in the sky. The star arrangement that makes up each one would look different from another location in the universe. Constellations also change over time because every star we see is moving through space. Over thousands of years, the stars in the Big Dipper, which is part of the larger constellation Ursa Major (the Great Bear), will move so far apart that the dipper pattern will disappear.

Sky Calendar 2022

Jupiter

Leonid meteor shower

Supermoon

JANUARY 3–4
QUADRANTIDS METEOR SHOWER PEAK. Featuring up to 40 meteors an hour, it is the first meteor shower of every new year.

MAY 6–7
ETA AQUARIDS METEOR SHOWER PEAK. View about 30 to 60 meteors an hour.

MAY 15–16
TOTAL LUNAR ECLIPSE. Look for the moon to darken and then take on a deep red color as it passes completely through Earth's umbra—or dark shadow. It will be visible in North America, Greenland, parts of western Europe, western Africa, and the Atlantic Ocean.

JUNE 14
SUPERMOON, FULL MOON. The moon will be full and at a close approach to Earth, likely appearing bigger and brighter than usual. Look for two more supermoons on July 13 and August 11.

AUGUST 12–13
PERSEID METEOR SHOWER PEAK. One of the best—see up to 90 meteors an hour! Best viewing is in the direction of the constellation Perseus.

AUGUST 14
SATURN AT OPPOSITION. This is your best chance to view the ringed planet in 2022.

AUGUST 27
MERCURY AT GREATEST EASTERN ELONGATION. Visible low in the western sky just after sunset, Mercury will be at its highest point above the horizon.

SEPTEMBER 26
JUPITER AT OPPOSITION. This is your best chance to view Jupiter in 2022. The gas giant will appear bright in the sky and be visible throughout the night. Got a pair of binoculars? You may be able to spot Jupiter's four largest moons as well.

OCTOBER 21–22
ORIONID METEOR SHOWER PEAK. View up to 20 meteors an hour. Look toward the constellation Orion for the best show.

NOVEMBER 8
TOTAL LUNAR ECLIPSE. The second total lunar eclipse of 2022 will be visible from Australia, Japan, eastern Russia, the Pacific Ocean, and some areas of western and central North America.

DECEMBER 13–14
GEMINID METEOR SHOWER PEAK. A spectacular show—see up to 120 multicolored meteors an hour!

2022—VARIOUS DATES
VIEW THE INTERNATIONAL SPACE STATION (ISS). Visit https://spotthestation .nasa.gov to find out when the ISS will be flying over your neighborhood.

Dates may vary slightly depending on your location. Check with a local planetarium for the best viewing times in your area.

QUIZ WHIZ

Are your space and Earth smarts out of this world? Take this quiz!

Write your answers on a piece of paper. Then check them below.

1 **True or false?** Salt is a type of crystal.

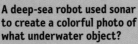

2 **How many moons does Mars have?**
a. 2   c. 6
b. 4   d. 12

3 **Fill in the blank.**
The world's strongest _____ resulted from activity along the Ring of Fire.

4 **True or false?** The gas in galaxy clusters can be as hot as 180 million degrees Fahrenheit (100 million degrees Celsius).

5 **A deep-sea robot used sonar to create a colorful photo of what underwater object?**
a. a trench
b. a ridge
c. a volcano
d. a coral reef

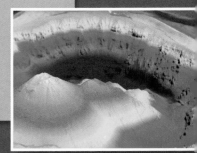

Not **STUMPED** yet? Check out the *NATIONAL GEOGRAPHIC KIDS QUIZ WHIZ* book collection for more crazy **SPACE AND EARTH** questions!

ANSWERS: 1. True; 2. a; 3. earthquake; 4. True; 5. c

HOMEWORK HELP

ACE YOUR SCIENCE FAIR

You can learn a lot about science from books, but to really experience it firsthand, you need to get into the lab and "do" some science. Whether you're entering a science fair or just want to learn more on your own, there are many scientific projects you can do. So put on your goggles and lab coat, and start experimenting.

Most likely, the topic of the project will be up to you. So remember to choose something that is interesting to you.

THE BASIS OF ALL SCIENTIFIC INVESTIGATION AND DISCOVERY IS THE SCIENTIFIC METHOD. CONDUCT YOUR EXPERIMENT USING THESE STEPS:

Observation/Research—Ask a question or identify a problem.

Hypothesis—Once you've asked a question, do some thinking and come up with some possible answers.

Experimentation—How can you determine if your hypothesis is correct? You test it. You perform an experiment. Make sure the experiment you design will produce an answer to your question.

Analysis—Gather your results, and use a consistent process to carefully measure the results.

Conclusion—Do the results support your hypothesis?

Report Your Findings—Communicate your results in the form of a paper that summarizes your entire experiment.

Bonus!
Take your project one step further. Your school may have an annual science fair, but there are also local, state, regional, and national science fair competitions. Compete with other students for awards, prizes, and scholarships!

EXPERIMENT DESIGN
There are three types of experiments you can do.

MODEL KIT—a display, such as an "erupting volcano" model. Simple and to the point.

DEMONSTRATION—shows the scientific principles in action, such as a tornado in a wind tunnel.

INVESTIGATION—the home run of science projects, and just the type of project for science fairs. This kind demonstrates proper scientific experimentation and uses the scientific method to reveal answers to questions.

AWESOME
EXPLORATION

Hot-air balloons soar above Cappadocia, Turkey.

10 COOL FACTS ABOUT THE GALÁPAGOS ISLANDS

As a marine scientist, National Geographic Explorer Salomé Buglass has spent countless hours studying the unique ecology of Ecuador's Galápagos Islands. Here, she reveals some intriguing things about her research there.

"IT'S FAIRLY COMMON TO SPOT A **GIANT TORTOISE** CROSSING THE ROAD OR A **MARINE IGUANA** SNEAKING INTO THE SUPERMARKET."

"When I have free time from work, I GO SURFING. I have to dodge turtles especially, or their hard shells will break my board!"

"**Blue-footed boobies are everywhere.** When they're diving for food, they travel at speeds up to **60 miles per hour** (97 km/h)."

"The **Galápagos penguins** are so adorable. They **mate for life,** and I like to look for my favorite couple."

"There is a **GREAT RESPECT FOR WILDLIFE** on the islands. We know to stay away from animals and **NOT PET OR FEED THEM.** We appreciate and admire nature from a distance."

"To study the oceans, we use robots with cameras, called **remotely operated vehicles (ROV),** to explore as far as **590 feet** (180 m) **below the water's surface."**

"Living on the Galápagos Islands is a unique experience. **Only a few locals can own a car,** SO EVERYONE RIDES BIKES."

"It's not unusual to spot some **whitetip reef sharks** basking in shallow water among mangroves."

"During a recent trip, we discovered **AN UNKNOWN SPECIES OF KELP. Finding this kind of kelp** in the tropical part of the world is like finding **A POLAR BEAR IN MIAMI!"**

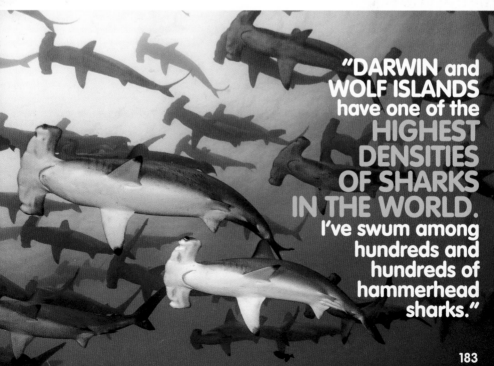

"**DARWIN** and **WOLF ISLANDS** have one of the **HIGHEST DENSITIES OF SHARKS IN THE WORLD.** I've swum among hundreds and hundreds of hammerhead sharks."

DARE TO EXPLORE

From listening to animals to reading the stars, three National Geographic explorers share secrets about communicating with the world.

"Don't be afraid to take things apart. Play with them, see how they work, and experiment on your own."

WHITE PREPARES TO MOUNT A LISTENING DEVICE TO A TREE THAT WILL HELP NAB ILLEGAL LOGGERS ON THE GROUND.

THE ENGINEER

Topher White attaches recycled cell phones to trees in remote rainforests around the world, hoping to pick up the sounds of illegal loggers. He describes trying to work while being swarmed by bees.

"Even though the forests can be home to illegal loggers, sometimes what's going on in the treetops is scarier than what's on the ground. One time I was installing a phone and bees kept landing on me. Eventually I was completely covered with them! But I had to finish the job, even if it meant getting a *lot* of bee stings.

"The phones I place each have an app that turns the phone into a listening device. They capture all the sounds of the rainforest. Listening to this noise can help us pick out the sounds of things like chain saws and logging trucks. If we can pinpoint the sounds of illegal logging, we can instantly send alerts to local authorities and tribes, who are then able to stop illegal loggers on the spot. In a way, the trees are telling us when they need help."

WANT TO BE AN ENGINEER?

STUDY	Mathematics, physics
WATCH	The documentary series *The Trials of Life*
READ	*The Wild Trees* by Richard Preston

WHITE ATTACHES A DEVICE TO A TREE IN INDONESIA, A COUNTRY IN SOUTHEAST ASIA.

FROM LEFT: ASTRONOMERS HALEY FICA, MUNAZZA ALAM, AND SARA CAMNASIO STAND IN FRONT OF A 21-FOOT (6.4-M)-WIDE TELESCOPE IN CHILE.

THE ASTRONOMER

Munazza Alam searches the sky for a planet that humans could live on one day. She discusses her hunt for what she calls the "Earth twin."

"I spend a lot of my nights at observatories atop mountain ranges, using high-resolution telescopes that are sometimes the size of a school bus. I'm observing faraway planets outside our solar system called exoplanets. By analyzing these exoplanets, I hope to discover if any of them have atmospheres similar to Earth that people could one day survive in. You could say I'm searching for Earth's twin. An 'Earth twin' would be a rocky planet with temperatures that would support liquid water. We haven't found one yet, but I do think we're getting closer. The more we study the stars and their planets, the more we can understand what they're like. As an astronomer, it's my job to keep examining the sky in the hopes that it'll reveal new things about our galaxy and beyond."

> "If you have a curiosity, don't let that flame go out. Never let go of that enthusiasm, because it will inspire you forever."

WANT TO BE AN ASTRONOMER?

STUDY	Physics, astronomy
WATCH	*Zathura: A Space Adventure*
READ	*The Magic School Bus: Lost in the Solar System* by Joanna Cole

THE VETERINARIAN

Jan Pol has helped nearly 500,000 animal patients in his 50 years as a veterinarian. His many amazing stories make it hard to choose just one, but here he recalls two supercute tales: a pair of injured hounds and a sick kitten.

> "I believe that every pet has the right to a good life."

"Dogs will chase anything that moves—including porcupines. One time two coonhounds came into the vet clinic with hundreds of porcupine quills stuck in their muzzles. Ouch! If we didn't remove the pointy spines, they could cause an infection that would make the dogs sick. So we sedated the pups and plucked the quills out one by one. They went back to their owner just fine, but dogs never learn their lesson—next time they meet a porcupine, I'm sure they'll be back!

"Another time a family brought in this stray kitten with a very infected eye. The family didn't want to give up on the kitten, so I wouldn't either. But I wasn't sure what was wrong until I started the surgery.

"I almost couldn't believe it—a huge insect larva was growing in the kitten's eye! We had to remove the eye, but the kitten was completely fine without it. Even better: The stray kitten found a home with the family who brought it in."

WANT TO BE A VETERINARIAN?

STUDY	Mathematics, biology
WATCH	*Beethoven*
READ	*All Creatures Great and Small* by James Herriot

DR. POL TREATS JUST ABOUT ANYTHING: HORSES, DOGS— EVEN HEDGEHOGS!

Keep Earth WILD

A National Geographic photographer gives you a behind-the-scenes look at his quest to save animals.

Joel Sartore has squealed like a pig, protected his camera from a parakeet, and suffered through a stink attack—all to help save animals through photography. "I hope people will look these animals in their eyes and then be inspired to protect them," says Sartore, a National Geographic photographer.

Sartore is on a mission to take pictures of more than 15,000 animal species living in captivity through his project, the National Geographic Photo Ark. During each photo shoot, he works with zookeepers, aquarists, and wildlife rehabbers to keep his subjects safe and comfortable. But things can still get a little, well, wild! Read on for some of Sartore's most memorable moments.

Moment of **SNOOZE**

GIANT PANDAS, *native to China*

Zoo Atlanta, Atlanta, Georgia, U.S.A.

These giant pandas were just a few months old when I put the football-size twins in a small, white photo tent and snapped a few pics as they tumbled on top of each other. But the youngsters were tiring out, and I knew I was losing my chance to get a memorable photo before they drifted off to sleep. One cub put his head on the back of the other, and I managed to capture an awesome shot just seconds before the two cubs fell asleep.

Some arctic fox dens are 300 years old.

Moment of **HA**

ARCTIC FOX, *native to the Arctic regions of Eurasia, North America, Greenland, and Iceland*

Great Bend Brit Spaugh Zoo, Great Bend, Kansas, U.S.A.

Todd the arctic fox wanted to sniff everything, but he was moving too quickly for me to get a good picture. I needed to do something surprising to get his attention, so I squealed like a pig! The weird sound made the fox stop, sit down, and tilt his head as if he were thinking, What's the matter with you? Good thing I was fast, because the pig noise only worked once. The next time I squealed, Todd completely ignored me.

More **WILDNESS!** Photo Ark spotlights all kinds of animals. Meet some of Joel Sartore's strangest subjects.

BUDGETT'S FROG

ORANGE SPOTTED FILEFISH

MEDITERRANEAN RED BUG

NORTH AMERICAN PORCUPINE

Sartore uses black or white backgrounds because he wants the focus to be on the animals. That way a mouse is as important as an elephant.

Newborn giant pandas are about the size of a stick of butter.

A single colony of gray-headed flying foxes can include a million bats.

Giraffes sometimes use their tongues to clean their ears.

Moment of YAY

GRAY-HEADED FLYING FOX, *native to southeastern Australia*

Australian Bat Clinic, Advancetown, Australia

When I arrived at the clinic, I was amazed to see all sorts of bats just hanging from laundry racks all over the rescue center. They sleepily watched me as I walked through the room and asked a staff member for a friendly flying fox to photograph. She scooped up a sweet bat and placed its feet on a wire rack in front of my backdrop. The calm bat didn't seem to mind being in front of the camera. The best part? This clinic rehabilitates bats that have torn their wings, and my subject was eventually released back into the wild.

Moment of YUM

RETICULATED GIRAFFE, *native to Africa*

Gladys Porter Zoo, Brownsville, Texas, U.S.A.

You definitely can't make a giraffe do anything it doesn't want to do. So to get this animal to be part of our photo shoot, we combined the activity with one of the giraffe's favorite things: lunch. We hung the huge black backdrop from the rafters in the part of the giraffe's enclosure where it gets fed. The giraffe ambled in, not minding me at all. For about 10 minutes, while the animal munched on bamboo leaves, I could take all the pictures I wanted. But as soon as lunch was over, the giraffe walked out, and our photo shoot was done.

SECRETS OF THE

DARING SCIENTISTS SEARCH FOR

A bizarre world lies under the sparkling Atlantic Ocean off the islands of the Bahamas, a world few have seen. Here, a system of superdeep underwater caves called blue holes contains odd-looking creatures, six-story-high rock formations, and even ancient human remains. Scuba-diving scientists must dodge whirlpools and squeeze through narrow tunnels to study blue holes—but their risky expeditions uncover amazing secrets.

FANGED CRUSTACEAN

NEON PINK CAVE WATER!

WEIRD WATER

Dive about 30 feet (9 m) into some blue holes, and the water turns pink. It looks nice—but it's poisonous. Because of a weak current here, rainwater and salt water mix in a way that traps a layer of toxic gas where pink bacteria thrive. To avoid getting ill, divers do not linger here.

In other blue holes, ocean tides can whip up whirlpools that look like giant bathtub drains. Scientists must circle carefully, or else risk being sucked in.

CREATURE FEATURE

Farther down, the caves become dark and twisty. Anthropologist and National Geographic Explorer Kenny Broad and his team have found many odd species here, including a tiny, transparent crustacean that is venomous (above).

Blue holes also contain fossils of animals— even birds. During the last ice age, these areas were dry and made perfect perches for the fliers. In one watery cave, a 12,000-year-old owl's nest was found surrounded by lizard bones—leftovers from the owl's meals.

BLUE HOLES

CLUES ABOUT UNDERWATER CAVES.

HOW BLUE HOLES FORMED

During past ice ages—the most recent about 18,000 years ago—water levels dropped and new land was exposed. Rain ate away at the land, forming holes that became deep caves. The caves filled with water after sea levels rose again. The deepest known blue hole is about 660 feet (200 m) deep.

BONE-CHILLING DISCOVERY

The most amazing find in the blue holes? Human skeletons. Scientists were able to trace the remains back 1,400 years to the time of the Lucayans—the first people believed to live in the Bahamas. No one is sure how the bones ended up in the submerged caves. But the team thinks the Lucayans might have used these areas as burial sites for their dead. With more investigation, the mystery of the skeletons may soon be solved. But scientists believe that other secrets are waiting to be uncovered in blue holes. "There are hundreds left that no human has seen," Broad says. "It's a whole other world for exploration."

A BLUE HOLE OFF BELIZE

SURVIVAL STORY

ORANGUTAN
TO THE RESCUE

After getting lost in the rainforest, National Geographic Explorer Agustín Fuentes received some very unlikely help. Read on to find out how Fuentes found his way home.

A ll Agustín Fuentes wanted to do was find the rare maroon leaf monkey. He'd been spending some time at Camp Leakey, an orangutan research camp on Borneo, a large, mountainous island in Southeast Asia, and he got the urge to take a day trip into the dense rainforest to seek one out. So he packed up his compass, headlamp, and small backpack, and off he went.

After four hours of following marked trails, Fuentes thought he caught a glimpse of a maroon leaf monkey. But then it scampered away into the rainforest. He had a decision to make: Should he stay on the trails and hope to see the monkey again? Or should he follow it?

"I took a risk and went off trail," Fuentes says.

Bad move. Forty-five minutes later, Fuentes found himself deep in the rainforest, with no maroon leaf monkey in sight. He used his compass to guess as to which direction he was heading and kept walking.

"Another 30 minutes passed, and I began to get a little nervous," says Fuentes. "Darkness was coming on quickly."

Fuentes tried to find comfort in the fact that he was in a place where another human had likely never been. As he looked around the rainforest, there was so much to admire.

"At one point, I spotted a shimmering metallic blue pool in an opening. I moved closer, and the blue image vibrated. Suddenly, hundreds of blue butterflies took flight before me," he says. "They had been feasting on wild pig droppings on the ground a few feet away."

Pulling out his compass, Fuentes headed south, thinking he'd eventually hit the river, if not a trail first. It paid off. After about 20 minutes, he saw an unmarked trail. Seconds later, he heard a rustling. He shone his headlight toward the sound. It was an orangutan! And not just any orangutan: Fuentes recognized right away that she was one of the apes being rehabilitated at camp.

"We looked at each other, and she held out her hand to me," he says. "Then she led me, hand in hand, to camp. Just like me, she was heading back for the evening."

Extreme Job!

There's not much normal about John Stevenson's job. A volcanologist, Stevenson evaluates eruptions, follows lava flow, and travels to remote locations to learn more about volcanoes. Read on for more details on his risky but rewarding career.

TESTING NEW RESEARCH EQUIPMENT

SCIENCE-MINDED "As a kid, I really liked science and nature, and in college I pursued chemical engineering but studied geology as well. Having a background in all of the sciences gave me a better understanding of the bigger picture, from volcano monitoring to understanding eruptions."

BIG DIG "I once spent ten days collecting pumice and ash samples from a 4,200-year-old eruption in Iceland. We'd dig in the soil until we found the layer of ash that we wanted, then spend up to two hours photographing and taking samples. At night, we'd find a nice spot by a stream, eat dinner, and camp out."

DANGER IN THE AIR "Being exposed to the edge of a lava flow can be dangerous. The air is hot and can be thick with poisonous sulfur dioxide gas. Once, while working at the active Bárðarbunga volcano in Iceland, we had to wear gas masks and use an electronic gas meter as dust swirled around us."

RAINING ASH "When I worked at Volcán de Colima in Mexico, we camped a few miles from the crater. One night, I woke up to a whooshing sound. This quickly changed to a *patter-patter-patter* that sounded like heavy rain falling on the tent. When I put my hand out to feel the rain, it was covered in coarse gray sand. The volcano had erupted, and ash was raining down on us. We quickly packed up our stuff and headed to a safer spot."

JOB PERKS "I get to play with fun gadgets in cool locations. If I didn't have to work, I would still go hiking and camping and play with gadgets and computers in my spare time anyway. I enjoy trying to solve the problems of getting the right data and finding a way to process it so that it can tell us about how the world works."

WORKING IN THE FIELD

Bet You Didn't Know!

⑧ deep facts about caves

1 **Certain ice caves** in Iceland are filled with **hot springs.**

2 1,000-year-old **popcorn** was found in a Utah, U.S.A., cave.

3 The world's largest cave— **Son Doong in Vietnam—** was discovered in 1990 by a local man seeking shelter from a storm.

4 **Speleology** is the **study of caves.**

5 **A cave in American Fork Canyon** was used as a **dance hall** during World War II.

6 Experts believe only about **1% of Earth's caves** have been discovered.

7 **Ancient** cave paintings in **Australia** show an almost **8-foot-tall** (2.4-m) **bird.**

8 In 2018, a **215**-mile (346-km) **underwater cave** was **discovered** near Tulum, Mexico.

A girl stands at the entrance of a cave in the French Alps.

HOW TO
SURVIVE A
KILLER BEE ATTACK!

1 Buzz Off
Killer bees—or Africanized honeybees—attack only when their hive is being threatened. If you see several bees buzzing near you, a hive is probably close by. Heed their "back off" attitude and slowly walk away.

2 Don't Join the Swat Team
Your first instinct might be to start swatting and slapping the bees. But that just makes the buzzers angry. Loud noises have the same effect, so don't start screaming, either. Just get away.

3 Don't Play Hide-and-Seek
Hives are often near water, but don't even think about outlasting the bees underwater. They'll hover and attack when you come up for air, even if you try to swim for it.

4 Run Like the Wind
Killer bees will chase you, but they'll give up when you're far enough away from the hive (usually about 200 yards [183 m]). Take off running and don't stop until the buzzing does.

5 Create a Cover-Up
Killer bees often go for the face and throat, which are the most dangerous places to be stung. While you're on the run, protect your face and neck with your hands, or pull your shirt over your head.

HOW TO
SURVIVE A
BEE STING!

1. De-Sting Yourself
First, get inside or to a cool place. Then, remove the stinger by scraping a fingernail over the area, like you would to get a splinter out. Do not squeeze the stinger or use tweezers unless you absolutely can't get it out any other way because squeezing it may release more venom.

2. Put It on Ice
Wash the area with soap and water and apply a cool compress to reduce swelling. Continue icing the spot for 20 minutes every hour. Place a washcloth or towel between the ice and your skin.

3. Treat It Right
With a parent's permission, take an antihistamine and gently rub a hydrocortisone cream on the sting site.

4. Hands Off
Make sure you don't scratch the sting. You'll just increase the pain and swelling.

5. Recognize Danger
If you experience severe burning and itching, swelling of the throat and/or mouth, difficulty breathing, weakness, or nausea, or if you already know you are allergic to bees, get to an emergency room immediately.

193

GETTING THE SHOT

Capturing good photographs of wild animals can be tough. To get amazing pictures of them, nature photographers often tap into their wild side, thinking and even acting like the creatures they're snapping. Whether tracking deadly snakes or swimming with penguins, the artists must be daring—but they also need to know when to keep their distance. Three amazing photographers tell their behind-the-scenes stories of how they got these incredible shots.

Check out this book!

GUIDE TO PHOTOGRAPHY

FANG FOCUS

PHOTOGRAPHER: Mattias Klum
ANIMAL: Jameson's mamba
SHOOT SITE: Cameroon, Africa

"The Jameson's mamba is beautiful but dangerous. It produces highly toxic venom. My team searched for weeks for the reptile, asking locals about the best spots to see one. At last we came across a Jameson's mamba peeking out from tree leaves. Carefully, I inched closer. It's important to make this kind of snake think that you don't see it. Otherwise it might feel threatened and strike you. At about four and a half feet (1.4 m) away, I took the picture. Then I backed up and the snake slid off."

SECRETS FROM AMAZING WILDLIFE PHOTOGRAPHERS

Usually solitary creatures, oceanic whitetip sharks have been observed swimming with pods of pilot whales.

SHARK TALE

PHOTOGRAPHER: Brian Skerry
ANIMAL: Oceanic whitetip shark
SHOOT SITE: The Bahamas

"I wanted to photograph an endangered oceanic whitetip shark. So I set sail with a group of scientists to an area where some had been sighted. Days later, the dorsal fin of a whitetip rose from the water near our boat. One scientist was lowered in a metal cage into the water to observe the fish. Then I dived in. Because I wasn't behind the protective bars, I had to be very careful. These nine-foot (2.7-m) sharks can be aggressive, but this one was just curious. She swam around us for two hours and allowed me to take pictures of her. She was the perfect model."

LEAPS and BOUNDS

PHOTOGRAPHER: Nick Nichols
ANIMAL: Bengal tiger
SHOOT SITE: Bandhavgarh National Park, India

"While following a tiger along a cliff, I saw him leap from the edge to his secret watering hole and take a drink. I wanted a close-up of the cat, but it wouldn't have been safe to approach him. Figuring he'd return to the spot, I set up a camera on the cliff that shoots off an infrared beam. Walking into the beam triggers the camera to click. The device was there for three months, but this was the only shot I got of the cat. Being near tigers makes the hair stand up on my arm. It was a gift to encounter such a magnificent creature."

Fewer than 2,500 Bengal tigers are left in the wild.

195

QUIZ WHIZ

Discover just how much you know about exploration with this quiz!

Write your answers on a piece of paper. Then check them below.

1 Where on Earth are you most likely to spot a blue-footed boobie?

a. Germany
b. Ghana
c. Galápagos Islands
d. Greece

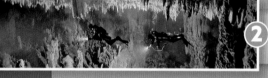

2 **True or false?** The deepest known blue hole is about 660 feet (200 m) deep.

3 This risky but rewarding job evaluates eruptions and follows lava flow.

a. volcanologist
b. conservationist
c. psychologist
d. agriculturalist

4 Giraffes sometimes use their tongues to clean their _____.

5 Which kind of animals does veterinarian Jan Pol treat in his practice?

a. horses
b. hedgehogs
c. kittens
d. all of the above

Not **STUMPED** yet? Check out the *NATIONAL GEOGRAPHIC KIDS QUIZ WHIZ* collection for more crazy **EXPLORATION** questions!

ANSWERS: 1. c; 2. True; 3. a; 4. ears; 5. d

HOMEWORK HELP

How to Write a Perfect Essay

Need to write an essay? Does the assignment feel as big as climbing Mount Everest? Fear not. You're up to the challenge! The following step-by-step tips will help you with this monumental task.

1 **BRAINSTORM.** Sometimes the subject matter of your essay is assigned to you, sometimes it's not. Either way, you have to decide what you want to say. Start by brainstorming some ideas, writing down any thoughts you have about the subject. Then read over everything you've come up with and consider which idea you think is the strongest. Ask yourself what you want to write about the most. Keep in mind the goal of your essay. Can you achieve the goal of the assignment with this topic? If so, you're good to go.

2 **WRITE A TOPIC SENTENCE.** This is the main idea of your essay, a statement of your thoughts on the subject. Again, consider the goal of your essay. Think of the topic sentence as an introduction that tells your readers what the rest of your essay will be about.

3 **OUTLINE YOUR IDEAS.** Once you have a good topic sentence, you then need to support that main idea with more detailed information, facts, thoughts, and examples. These supporting points answer one question about your topic sentence—"Why?" This is where research and perhaps more brainstorming come in. Then organize these points in the way you think makes the most sense, probably in order of importance. Now you have an outline for your essay.

4 **ON YOUR MARK, GET SET, WRITE!** Follow your outline, using each of your supporting points as the topic sentence of its own paragraph. Use descriptive words to get your ideas across to the readers. Go into detail, using specific information to tell your story or make your point. Stay on track, making sure that everything you include is somehow related to the main idea of your essay. Use transitions to make your writing flow.

5 **WRAP IT UP.** Finish your essay with a conclusion that summarizes your entire essay and restates your main idea.

6 **PROOFREAD AND REVISE.** Check for errors in spelling, capitalization, punctuation, and grammar. Look for ways to make your writing clear, understandable, and interesting. Use descriptive verbs, adjectives, or adverbs when possible. It also helps to have someone else read your work to point out things you might have missed. Then make the necessary corrections and changes in a second draft. Repeat this revision process once more to make your final draft as good as you can.

WONDERS of NATURE

Tiny bioluminescent shrimp known as sea fireflies glitter on the rocks and sand in Okayama, Japan.

Biomes

A BIOME, OFTEN CALLED A MAJOR LIFE ZONE,

is one of the natural world's major communities where plants and animals adapt to their specific surroundings. Biomes are classified depending on the predominant vegetation, climate, and geography of a region. They can be divided into six major types: forest, freshwater, marine, desert, grassland, and tundra. Each biome consists of many ecosystems.

Biomes are extremely important. Balanced ecological relationships among biomes help to maintain the environment and life on Earth as we know it. For example, an increase in one species of plant, such as an invasive one, can cause a ripple effect throughout a whole biome.

FOREST

Forests occupy about one-third of Earth's land area. There are three major types of forests: tropical, temperate, and boreal (taiga). Forests are home to a diversity of plants, some of which may hold medicinal qualities for humans, as well as thousands of animal species, some still undiscovered. Forests can also absorb carbon dioxide, a greenhouse gas, and give off oxygen.

The rabbit-size royal antelope lives in West Africa's dense forests.

FRESHWATER

Most water on Earth is salty, but freshwater ecosystems—including lakes, ponds, wetlands, rivers, and streams—usually contain water with less than one percent salt concentration. The countless animal and plant species that live in freshwater biomes vary from continent to continent, but they include algae, frogs, turtles, fish, and the larvae of many insects.

The place where freshwater and salt water meet is called an estuary.

MARINE

The marine biome covers almost three-fourths of Earth's surface, making it the largest habitat on our planet. Oceans make up the majority of the saltwater marine biome. Coral reefs are considered to be the most biodiverse of any of the biome habitats. The marine biome is home to more than one million plant and animal species.

Estimated to be up to 100,000 years old, seagrass growing in the Mediterranean Sea may be the oldest living thing on Earth.

DESERT

Covering about one-fifth of Earth's surface, deserts are places where precipitation is less than 10 inches (25 cm) a year. Although most deserts are hot, there are other kinds as well. The four major kinds of deserts are hot, semiarid, coastal, and cold. Far from being barren wastelands, deserts are biologically rich habitats.

Some sand dunes in the Sahara are tall enough to bury a 50-story building.

GRASSLAND

Biomes called grasslands are characterized by having grasses instead of large shrubs or trees. Grasslands generally have precipitation for only about half to three-fourths of the year. If it were more, they would become forests. Grasslands can be divided into two types: tropical (savannas) and temperate. Some of the world's largest land animals, such as elephants, live there.

Grasslands in North America are called prairies; in South America, they're called pampas.

TUNDRA

The coldest of all biomes, a tundra is characterized by an extremely cold climate, simple vegetation, little precipitation, poor nutrients, and a short growing season. There are two types of tundra: Arctic and alpine. A tundra is home to few kinds of vegetation. Surprisingly, though, quite a few animal species can survive the tundra's extremes, such as wolves, caribou, and even mosquitoes.

Formed 10,000 years ago, the Arctic tundra is the world's youngest biome.

10 WILD FACTS ABOUT THE AMAZON

The **AMAZON'S BLUE MORPHO BUTTERFLY** appears in **DIFFERENT COLORS** when observed from **DIFFERENT ANGLES.**

The Amazon BIOME spans eight countries: **BRAZIL, BOLIVIA, PERU, ECUADOR, COLOMBIA, VENEZUELA, GUYANA,** and **SURINAME,** plus the territory of **FRENCH GUIANA.**

The Amazon isn't just a **RAINFOREST.** Its other **ECOSYSTEMS INCLUDE FLOODPLAIN FORESTS, SAVANNAS, AND RIVERS.**

The **FLOODED FORESTS** of the **AMAZON** are among the only **PLACES ON EARTH** where **FISH FEED** on **FRUITS** and **SEEDS.**

Scientists think that some **PLANTS** in the Amazon can be **USED TO FIGHT CANCER.**

The Amazon is home to BOLDLY COLORED MACAWS, which mate for life and can LIVE FOR UP TO 60 YEARS.

15 PERCENT of all the **FRESHWATER ON EARTH** can be **FOUND** in the **AMAZON BASIN.**

RUBBER is made from **THE SAP** of the **RUBBER TREE,** which grows in the **AMAZON.**

The **AMAZON BIOME** is HOME to **10 percent** of the **WORLD'S KNOWN SPECIES**—including the endangered GIANT OTTER.

SPANNING MORE THAN 1.5 BILLION ACRES (6 million sq km), the **Amazon BIOME** is about **TWICE THE SIZE OF INDIA.**

THE OC

PACIFIC OCEAN

STATS

Surface area
65,436,200 sq mi (169,479,000 sq km)

Portion of Earth's water area
47 percent

Greatest depth
**Challenger Deep
(in the Mariana Trench)
-36,037 ft (-10,984 m)**

Surface temperatures
**Summer high: 90°F (32°C)
Winter low: 28°F (-2°C)**

Tides
**Highest: 30 ft (9 m) near Korean Peninsula
Lowest: 1 ft (0.3 m) near Midway Islands**

Cool creatures: **giant Pacific octopus,
bottlenose whale, clownfish, great
white shark**

Clownfish

ATLANTIC OCEAN

STATS

Surface area
35,338,500 sq mi (91,526,300 sq km)

Portion of Earth's water area
25 percent

Greatest depth
**Puerto Rico Trench
-28,232 ft (-8,605 m)**

Surface temperatures
**Summer high: 90°F (32°C)
Winter low: 28°F (-2°C)**

Tides
**Highest: 52 ft (16 m)
Bay of Fundy, Canada
Lowest: 1.5 ft (0.5 m)
Gulf of Mexico and Mediterranean Sea**

Cool creatures: **blue whale, Atlantic spotted
dolphin, sea turtle, bottlenose dolphin**

Bottlenose dolphin

EANS

INDIAN OCEAN

STATS

Surface area
28,839,800 sq mi (74,694,800 sq km)

Portion of Earth's water area
21 percent

Greatest depth
**Java Trench
-23,376 ft (-7,125 m)**

Surface temperatures
**Summer high: 93°F (34°C)
Winter low: 28°F (-2°C)**

Tides
**Highest: 36 ft (11 m)
Lowest: 2 ft (0.6 m)
Both along Australia's west coast**

Cool creatures: **humpback whale, Portuguese man-of-war, dugong (sea cow), leatherback turtle**

ARCTIC OCEAN

STATS

Surface area
5,390,000 sq mi (13,960,100 sq km)

Portion of Earth's water area
4 percent

Greatest depth
**Molloy Deep
-18,599 ft (-5,669 m)**

Surface temperatures
**Summer high: 41°F (5°C)
Winter low: 28°F (-2°C)**

Tides
Less than 1 ft (0.3 m) variation throughout the ocean

Cool creatures: **beluga whale, orca, harp seal, narwhal**

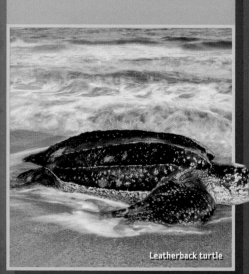

Leatherback turtle

Narwhal

To see the major oceans and bays in relation to landmasses, look at the map on pages 256 and 257.

Weather and Climate

Weather is the condition of the atmosphere—temperature, wind, humidity, and precipitation—at a given place at a given time. Climate, however, is the average weather for a particular place over a long period of time. Different places on Earth have different climates, but climate is not a random occurrence. It is a pattern that is controlled by factors such as latitude, elevation, prevailing winds, the temperature of ocean currents, and location on land relative to water. Climate is generally constant, but evidence indicates that human activity is causing a change in its patterns.

WEATHER EXTREMES

MOST SNOW RECORDED IN ONE SEASON: 1,140 inches (29 m) in Mount Baker, Washington, U.S.A.

FASTEST TEMPERATURE RISE: 49 degrees in two minutes, in Rapid City, South Dakota, U.S.A.

HEAVIEST HAILSTONE: 2.25 pounds (1 kg) in Gopalganj, Bangladesh

GLOBAL CLIMATE ZONES

Climatologists, people who study climate, have created different systems for classifying climates. One that is often used is called the Köppen system, which classifies climate zones according to precipitation, temperature, and vegetation. It has five major categories—tropical, dry, temperate, cold, and polar—with a sixth category for locations where high elevations override other factors.

ARCTIC OCEAN
ARCTIC CIRCLE
TROPIC OF CANCER
ATLANTIC OCEAN
PACIFIC OCEAN
EQUATOR
PACIFIC OCEAN
INDIAN OCEAN
TROPIC OF CAPRICORN
ANTARCTIC CIRCLE

Climate
Tropical Dry Temperate Cold Polar

Climate CHANGE

A POLAR BEAR ON A PIECE OF MELTING ICEBERG

Rising Temperatures, Explained

Fact: The world is getting warmer.
Earth's surface temperature has been increasing. In the past 50 years, our planet has warmed twice as fast as in the 50 years before that. This is the direct effect of climate change, which refers not only to the increase in Earth's average temperature (known as global warming), but also to its long-term effects on winds, rain, and ocean currents. Global warming is the reason glaciers and polar ice sheets are melting—resulting in rising sea levels and shrinking habitats. This makes survival for some animals a big challenge. Warming also means more flooding along the coasts and drought for inland areas.

Why are temperatures climbing?
While some of the recent climate changes can be tied to natural causes—such as changes in the sun's intensity, the unusually warm ocean

SCIENTISTS ARE CONCERNED THAT GREENLAND'S ICE SHEET HAS BEGUN TO MELT IN SUMMER. BIRTHDAY CANYON, SHOWN HERE, WAS CARVED BY MELTWATER.

currents of El Niño, and volcanic activity—human activities are the greatest contributor.

Everyday activities that require burning fossil fuels, such as driving gasoline-powered cars, contribute to global warming. These activities produce greenhouse gases, which enter the atmosphere and trap heat. At the current rate, Earth's global average temperature is projected to rise some 5.4°F (3°C) by the year 2100, and it will get even warmer after that. And as the climate continues to warm, it will unfortunately continue to affect the environment and our society in many ways.

WATER CYCLE

Precipitation falls

Water storage in ice and snow

Water vapor condenses in clouds

Water filters into the ground

Meltwater and surface runoff

Freshwater storage

Evaporation

Groundwater discharge

Water storage in ocean

The amount of water on Earth is more or less constant—

only the form changes. As the sun warms Earth's surface, liquid water is changed into water vapor in a process called **evaporation.** Water on the surface of plants' leaves turns into water vapor in a process called **transpiration.** As water vapor rises into the air, it cools and changes form again. This time, it becomes clouds in a process called **condensation.** Water droplets fall from the clouds as **precipitation,** which then travels as groundwater or runoff back to the lakes, rivers, and oceans, where the cycle (shown above) starts all over again.

To a meteorologist— a person who studies the weather—a "light rain" is less than 1/48 inch (0.5 mm). A "heavy rain" is more than 1/6 inch (4 mm).

You drink the same water as the dinosaurs! Earth has been recycling water for more than four billion years.

A MELTING WORLD

If all the ice on Earth melted, the world's oceans would rise 216 feet (66 m). But how high is that exactly? Check out this chart to see what might end up underwater.

THE STATUE OF LIBERTY 305 feet (93 m)

12 GIRAFFES 216 feet (66 m)

5 SCHOOL BUSES 200 feet (61 m)

6 ORCAS 192 feet (59 m)

THE SKY IS FALLING

THE SKY CAN'T ACTUALLY FALL, BUT MOISTURE IN THE AIR CAN AND DOES.

"PRECIPITATION" IS A FANCY WORD FOR THE WET STUFF THAT FALLS FROM THE SKY.

Precipitation is rain, freezing rain, sleet, snow, or hail. It forms when water vapor in the air condenses into clouds, gets heavier, and drops to the ground. Precipitation can ruin a picnic, but life on Earth couldn't exist without it.

Develops when ice crystals fall toward the ground, partly melt, and then refreeze. This happens mainly in winter when air near the ground is below freezing temperatures.

SLEET

RAIN

Formed when ice crystals in high, cold clouds get heavy and fall. Even in summer, falling ice crystals could remain frozen, but warm air near the ground melts them into raindrops.

FREEZING RAIN

Falls during the winter when rain freezes immediately as it hits a surface. Freezing rain creates layers of ice on the roads and causes dangerous driving conditions.

Produced when ice crystals in clouds get heavy enough to fall. The air has to be cold enough all the way down for the crystals to stay frozen.

SNOW

HAIL

Formed inside thunderstorms when ice crystals covered in water pass through patches of freezing air in the tops of cumulonimbus clouds. The water on the ice crystals freezes. The crystals become heavy and fall to the ground.

Types of Clouds

If you want a clue about the weather, look up at the clouds. They'll tell a lot about the condition of the air and what weather might be on the way. Clouds are made of both air and water. On fair days, warm air currents rise up and push against the water in clouds, keeping it from falling. But as the raindrops in a cloud get bigger, it's time to set them free. The bigger raindrops become too heavy for the air currents to hold up, and they fall to the ground.

1 STRATUS These clouds make the sky look like a bowl of thick gray porridge. They hang low in the sky, blanketing the day in dreary darkness. Stratus clouds form when cold, moist air close to the ground moves over a region.

2 CIRRUS These wispy tufts of clouds are thin and hang high up in the atmosphere where the air is extremely cold. Cirrus clouds are made of tiny ice crystals.

3 CUMULONIMBUS These are the monster clouds. Rising air currents force fluffy cumulus clouds to swell and shoot upward, as much as 70,000 feet (21,000 m). When these clouds bump against the top of the troposphere, or the tropopause, they flatten out on top like tabletops.

4 CUMULUS These white, fluffy clouds make people sing, "Oh, what a beautiful morning!" They form low in the atmosphere and look like marshmallows. They often mix with large patches of blue sky. Formed when hot air rises, cumulus clouds usually disappear when the air cools at night.

How Much Does a Cloud Weigh?

A light, fluffy cumulus cloud typically weighs about 216,000 pounds (98,000 kg). That's about the weight of 18 elephants. A rain-soaked cumulonimbus cloud typically weighs 105.8 million pounds (48 million kg), or about the same as 9,000 elephants.

Lightning!

There are about 3,000 **LIGHTNING FLASHES** on Earth every minute.

⚡ LIGHTNING SAFETY TIPS

INSIDE

Stay inside for 30 minutes after the last lightning or thunder.

Don't take baths or showers or wash dishes.

Avoid using landline phones (cell phones are okay), computers, TVs, and other electrical equipment.

OUTSIDE

Get into an enclosed structure or vehicle and shut the windows.

Stay away from bodies of water.

Avoid tall objects such as trees.

If you're in the open, crouch down (but do not lie flat) in the lowest place you can find.

Clouds suddenly appeared on the horizon, the sky turned dark, and it started to rain as Sabrina was hiking through the Grand Canyon with her parents.

As lightning flashed around them, Sabrina and her parents ran for cover. "When it stopped raining, we thought it was safe," says Sabrina. They started to hike back to their car along the trail. Then *zap!* A lightning bolt struck nearby. It happened so fast that the family didn't know what hit them. A jolt of electricity shot through their bodies. "It felt like a strong tingling over my whole body," says Sabrina. "It really hurt."

Sabrina and her family were lucky. The lightning didn't zap them directly, and they recovered within minutes. Some people aren't so lucky. Lightning kills thousands of people each year.

Lightning is a giant electric spark similar to the small spark you get when you walk across a carpet and touch a metal doorknob—but much stronger. One flash can contain a billion volts of electricity—enough to light a 100-watt incandescent bulb for three months. Lightning crackles through the air at a temperature five times hotter than the surface of the sun. The intense heat makes the surrounding air expand rapidly, creating a sound we know as thunder. Getting hit by lightning is rare, but everyone must be careful.

"For the first few years after I was struck, I was so scared every time there was a storm," says Sabrina. "Now I'm not scared. But I'm always cautious."

THE ENHANCED FUJITA SCALE

The Enhanced Fujita (EF) Scale, named after tornado expert T. Theodore Fujita, classifies tornadoes based on wind speed and the intensity of damage that they cause.

What Is a
Tornado?

EF0
65–85 mph winds
(105–137 km/h)
Slight damage

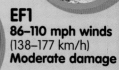

EF1
86–110 mph winds
(138–177 km/h)
Moderate damage

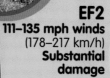

EF2
111–135 mph winds
(178–217 km/h)
Substantial damage

EF3
136–165 mph winds
(218–266 km/h)
Severe damage

EF4
166–200 mph winds
(267–322 km/h)
Massive damage

EF5
More than 200 mph winds
(322+ km/h)
Catastrophic damage

TORNADOES, ALSO KNOWN AS TWISTERS, are funnels of rapidly rotating air that are created during a thunderstorm. With wind speeds that can exceed 300 miles an hour (483 km/h), tornadoes have the power to pick up and destroy everything in their path.

THIS ROTATING FUNNEL OF AIR, formed in a cumulus or cumulonimbus cloud, became a tornado when it touched the ground.

TORNADOES HAVE OCCURRED IN ALL 50 U.S. STATES AND ON EVERY CONTINENT EXCEPT ANTARCTICA.

HURRICANE
HAPPENINGS

A storm is coming! But is this a tropical cyclone, a hurricane, or a typhoon? These weather events go by different names depending on where they form and how fast their winds get. Strong tropical cyclones are called hurricanes in the Atlantic and parts of the Pacific Ocean; in the western Pacific they are called typhoons. But any way you look at it, these storms pack a punch.

1,380 MILES (2,221 km)
Diameter of the most massive tropical cyclone ever recorded, 1979's Typhoon Tip

82°F (27.8°C)
Water surface temperature necessary for a tropical cyclone to form

16.6
Average number of tropical storms each year in the Northeast and Central Pacific Basins

164 FEET (50 m)
Depth of warm ocean water needed to fuel the storm

31
Number of days Hurricane John lasted in 1994

12.1

Average number of tropical storms in the Atlantic Basin each year

254
(408 km/h)
MILES AN HOUR

Strongest gust of storm wind ever recorded

12–25
(20–40 km)
MILES

Diameter of a hurricane eye

HURRICANE NAMES FOR 2022

Hurricane names come from six official international lists. The names alternate between male and female. When a storm becomes a hurricane, a name from the list is used, in alphabetical order. Each list is reused every six years. A name is "retired" if that hurricane caused a lot of damage or many deaths. Check out the names for Atlantic hurricanes in 2022:

Alex	Hermine	Owen
Bonnie	Ian	Paula
Colin	Julia	Richard
Danielle	Karl	Shary
Earl	Lisa	Tobias
Fiona	Martin	Virginie
Gaston	Nicole	Walter

SCALE OF HURRICANE INTENSITY

CATEGORY	ONE	TWO	THREE	FOUR	FIVE
DAMAGE	Minimal	Moderate	Extensive	Extreme	Catastrophic
WINDS	74–95 mph (119–153 km/h)	96–110 mph (154–177 km/h)	111–129 mph (178–208 km/h)	130–156 mph (209–251 km/h)	157 mph or higher (252+ km/h)

(DAMAGE refers to wind and water damage combined.)

Avalanche!

A million tons (907,184 t) of snow rumble eight miles (13 km) downhill, kicking up a cloud of snow dust visible a hundred miles (161 km) away.

This is not a scene from a disaster movie—this describes reality one day in April 1981. The mountain was Mount Sanford in Alaska, U.S.A., and the event was one of history's biggest avalanches. Amazingly, no one was hurt, and luckily, avalanches this big are rare.

An avalanche is a moving mass of snow that may contain ice, soil, rocks, and uprooted trees. The height of a mountain, the steepness of its slope, and the type of snow lying on it all help determine the likelihood of an avalanche. Avalanches begin when an unstable mass of snow breaks away from a mountainside and moves downhill. The growing river of snow picks up speed as it rushes down the mountain. Avalanches have been known to reach speeds of 155 miles an hour (249 km/h)—about the same as the record for downhill skiing.

To protect yourself and stay safe while playing in the mountains, follow our safety tips.

90 percent of AVALANCHE INCIDENTS are triggered by humans.

Safety TIPS

SAFETY FIRST
Before heading out, check for avalanche warnings.

EQUIPMENT
When hiking, carry safety equipment, including a long probe, a small shovel, and an emergency avalanche rescue beacon that signals your location.

NEVER GO IT ALONE
Don't hike in the mountain wilderness without a companion.

IF CAUGHT
If caught in the path of an avalanche, try to get to the side of it. If you can't, grab a tree as an anchor.

Wildfires!

or injured even more people and animals, including an estimated 5,000 koalas.

Although the impact of the wildfires was devastating, Australia has worked its way toward recovery. Massive financial contributions from the Australian government, as well as private donations, have helped to rebuild homes and habitats for animals, especially koalas, which are a vulnerable species. One welcome sign of renewal and recovery? The birth of a healthy baby koala, born at the Australian Reptile Park outside of Sydney. The baby (above) was part of their breeding program, aimed to replenish the animal's population. The joey, appropriately named "Ash," served as a beacon of hope for the future of Australia's native wildlife.

A deadly combination of drought and lightning sparked one of the worst ecological disasters in Australia. The recent wildfires, which burned for several months between late 2019 and early 2020, devastated parts of the country, charring a total of 42 million acres (17 million ha) of land across the country—an area about the size of the state of Florida, U.S.A. A collective effort of firefighters targeting the blaze from the ground and the air—as well as welcome rain— finally contained the flames. But not before the fires destroyed thousands of homes and killed

Locusts!

T ypically, locusts, a type of grasshopper, are harmless. They don't sting, bite, or cause much destruction on their own. But in large numbers, they can cause a lot of damage. Case in point: the swarms of locusts that descended upon Pakistan in 2020. Considered the worst infestation in decades, billions of locusts feasted on fields of crops. And because each locust can eat its own bodyweight in food daily, these massive swarms can consume as much food as 35,000 people in a 24-hour period. These effects were catastrophic for farmers, who lost entire harvests to the hungry insects, and have raised concerns about food shortages.

Why were the bugs so bad? Experts say dampness from heavy rains and cyclones sparked unusually active breeding among the locusts, causing their population to skyrocket in Pakistan as well as East Africa, India, and parts of the Arabian Peninsula. Things got so grim that Pakistan declared a state of emergency to secure funding to help farmers. Authorities in Pakistan and India also agreed to work together to fight the locusts. By sharing data and resources, they were able to work to put this plague behind them.

QUIZ WHIZ

Quiz yourself to find out if you're a natural when it comes to nature knowledge!

Write your answers on a piece of paper. Then check them below.

1 **True or false?** The Pacific Ocean covers 15 percent of Earth's water area.

2 If all the ice on Earth melted, the world's oceans would rise as high as _____.

a. five school buses
b. the Statue of Liberty
c. six orcas
d. all of the above

3 The birth of a baby _____ at the Australian Reptile Park was a sign of hope after the Australian wildfires of 2019 and 2020.

a. kangaroo
b. crocodile
c. koala
d. wombat

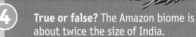

4 **True or false?** The Amazon biome is about twice the size of India.

5 Snow is produced when ice crystals in clouds get heavy enough to _____.

a. melt
b. fall
c. evaporate
d. freeze

Not **STUMPED** yet? Check out the *NATIONAL GEOGRAPHIC KIDS QUIZ WHIZ* collection for more crazy **NATURE** questions!

ANSWERS: 1. False. It covers 47 percent of Earth's water area.; **2.** d; **3.** c; **4.** True; **5.** b

Oral Reports Made Easy

TIP: Make sure you practice your presentation a few times. Stand in front of a mirror or have a parent record you so you can see if you need to work on anything, such as eye contact.

Does the thought of public speaking start your stomach churning like a tornado? Would you rather get caught in an avalanche than give a speech?

Giving an oral report does not have to be a natural disaster. The basic format is very similar to that of a written essay. There are two main elements that make up a good oral report—the writing and the presentation. As you write your oral report, remember that your audience will be hearing the information as opposed to reading it. Follow the guidelines below, and there will be clear skies ahead.

Writing Your Material

Follow the steps in the "How to Write a Perfect Essay" section on page 197, but prepare your report to be spoken rather than written.

Try to keep your sentences short and simple. Long, complex sentences are harder to follow. Limit yourself to just a few key points. You don't want to overwhelm your audience with too much information. To be most effective, hit your key points in the introduction, elaborate on them in the body, and then repeat them once again in your conclusion.

AN ORAL REPORT HAS THREE BASIC PARTS:

- Introduction—This is your chance to engage your audience and really capture their interest in the subject you are presenting. Use a funny personal experience or a dramatic story, or start with an intriguing question.

- Body—This is the longest part of your report. Here you elaborate on the facts and ideas you want to convey. Give information that supports your main idea, and expand on it with specific examples or details. In other words, structure your oral report in the same way you would a written essay, so that your thoughts are presented in a clear and organized manner.

- Conclusion—This is the time to summarize the information and emphasize your most important points to the audience one last time.

Preparing Your Delivery

1 Practice makes perfect. Practice! Practice! Practice! Confidence, enthusiasm, and energy are key to delivering an effective oral report, and they can best be achieved through rehearsal. Ask family and friends to be your practice audience and give you feedback when you're done. Were they able to follow your ideas? Did you seem knowledgeable and confident? Did you speak too slowly or too fast, too softly or too loudly? The more times you practice giving your report, the more you'll master the material. Then you won't have to rely so heavily on your notes or papers, and you will be able to give your report in a relaxed and confident manner.

2 Present with everything you've got. Be as creative as you can. Incorporate videos, sound clips, slide presentations, charts, diagrams, and photos. Visual aids help stimulate your audience's senses and keep them intrigued and engaged. They can also help to reinforce your key points. And remember that when you're giving an oral report, you're a performer. Take charge of the spotlight and be as animated and entertaining as you can. Have fun with it.

3 Keep your nerves under control. Everyone gets a little nervous when speaking in front of a group. That's normal. But the more preparation you've done— meaning plenty of researching, organizing, and rehearsing—the more confident you'll be. Preparation is the key. And if you make a mistake or stumble over your words, just regroup and keep going. Nobody's perfect, and nobody expects you to be.

HISTORY
HAPPENS

Massive 32-foot (10-m)-tall sandstone
pillar statues line the interior of the temple
of Ramses II in Abu Simbel, Egypt.

Ancient World
ADVENTURE

KOURION

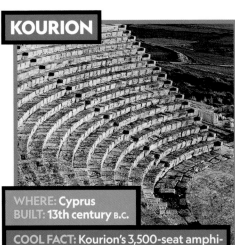

WHERE: Cyprus
BUILT: 13th century B.C.

COOL FACT: Kourion's 3,500-seat amphi-theater survived an earthquake in A.D. 364 that leveled the rest of the city. It's still used for performances today.

AYUTTHAYA

WHERE: Thailand
BUILT: About A.D. 1350

COOL FACT: Home to hundreds of thousands of people at the end of the 17th century, this former capital of the Siamese Kingdom was one of the world's largest cities.

FORBIDDEN CITY

WHERE: China
BUILT: Between A.D. 1406 and A.D. 1420

COOL FACT: The 180-acre (73-ha) imperial compound in Beijing is rumored to have more than 9,999 rooms and was home to 24 Chinese emperors over a nearly 500-year span.

*E*ver wonder what it was like on Earth hundreds of years ago? Check out these amazing ancient sites. Visiting them is like taking a time machine into the past!

PAMUKKALE

WHERE: **Turkey**
BUILT: **About 200 B.C.**

COOL FACT: People flocked to this ancient spa town to bathe in its hot springs, which are said to have healing powers. Today, tourists still visit, floating above submerged ruins of ancient columns.

PALENQUE

WHERE: **Mexico**
BUILT: **About A.D. 500**

COOL FACT: This ancient Maya city-state's buildings, including temples and tombs, were built without the use of metal tools, pack animals, or even the wheel.

TIMBUKTU

WHERE: **Mali**
BUILT: **About A.D. 1100**

COOL FACT: Once known as the fabled "City of Gold," Africa's Timbuktu was a center of learning and culture in the 15th and 16th centuries and is home to a still standing university.

THE LOST CITY OF POMPEII

When will the volcano that buried this ancient civilization blow again?

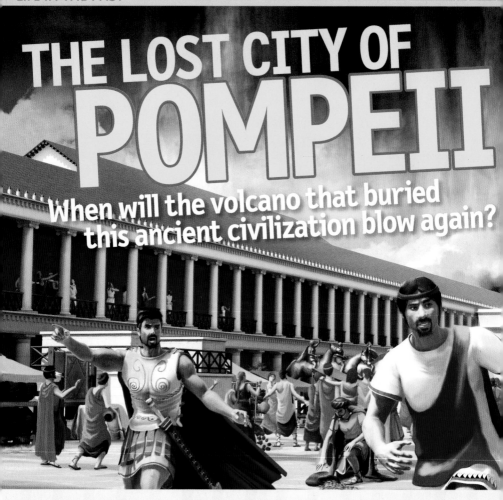

A deafening boom roars through Pompeii's crowded marketplace. The ground shakes violently, throwing the midday shoppers off balance and toppling stands of fish and meat. People start screaming and pointing toward Mount Vesuvius, a massive volcano that rises above the bustling city, located in what is now southern Italy.

Vesuvius has been silent for nearly 2,000 years, but it roars back to life, shooting ash and smoke into the air. Almost overnight, the city and most of its residents have vanished under a blanket of ash and lava.

Now, almost 2,000 years later, scientists agree that Vesuvius is overdue for another major eruption—but no one knows when it will happen. Three million people live in the volcano's shadow, in the modern-day city of Naples, Italy. Correctly predicting when the eruption might take place will mean the difference between life and death for many.

THE SKY IS FALLING

Thanks to excavations that started in 1748 and continue to this day, scientists have been able to re-create almost exactly what happened in Pompeii on that terrible day in A.D. 79.

"The thick ash turned everything black," says Pompeii expert Andrew Wallace-Hadrill.

"People couldn't see the sun. All the landmarks disappeared. They didn't have the foggiest idea which way they were going."

Some people ran for their lives, clutching their valuable coins and jewelry. Other people took shelter in their homes. But the debris kept falling. Piles grew as deep as nine feet (2.7 m) in some places, blocking doorways and caving in roofs.

Around midnight, the first of four searing-hot clouds, or surges, of ash, pumice, rock, and toxic gas rushed down the mountainside. Traveling toward Pompeii at up to 180 miles an hour (290 km/h), it scorched everything in its path. Around 7 a.m., 18 hours after the

TODAY, MILLIONS OF TOURISTS VISIT THE RUINS OF POMPEII, INCLUDING THE FORUM, BELOW.

THIS ARTIST'S CONCEPT RE-CREATES THE FORUM AT POMPEII AS IT LOOKED THE DAY OF THE ERUPTION IN A.D. 79. THE FORUM WAS THE CENTER OF PUBLIC LIFE.

eruption, the last fiery surge buried the city.

LOST AND FOUND

Visiting the ruins of Pompeii today is like going back in time. The layers of ash actually helped preserve buildings, artwork, and even the forms of bodies. "It gives you the feeling you can reach out and touch the ancient world," Wallace-Hadrill says.

There are kitchens with pots on the stove and bakeries with loaves of bread—now turned to charcoal—still in the ovens. Narrow corridors lead to magnificent mansions with elaborate gardens and fountains. Mosaics, or designs made out of tiles, decorate the walls and floors.

WARNING SIGNS

Pompeii's destruction may be ancient history, but there's little doubt that disaster will strike again. Luckily, people living near Vesuvius today will likely receive evacuation warnings before the volcano blows.

Scientists are closely monitoring Vesuvius for shifts in the ground, earthquakes, and rising levels of certain gases, which could be signs of an upcoming eruption. The Italian government is also working on a plan to help people flee the area in the event of a natural disaster.

CREEPY CASTS

Volcanic ash settled around many of the victims at the moment of death. When the bodies decayed, holes remained inside the solid ash. Scientists poured plaster into the holes to preserve the shapes of the victims.

10 ENDURING FACTS ABOUT THE GREAT WALL OF CHINA

Workers layered local soil to create the wall's bricks, which they'd mix with water and bake in a kiln for up to 15 hours.

In the 13th century, Mongolian Genghis Khan led the first—and only—army to breach the wall in its history.

The wall—designed to keep invaders from the north out of China—**was built over a period of nearly 2,000 years.**

You can **ride a TOBOGGAN** from the top of the Great Wall to the ground below.

Some **10 million** people visit the Great Wall of China each year.

MORTAR CREATED WITH STICKY RICE FLOUR WAS USED TO HOLD THE WALL'S BRICKS TOGETHER AND MAKE IT STRONGER.

Smoke signals from the wall's watchtowers **alerted troops** if an enemy was spotted approaching.

ARCHERS SHOT ARROWS **THROUGH NOCKS—** SPECIALLY DESIGNED HOLES IN THE WALL'S WATCHTOWERS.

You can camp out on certain portions of the Great Wall.

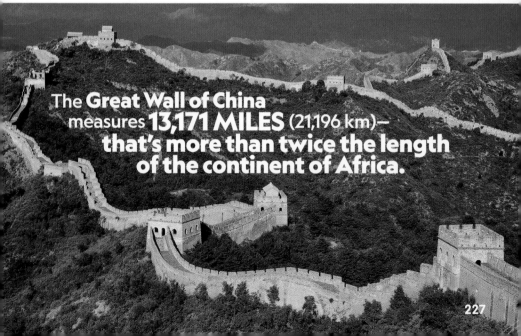

The **Great Wall of China** measures **13,171 MILES** (21,196 km)— **that's more than twice the length of the continent of Africa.**

PiRATES!

MEET THREE OF HISTORY'S MOST FEARSOME HIGH-SEAS BADDIES.

Yo-ho, yo-ho—*uh-oh!* A mysterious ship on the horizon flying a skull-and-crossbones flag wasn't a welcome sight to sailors in the 18th and 19th centuries. That flag meant one thing: pirates. Faced with faster, cannon-crammed vessels typically crewed by pirates, a ship captain was left with two choices: lower their sails and surrender—or turn and fight.

Life wasn't one big swashbuckling adventure for the pirates, however. Lousy food, cramped quarters, stinky crewmates, and hurricanes were all part of the job. Still, a handful of pirates managed to enjoy success at sea ... and inspired fear in those who were unfortunate enough to meet them face-to-face. Check out some of history's most famous pirates.

RACHEL WALL

REIGN OF TERROR New England coast, U.S.A., late 1700s

Rachel Wall and her husband, George, worked together as pirates, targeting small islands off the coast of Maine in the Atlantic Ocean. After storms, they'd stop their sailboat and raise a distress flag. When passersby responded to Rachel's screams for help, they were robbed—or worse—for their trouble. After just two summers of piracy, Rachel and George killed at least 24 men and raked in about $6,000, plus an unknown amount of valuable goods. They later sold their loot, pretending they found it washed up on a beach.

CRIME DOESN'T PAY Eventually the law caught up with Rachel Wall. In 1789, she made history when she was the last woman to be hanged in the state of Massachusetts.

CHENG I SAO

REIGN OF TERROR South China Sea, 1801–1810

Cheng I Sao ruled a pirate fleet of nearly 2,000 ships. Sometimes called Madame Cheng, she turned to crime after she married a famous pirate. More than 80,000 buccaneers—men, women, and even children—reported to Madame Cheng. They seized loot in all sorts of ways: selling "protection" from pirate attacks, raiding ships, and kidnapping for ransom. Madame Cheng was best known for paying her pirates cash for each head they brought back from their assaults. (Yikes!)

CRIME DOESN'T PAY—USUALLY Every government attempt to stop Madame Cheng was a failure. Rumor has it that after she retired from piracy, she started a second career as a smuggler. She died peacefully at age 69.

BLACKBEARD

REIGN OF TERROR North America's East Coast and the Caribbean, 1713–1718

Nobody knows Blackbeard's real name—historians think it might've been Edward Teach—but he's arguably history's most famous pirate. He began his career as a privateer, or a kind of legal pirate, who was hired by the British government to attack enemy fleets and steal their goods.

Blackbeard abandoned privateering in 1713 and went full-pirate when he sailed to the Caribbean on a French ship that was gifted to him by another pirate, adding cannons to the vessel and renaming it *Queen Anne's Revenge*. He terrified his enemies by strapping pistols and knives across his chest and sticking smoking cannon fuses in his beard. According to legend, Blackbeard hid a treasure somewhere ... but it's never been found.

CRIME DOESN'T PAY A few years into Blackbeard's time as a pirate, he was nabbed by the British Navy. They executed him and stuck his head on the front of a ship as a way to warn wannabe pirates to stay away from seafaring crime.

ROYAL

Check out what some of history's most

FIT FOR A QUEEN

Though militaries of the past were made up mostly of men, a few notable women—royal and otherwise—rode into battle, leading troops to victory. Not much is known about many of them. Check out what we *do* know about fierce females on the battlefield.

Armor for All

The few historical accounts of royal women in battle say that they likely donned the same gear as men. They're usually described as wearing hauberks: garments made of metal that covered the arms, torso, and upper legs.

Legendary Look

Many images of armor-clad women depict fictional figures like Minerva, the Roman goddess of women and warfare. According to legend, Minerva's father, Jupiter, swallowed her pregnant mother after a prophecy foretold that their unborn child would grow up to defeat him. When Minerva eventually escaped from inside Jupiter, she was wearing full battle armor and ready to fight her father.

MINERVA

Secret Suit

Though some historical paintings depict women in metal armor, no one knows for sure how accurate these illustrations are. That means the exact appearance of women's armor in the past is still a mystery, but historians think it looked similar to what men wore, like the suit above worn by English nobility during the 16th century.

Knight Me

In 1149, when invaders threatened to take over the town of Tortosa, Spain, local women threw on men's clothing and fought off the enemy. Spanish count Ramon Berenguer IV was so impressed that he created the Order of the Hatchet, granting the women rights similar to those of knights, such as not having to pay taxes.

CHECK OUT THE BOOK!

THE BOOK OF **Queens**

Custom Fit

Joan of Arc is one of history's most famous warriors. During the 15th century, France's King Charles VII presented the military leader with armor tailored to fit her perfectly.

RUMBLE

fearsome fighters wore on the battlefield.

So Much Metal

Being a knight sounds exciting, but wearing armor was not. Mail armor, invented around the third century B.C., was made of interlocking metal circles layered over quilted fabric to protect against arrows. Plate armor, invented around the late 1300s, was heavy and hard to see out of. But because it was made of bands of steel over leather, it defended against heavy blows while allowing for movement. The best protection? Probably a combination of both.

MAIL ARMOR

PLATE ARMOR

FIT FOR A KING

On the battlefield, sturdy armor meant the difference between life and death. Good armor protected its wearer against a variety of weapons while still allowing them to move easily. Discover what kings and their soldiers wore throughout history.

Works of Art

Today, Japanese samurai are famous for their long blades known as *katanas*, but their armor during the Heian period (A.D. 794–1185) was just as well known. Samurai armor, called *o-yoroi* (pronounced oh-YO-roy, above), was made of metal and leather, and designed to deflect blades and arrows. It consisted of multiple pieces laced together, including the *kabuto* (helmet), the *menpo* (face mask), and extra leg and arm guards. Some pieces were decorated so beautifully that today they're regarded as works of art.

Cat Fight

The Aztec Empire, which reigned over central Mexico from 1345 to 1521, was known for a group of warriors called the *ocelotl* (pronounced oh-seh-LO-tl), meaning "jaguars." In addition to wearing regular armor in battle, these jaguar fighters donned symbols of their namesake. One example was a helmet shaped like a jaguar head, with room for the soldier to peek out from below the teeth. And they sometimes wore capes made from real jaguar pelts. These outfits were thought to transfer the fierceness of the jaguar to the wearer.

SIXTH-CENTURY STATUE OF A JAGUAR WARRIOR

Animal Armor

Throughout history, some animals donned armor along with their soldiers, including battle horses and even elephants. War elephants, first used in what is now India during the 12th century, were sometimes dressed in fancy sets of metal armor weighing more than 350 pounds (159 kg). A few were also adorned with "tusk swords," which were metal weapons mounted on the elephants' tusks. Other elephants were saddled with carriages where archers could sit and fire on their enemies.

THE BOOK OF KINGS

CHECK OUT THE BOOK!

7 COOL THINGS ABOUT THE TOWER OF LONDON

As a palace, the Tower of London was a great place to live. As a prison, it wasn't so nice—especially because so many prisoners lost their lives. The place has been a lot of things in its nearly 1,000-year history. Today tourists can explore the Tower, in England, in the United Kingdom. Here are seven reasons why the Tower was—and still is—a cool place to be (as long as you weren't a prisoner, that is).

1

Ravens are like local superheroes. Well, sort of. Legend says if the ravens that live on the Tower grounds ever leave, the Tower will crumble and a disaster will befall England. No one knows when the ravens first showed up, but Charles II took the legend so seriously that in the 1670s he decreed that six ravens be kept there all the time. Today there are still always six—plus a couple of spares, just in case.

2

If you lived at the Tower today, your mom or dad might be in charge. The 35 Yeoman Warders and their families are among the few still allowed to live at the Tower. Established in 1509 as bodyguards for the king, today they give tours and manage the day-to-day details of the Tower. They're called "beefeaters," possibly because their job once allowed them to eat beef from the king's table.

3

You need a secret password at night. Called the "Word," the password changes every 24 hours and is a must-have to enter the Tower after hours. It's written on a piece of paper and delivered to the yeoman on duty for the night.

4

You might see a ghost. Queen Anne Boleyn, who was executed on orders from her husband, King Henry VIII, is said to wander the grounds without her head. One building is believed to be so haunted that dogs refuse to enter.

5

You'd have lots of bling. England's crown jewels are still guarded in the Tower's Jewel House, a dazzling display of crowns, robes, jewelry, and scepters that dates back hundreds of years. More than 23,500 diamonds, sapphires, rubies, and other gems adorn the royal collection.

6

You'd never have to worry about a prison break. The Tower was so secure that only a few escape attempts succeeded. In 1716, one man sneaked out dressed in women's clothing. In 1100, a prisoner threw such a wild party for the guards that they didn't notice him climbing over the wall to meet a waiting boat!

7

You could find buried gold. In 1662, a goldsmith named John Barkstead supposedly hid more than $40,000 worth of stolen gold somewhere on Tower grounds. Many have searched for the loot, but it has never been found.

GOING TO WAR

Since the beginning of time, different countries, territories, and cultures have feuded with each other over land, power, and politics. Major military conflicts include the following wars:

1095-1291 THE CRUSADES
Starting late in the 11th century, these wars over religion were fought in the Middle East for nearly 200 years.

1337-1453 HUNDRED YEARS' WAR
France and England battled over rights to land for more than a century before the French eventually drove the English out in 1453.

1754-1763 FRENCH AND INDIAN WAR (part of Europe's Seven Years' War)
A nine-year war between the British and French for control of North America.

1775-1783 AMERICAN REVOLUTION
Thirteen British colonies in America united to reject the rule of the British government and to form the United States of America.

1861-1865 AMERICAN CIVIL WAR
This war occurred when the northern states (the Union) went to war with the southern states, which had seceded, or withdrawn, to form the Confederate States of America. Slavery was one of the key issues in the Civil War.

1910-1920 MEXICAN REVOLUTION
The people of Mexico revolted against the rule of dictator President Porfirio Díaz, leading to his eventual defeat and to a democratic government.

1914-1918 WORLD WAR I
The assassination of Austria's Archduke Ferdinand by a Serbian nationalist sparked this wide-spreading war. The U.S. entered after Germany sank the British ship *Lusitania,* killing more than 120 Americans.

1918-1920 RUSSIAN CIVIL WAR
Following the 1917 Russian Revolution, this conflict pitted the Communist Red Army against the foreign-backed White Army. The Red Army won, leading to the establishment of the Union of Soviet Socialist Republics (U.S.S.R.) in 1922.

1936-1939 SPANISH CIVIL WAR
Aid from Italy and Germany helped Spain's Nationalists gain victory over the Communist-supported Republicans. The war resulted in the loss of more than 300,000 lives and increased tension in Europe leading up to World War II.

1939-1945 WORLD WAR II
This massive conflict in Europe, Asia, and North Africa involved many countries that aligned with the two sides: the Allies and the Axis. After the bombing of Pearl Harbor in Hawaii in 1941, the U.S. entered the war on the side of the Allies. More than 50 million people died during the war.

1946-1949 CHINESE CIVIL WAR
Also known as the "War of Liberation," this war pitted the Communist and Nationalist Parties in China against each other. The Communists won.

1950-1953 KOREAN WAR
Kicked off when the Communist forces of North Korea, with backing from the Soviet Union, invaded their democratic neighbor to the south. A coalition of 16 countries from the United Nations stepped in to support South Korea. An armistice, or temporary truce, ended active fighting in 1953.

1950s-1975 VIETNAM WAR
This war was fought between the Communist North, supported by allies including China, and the government of South Vietnam, supported by the United States and other anticommunist nations.

1967 SIX-DAY WAR
This was a battle for land between Israel and the states of Egypt, Jordan, and Syria. The outcome resulted in Israel's gaining control of coveted territory, including the Gaza Strip and the West Bank.

1991-PRESENT SOMALI CIVIL WAR
The war began when Somalia's last president, a dictator named Mohamed Siad Barre, was overthrown. It has led to years of fighting and anarchy.

2001-2014 WAR IN AFGHANISTAN
After attacks in the U.S. by the terrorist group al Qaeda, a coalition that eventually included more than 40 countries invaded Afghanistan to find Osama bin Laden and other al Qaeda members and to dismantle the Taliban. Bin Laden was killed in a U.S. covert operation in 2011. The North Atlantic Treaty Organization (NATO) took control of the coalition's combat mission in 2003. That combat mission officially ended in 2014.

2003-2011 WAR IN IRAQ
A coalition led by the U.S., and including Britain, Australia, and Spain, invaded Iraq over suspicions that Iraq had weapons of mass destruction.

SPY TREES

Picture this: You're tossed onto the front lines of World War I. Up ahead, you spot a tree towering over the barren countryside. Ravaged by bullets and bombs and stripped of its leaves, the tree has certainly seen better days. But look closely and you just may see that it's not a real tree, but a replica made of iron and steel.

On the battlefield, it's not uncommon to use extreme tactics to gain an advantage on the enemy—even constructing fake trees to use as the ultimate observation post for sneaky spies.

That's just what both the British and Germans did during World War I to spy on one another. After measuring, sketching, and photographing real trees on the battlefield, artists would then create lifelike, hollow towers using painted steel and iron. Then, in the middle of the night, troops would cut down the actual tree and replace it with the fake one. By the next morning, a soldier would be hidden inside the camouflaged tower. Offering a perfect vantage point to observe any movement on the enemy's front, these spy trees no doubt elevated the war to a new level.

THE CONSTITUTION & THE BILL OF RIGHTS

The United States Constitution was written in 1787 by a group of political leaders from the 13 states that made up the United States at the time. Thirty-nine men, including Benjamin Franklin and James Madison, signed the document to create a national government. While some feared the creation of a strong federal government, all 13 states eventually ratified, or approved, the Constitution, making it the law of the land. The Constitution has three major parts: the preamble, the articles, and the amendments.

Here's a summary of what topics are covered in each part of the Constitution. Check out the Constitution online or at your local library for the full text.

THE PREAMBLE outlines the basic purposes of the government: *We the People of the United States, in order to form a more perfect Union, establish justice, insure domestic tranquility, provide for the common defense, promote the general welfare, and secure the blessings of liberty to ourselves and our posterity, do ordain and establish this Constitution for the United States of America.*

SEVEN ARTICLES outline the powers of Congress, the president, and the court system:

Article I outlines the legislative branch—the Senate and the House of Representatives—and its powers and responsibilities.

Article II outlines the executive branch—the presidency—and its powers and responsibilities.

Article III outlines the judicial branch—the court system—and its powers and responsibilities.

Article IV describes the individual states' rights and powers.

Article V outlines the amendment process.

Article VI establishes the Constitution as the law of the land.

Article VII gives the requirements for the Constitution to be approved.

THE AMENDMENTS, or additions to the Constitution, were put in later as needed. In 1791, the first 10 amendments, known as the Bill of Rights, were added. Since then, another 17 amendments have been added. This is the Bill of Rights:

1st Amendment: guarantees freedom of religion, speech, and the press, and the right to assemble and petition. The U.S. may not have a national religion.

2nd Amendment: discusses the militia and the right of people to bear arms

3rd Amendment: prohibits the military or troops from using private homes without consent

4th Amendment: protects people and their homes from search, arrest, or seizure without probable cause or a warrant

5th Amendment: grants people the right to have a trial and prevents punishment before prosecution; protects private property from being taken without compensation

6th Amendment: guarantees the right to a speedy and public trial

7th Amendment: guarantees a trial by jury in certain cases

8th Amendment: forbids "cruel and unusual punishments"

9th Amendment: states that the Constitution is not all-encompassing and does not deny people other, unspecified rights

10th Amendment: grants the powers not covered by the Constitution to the states and the people

Read the full text version of the United States Constitution at constitutioncenter.org/constitution/full-text

White House

BRANCHES OF GOVERNMENT

The **UNITED STATES GOVERNMENT** is divided into three branches: executive, legislative, and judicial. The system of checks and balances is a way to control power and to make sure one branch can't take the reins of government. For example, most of the president's actions require the approval of Congress. Likewise, the laws passed in Congress must be signed by the president before they can take effect.

Executive Branch

The Constitution lists the central powers of the president: to serve as commander in chief of the armed forces; make treaties with other nations; grant pardons; inform Congress on the state of the union; and appoint ambassadors, officials, and judges. The executive branch includes the president and the 15 governmental departments.

Legislative Branch

This branch is made up of Congress—the Senate and the House of Representatives. The Constitution grants Congress the power to make laws. Congress is made up of elected representatives from each state. Each state has two representatives in the Senate, while the number of representatives in the House is determined by the size of the state's population. Washington, D.C., and the territories elect nonvoting representatives to the House of Representatives. The Founding Fathers set up this system as a compromise between big states—which wanted representation based on population—and small states—which wanted all states to have equal representation rights.

The U.S. Capitol in Washington, D.C.

Judicial Branch

The judicial branch is composed of the federal court system—the U.S. Supreme Court, the courts of appeals, and the district courts. The Supreme Court is the most powerful court. Its motto is "Equal Justice Under Law." This influential court is responsible for interpreting the Constitution and applying it to the cases that it hears. The decisions of the Supreme Court are absolute—they are the final word on any legal question.

The U.S. Supreme Court Building in Washington, D.C.

There are nine justices on the Supreme Court. They are appointed by the president of the United States and confirmed by the Senate.

237

GEORGE WASHINGTON'S RULES TO LIVE BY

REAL-LIFE ADVICE FROM THE FIRST U.S. PRESIDENT

Starting as a boy, George Washington followed a set of 110 dos and don'ts on everything from public tooth picking to freaking out friends. Check out three of G.W.'s polite practices.

These rules have not been edited; this is how George actually wrote them.

RULE 2

"In visiting the Sick, do not Presently play the Physicion if you be not Knowing therein."

MODERN-DAY MEANING: You probably don't want to give your friends advice on medicine. Best leave that to the doc and your pals' parents.

WAY BACK FACT: One 18th-century recipe for homemade cold medicine included the tips of crab claws and the "jelly" of vipers.

RULE 3

"Shew Nothing to your Freind that may affright him."

MODERN-DAY MEANING: Scaring a friend is a no-no, and yelling "Boo!" may get *you* booed. So don't jump out of a dark hallway in front of your little brother or put a fake snake under your friend's pillow.

WAY BACK FACT: As a general in the Revolutionary War, George Washington tried not to "affright" troops by telling them how bad things were. But in 1775, the war's first year, he was very worried about keeping the army calm and finding food for his thousands of soldiers.

RULE 1

"Cleanse not your teeth with the Table Cloth Napkin Fork or Knife but if Others do it let it be done wt. a Pick Tooth."

MODERN-DAY MEANING: Gross! Who wants to watch somebody rub their teeth clean with table linens or pick at them with silverware? But back in Washington's day, this was okay as long as everybody else was doing the same. According to the rule, you should just trade in the utensils and table linens for toothpicks when spiffing up your pearly whites.

WAY BACK FACT: George Washington had problems with his teeth. He used all kinds of tooth powders, a silver tooth-brush, and a tongue scraper.

George Washington's
Rules
TO LIVE BY

A GOOD MANNERS GUIDE FROM THE FATHER OF OUR COUNTRY

Check out this boo

On the Money Quiz!

George Washington has been featured on the dollar bill since 1869, seven years after it was first put into print. In 1909, Teddy Roosevelt commissioned the penny featuring Abraham Lincoln to celebrate the popular president's 100th birthday. Today, more than 30 presidents and other prominent historical figures are featured on various bills and coins. So, do you know which president's face appears on each bill—or coin? See if you can match the president to the correct currency.

 **A**
 **B**
 **C**
 **D**
 **E**
 **F**

1. Thomas Jefferson
2. George Washington
3. Andrew Jackson
4. Alexander Hamilton
5. Franklin D. Roosevelt
6. Ulysses S. Grant

A. quarter
B. dime
C. $20 bill
D. $10 bill
E. $2 bill
F. $50 bill

ANSWERS: 1. E; 2. A; 3. C; 4. D; 5. B; 6. F

The Native American Experience

Native Americans are indigenous

to North and South America—they are the people who were here before Columbus and other European explorers came to these lands. They live in nations, tribes, and bands across both continents. For decades following the arrival of Europeans in 1492, Native Americans clashed with the newcomers who had ruptured the indigenous people's ways of living.

Tribal Land

During the 19th century, both United States legislation and military action restricted the movement of Native Americans, forcing them to live on reservations and attempting to dismantle tribal structures. For centuries, Native Americans were displaced or killed, or became assimilated into the general U.S. population. In 1924 the Indian Citizenship Act granted citizenship to all Native Americans. Unfortunately, this was not enough to end the social discrimination and mistreatment that many indigenous people have faced. Today, Native Americans living in the U.S. still face many challenges.

Healing the Past

Many members of the 560-plus recognized tribes in the United States live primarily on reservations. Some tribes have more than one reservation, while others have none. Together these reservations make up less than 3 percent of the nation's land area. The tribal governments on reservations have the right to form their own governments and to enforce laws, similar to individual states. Many feel that this sovereignty is still not enough to right the wrongs of the past: They hope for a change in the U.S. government's relationship with Native Americans.

An annual powwow in New Mexico features more than 3,000 dancers from more than 500 North American tribes.

Navajo is the most commonly spoken Native American language in the United States.

Top: A Navajo teenager holds her pet lamb.

Middle: A Monacan girl dances in a traditional jingle dress.

Bottom: Little Shell men in traditional costume

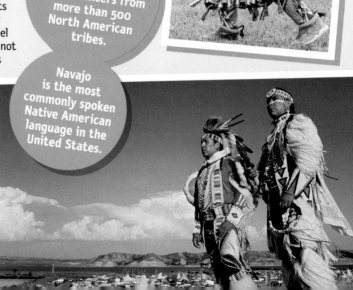

The president of the United States is the chief of the executive branch, the commander in chief of the U.S. armed forces, and head of the federal government. Elected every four years, the president is the highest policy-maker in the nation. The 22nd Amendment (1951) says that no person may be elected to the office of president more than twice. There have been 46 presidencies and 45 presidents.

GEORGE WASHINGTON
1st President of the United States ★ 1789–1797
BORN Feb. 22, 1732, in Pope's Creek, Westmoreland County, VA
POLITICAL PARTY Federalist
NO. OF TERMS two
VICE PRESIDENT John Adams
DIED Dec. 14, 1799, at Mount Vernon, VA

JOHN ADAMS
2nd President of the United States ★ 1797–1801
BORN Oct. 30, 1735, in Braintree (now Quincy), MA
POLITICAL PARTY Federalist
NO. OF TERMS one
VICE PRESIDENT Thomas Jefferson
DIED July 4, 1826, in Quincy, MA

THOMAS JEFFERSON
3rd President of the United States ★ 1801–1809
BORN April 13, 1743, at Shadwell, Goochland (now Albemarle) County, VA
POLITICAL PARTY Democratic-Republican
NO. OF TERMS two
VICE PRESIDENTS 1st term: Aaron Burr
2nd term: George Clinton
DIED July 4, 1826, at Monticello, Charlottesville, VA

THOMAS JEFFERSON HAD A **PET MOCKINGBIRD** THAT **FLEW FREELY** AROUND THE **WHITE HOUSE.**

JAMES MADISON
4th President of the United States ★ 1809–1817
BORN March 16, 1751, at Belle Grove, Port Conway, VA
POLITICAL PARTY Democratic-Republican
NO. OF TERMS two
VICE PRESIDENTS 1st term: George Clinton
2nd term: Elbridge Gerry
DIED June 28, 1836, at Montpelier, Orange County, VA

JAMES MONROE
5th President of the United States ★ 1817–1825
BORN April 28, 1758, in Westmoreland County, VA
POLITICAL PARTY Democratic-Republican
NO. OF TERMS two
VICE PRESIDENT Daniel D. Tompkins
DIED July 4, 1831, in New York, NY

JOHN QUINCY ADAMS
6th President of the United States ★ 1825–1829
BORN July 11, 1767, in Braintree (now Quincy), MA
POLITICAL PARTY Democratic-Republican
NO. OF TERMS one
VICE PRESIDENT John Caldwell Calhoun
DIED Feb. 23, 1848, at the U.S. Capitol, Washington, D.C.

ANDREW JACKSON
7th President of the United States ★ 1829–1837
BORN March 15, 1767, in the Waxhaw region, NC and SC
POLITICAL PARTY Democrat
NO. OF TERMS two
VICE PRESIDENTS 1st term: John Caldwell Calhoun
2nd term: Martin Van Buren
DIED June 8, 1845, in Nashville, TN

MARTIN VAN BUREN
8th President of the United States ★ 1837–1841
BORN Dec. 5, 1782, in Kinderhook, NY
POLITICAL PARTY Democrat
NO. OF TERMS one
VICE PRESIDENT Richard M. Johnson
DIED July 24, 1862, in Kinderhook, NY

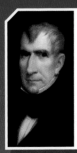

WILLIAM HENRY HARRISON

9th President of the United States ★ *1841*

BORN Feb. 9, 1773, in Charles City County, VA
POLITICAL PARTY Whig
NO. OF TERMS one (died while in office)
VICE PRESIDENT John Tyler
DIED April 4, 1841, in the White House, Washington, D.C.

JOHN TYLER

10th President of the United States ★ *1841–1845*

BORN March 29, 1790, in Charles City County, VA
POLITICAL PARTY Whig
NO. OF TERMS one (partial)
VICE PRESIDENT none
DIED Jan. 18, 1862, in Richmond, VA

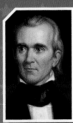

JAMES K. POLK

11th President of the United States ★ *1845–1849*

BORN Nov. 2, 1795, near Pineville, Mecklenburg County, NC
POLITICAL PARTY Democrat
NO. OF TERMS one
VICE PRESIDENT George Mifflin Dallas
DIED June 15, 1849, in Nashville, TN

ZACHARY TAYLOR

12th President of the United States ★ *1849–1850*

BORN Nov. 24, 1784, in Orange County, VA
POLITICAL PARTY Whig
NO. OF TERMS one (died while in office)
VICE PRESIDENT Millard Fillmore
DIED July 9, 1850, in the White House, Washington, D.C.

MILLARD FILLMORE

13th President of the United States ★ *1850–1853*

BORN Jan. 7, 1800, in Cayuga County, NY
POLITICAL PARTY Whig
NO. OF TERMS one (partial)
VICE PRESIDENT none
DIED March 8, 1874, in Buffalo, NY

FRANKLIN PIERCE

14th President of the United States ★ *1853–1857*

BORN Nov. 23, 1804, in Hillsborough (now Hillsboro), NH
POLITICAL PARTY Democrat
NO. OF TERMS one
VICE PRESIDENT William Rufus De Vane King
DIED Oct. 8, 1869, in Concord, NH

JAMES BUCHANAN

15th President of the United States ★ *1857–1861*

BORN April 23, 1791, in Cove Gap, PA
POLITICAL PARTY Democrat
NO. OF TERMS one
VICE PRESIDENT John Cabell Breckinridge
DIED June 1, 1868, in Lancaster, PA

ABRAHAM LINCOLN

16th President of the United States ★ *1861–1865*

BORN Feb. 12, 1809, near Hodgenville, KY
POLITICAL PARTY Republican (formerly Whig)
NO. OF TERMS two (assassinated)
VICE PRESIDENTS 1st term: Hannibal Hamlin
2nd term: Andrew Johnson
DIED April 15, 1865, in Washington, D.C.

ABRAHAM LINCOLN KEPT LETTERS IN HIS STOVEPIPE HAT.

ANDREW JOHNSON

17th President of the United States ★ *1865–1869*

BORN Dec. 29, 1808, in Raleigh, NC
POLITICAL PARTY Democrat
NO. OF TERMS one (partial)
VICE PRESIDENT none
DIED July 31, 1875, in Carter's Station, TN

ULYSSES S. GRANT
18th President of the United States ★ 1869–1877

BORN April 27, 1822,
in Point Pleasant, OH

POLITICAL PARTY Republican

NO. OF TERMS two

VICE PRESIDENTS 1st term: Schuyler Colfax
2nd term: Henry Wilson

DIED July 23, 1885, in Mount
McGregor, NY

RUTHERFORD B. HAYES
19th President of the United States ★ 1877–1881

BORN Oct. 4, 1822,
in Delaware, OH

POLITICAL PARTY Republican

NO. OF TERMS one

VICE PRESIDENT William Almon Wheeler

DIED Jan. 17, 1893, in Fremont, OH

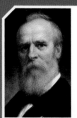

JAMES A. GARFIELD
20th President of the United States ★ 1881

BORN Nov. 19, 1831, near
Orange, OH

POLITICAL PARTY Republican

NO. OF TERMS one (assassinated)

VICE PRESIDENT Chester A. Arthur

DIED Sept. 19, 1881, in Elberon, NJ

CHESTER A. ARTHUR
21st President of the United States ★ 1881–1885

BORN Oct. 5, 1829, in Fairfield, VT

POLITICAL PARTY Republican

NO. OF TERMS one (partial)

VICE PRESIDENT none

DIED Nov. 18, 1886, in New York, NY

GROVER CLEVELAND
22nd and 24th President of the United States
1885–1889 ★ 1893–1897

BORN March 18, 1837, in Caldwell, NJ

POLITICAL PARTY Democrat

NO. OF TERMS two (nonconsecutive)

VICE PRESIDENTS 1st administration:
Thomas Andrews Hendricks
2nd administration:
Adlai Ewing Stevenson

DIED June 24, 1908, in Princeton, NJ

BENJAMIN HARRISON
23rd President of the United States ★ 1889–1893

BORN Aug. 20, 1833, in North Bend, OH

POLITICAL PARTY Republican

NO. OF TERMS one

VICE PRESIDENT Levi Parsons Morton

DIED March 13, 1901, in Indianapolis, IN

WILLIAM MCKINLEY
25th President of the United States ★ 1897–1901

BORN Jan. 29, 1843, in Niles, OH

POLITICAL PARTY Republican

NO. OF TERMS two (assassinated)

VICE PRESIDENTS 1st term:
Garret Augustus Hobart
2nd term:
Theodore Roosevelt

DIED Sept. 14, 1901, in Buffalo, NY

THEODORE ROOSEVELT
26th President of the United States ★ 1901–1909

BORN Oct. 27, 1858, in New York, NY

POLITICAL PARTY Republican

NO. OF TERMS one, plus balance of
McKinley's term

VICE PRESIDENTS 1st term: none
2nd term: Charles
Warren Fairbanks

DIED Jan. 6, 1919, in Oyster Bay, NY

WILLIAM HOWARD TAFT
27th President of the United States ★ 1909–1913

BORN Sept. 15, 1857, in Cincinnati, OH

POLITICAL PARTY Republican

NO. OF TERMS one

VICE PRESIDENT James Schoolcraft
Sherman

DIED March 8, 1930, in Washington, D.C.

WOODROW WILSON
28th President of the United States ★ 1913–1921

BORN Dec. 29, 1856, in Staunton, VA

POLITICAL PARTY Democrat

NO. OF TERMS two

VICE PRESIDENT Thomas Riley Marshall

DIED Feb. 3, 1924, in Washington, D.C.

WARREN G. HARDING
29th President of the United States ★ 1921–1923

BORN Nov. 2, 1865, in Caledonia
(now Blooming Grove), OH
POLITICAL PARTY Republican
NO. OF TERMS one (died while in office)
VICE PRESIDENT Calvin Coolidge
DIED Aug. 2, 1923, in San Francisco, CA

CALVIN COOLIDGE
30th President of the United States ★ 1923–1929

BORN July 4, 1872, in Plymouth, VT
POLITICAL PARTY Republican
NO. OF TERMS one, plus balance of
Harding's term
VICE PRESIDENTS 1st term: none
2nd term:
Charles Gates Dawes
DIED Jan. 5, 1933, in Northampton, MA

HERBERT HOOVER
31st President of the United States ★ 1929–1933

BORN Aug. 10, 1874,
in West Branch, IA
POLITICAL PARTY Republican
NO. OF TERMS one
VICE PRESIDENT Charles Curtis
DIED Oct. 20, 1964, in New York, NY

FRANKLIN D. ROOSEVELT
32nd President of the United States ★ 1933–1945

BORN Jan. 30, 1882, in Hyde Park, NY
POLITICAL PARTY Democrat
NO. OF TERMS four (died while in office)
VICE PRESIDENTS 1st & 2nd terms: John
Nance Garner; 3rd term:
Henry Agard Wallace;
4th term: Harry S. Truman
DIED April 12, 1945,
in Warm Springs, GA

HARRY S. TRUMAN
33rd President of the United States ★ 1945–1953

BORN May 8, 1884, in Lamar, MO
POLITICAL PARTY Democrat
NO. OF TERMS one, plus balance of
Franklin D. Roosevelt's term
VICE PRESIDENTS 1st term: none
2nd term:
Alben William Barkley
DIED Dec. 26, 1972, in Independence, MO

DWIGHT D. EISENHOWER
34th President of the United States ★ 1953–1961

BORN Oct. 14, 1890, in Denison, TX
POLITICAL PARTY Republican
NO. OF TERMS two
VICE PRESIDENT Richard Nixon
DIED March 28, 1969,
in Washington, D.C.

JOHN F. KENNEDY
35th President of the United States ★ 1961–1963

BORN May 29, 1917, in Brookline, MA
POLITICAL PARTY Democrat
NO. OF TERMS one (assassinated)
VICE PRESIDENT Lyndon B. Johnson
DIED Nov. 22, 1963, in Dallas, TX

LYNDON B. JOHNSON
36th President of the United States ★ 1963–1969

BORN Aug. 27, 1908, near Stonewall, TX
POLITICAL PARTY Democrat
NO. OF TERMS one, plus balance of
Kennedy's term
VICE PRESIDENTS 1st term: none
2nd term: Hubert
Horatio Humphrey
DIED Jan. 22, 1973, near San Antonio, TX

RICHARD NIXON
37th President of the United States ★ 1969–1974

BORN Jan. 9, 1913, in Yorba Linda, CA
POLITICAL PARTY Republican
NO. OF TERMS two (resigned)
VICE PRESIDENTS 1st term & 2nd term
(partial): Spiro Theodore
Agnew; 2nd term
(balance): Gerald R. Ford
DIED April 22, 1994, in New York, NY

HARRY S. TRUMAN OFFICIALLY OPENED THE FIRST WHITE HOUSE BOWLING ALLEY IN 1947.

GERALD R. FORD
38th President of the United States ★ 1974–1977
BORN July 14, 1913, in Omaha, NE
POLITICAL PARTY Republican
NO. OF TERMS one (partial)
VICE PRESIDENT Nelson Aldrich Rockefeller
DIED Dec. 26, 2006, in Rancho Mirage, CA

BILL CLINTON
42nd President of the United States ★ 1993–2001
BORN Aug. 19, 1946, in Hope, AR
POLITICAL PARTY Democrat
NO. OF TERMS two
VICE PRESIDENT Albert Arnold Gore, Jr.

JIMMY CARTER
39th President of the United States ★ 1977–1981
BORN Oct. 1, 1924, in Plains, GA
POLITICAL PARTY Democrat
NO. OF TERMS one
VICE PRESIDENT Walter Frederick (Fritz) Mondale

GEORGE W. BUSH
43rd President of the United States ★ 2001–2009
BORN July 6, 1946, in New Haven, CT
POLITICAL PARTY Republican
NO. OF TERMS two
VICE PRESIDENT Richard Bruce Cheney

RONALD REAGAN
40th President of the United States ★ 1981–1989
BORN Feb. 6, 1911, in Tampico, IL
POLITICAL PARTY Republican
NO. OF TERMS two
VICE PRESIDENT George H. W. Bush
DIED June 5, 2004, in Los Angeles, CA

BARACK OBAMA
44th President of the United States ★ 2009–2017
BORN Aug. 4, 1961, in Honolulu, HI
POLITICAL PARTY Democrat
NO. OF TERMS two
VICE PRESIDENT Joe Biden

GEORGE H. W. BUSH
41st President of the United States ★ 1989–1993
BORN June 12, 1924, in Milton, MA
POLITICAL PARTY Republican
NO. OF TERMS one
VICE PRESIDENT James Danforth (Dan) Quayle III
DIED November 30, 2018, in Houston, TX

DONALD TRUMP
45th President of the United States ★ 2017–2021
BORN June 14, 1946, in Queens, NY
POLITICAL PARTY Republican
NO. OF TERMS one
VICE PRESIDENT Mike Pence

JOE BIDEN
46th President of the United States ★ 2021–
BORN November 20, 1942, in Scranton, PA
POLITICAL PARTY Democrat
VICE PRESIDENT Kamala Harris

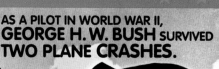

AS A PILOT IN WORLD WAR II, GEORGE H. W. BUSH SURVIVED TWO PLANE CRASHES.

Check out this book!

OUR COUNTRY'S **PRESIDENTS**
A COMPLETE ENCYCLOPEDIA OF THE U.S. PRESIDENCY

CIVIL RIGHTS

Although the Constitution protects the civil rights of American citizens, it has not always been able to protect all Americans from persecution or discrimination. During the first half of the 20th century, many Americans, particularly African Americans, were subjected to widespread discrimination and racism. By the mid-1950s, many people were eager to end the barriers caused by racism and bring freedom to all men and women.

The civil rights movement of the 1950s and 1960s sought to end racial discrimination against African Americans, especially in the southern states. The movement wanted to restore the fundamentals of economic and social equality to those who had been oppressed.

Woolworth Counter Sit-in

On February 1, 1960, four African-American college students strolled into a Woolworth's "five-and-dime" store in Greensboro, North Carolina. They planned to have lunch there, but were refused service as soon as they sat down at the counter. In a time of heightened racial tension, the Woolworth's manager had a strict whites-only policy. But the students wouldn't take no for an answer. The men—later dubbed the "Greensboro Four"—stayed seated, peacefully and quietly, at the lunch counter until closing. The next day, they returned with 15 additional college students. The following day, even more. By February 5, some 300 students gathered at Woolworth's, forming one of the most famous sit-ins of the civil rights movement. The protest—which sparked similar sit-ins throughout the country—worked: Just six months later, restaurants across the South began to integrate.

Key Events in the Civil Rights Movement

1954	The Supreme Court case *Brown v. Board of Education* declares school segregation illegal.
1955	Rosa Parks refuses to give up her bus seat to a white passenger and spurs a bus boycott.
1957	The Little Rock Nine help to integrate schools.
1960	Four black college students begin sit-ins at a restaurant in Greensboro, North Carolina.
1961	Freedom Rides to southern states begin as a way to protest segregation in transportation.
1963	Martin Luther King, Jr., leads the famous March on Washington.
1964	The Civil Rights Act, signed by President Lyndon B. Johnson, prohibits discrimination based on race, color, religion, sex, and national origin.
1967	Thurgood Marshall becomes the first African American to be named to the Supreme Court.
1968	President Lyndon B. Johnson signs the Civil Rights Act of 1968, which prohibits discrimination in the sale, rental, and financing of housing.

STONE OF HOPE:
THE LEGACY OF MARTIN LUTHER KING, JR.

On April 4, 1968, Dr. Martin Luther King, Jr., was shot by James Earl Ray while standing on a hotel balcony in Memphis, Tennessee, U.S.A. The news of his death sent shock waves throughout the world: Dr. King, a Baptist minister and founder of the Southern Christian Leadership Conference, was the most prominent civil rights leader of his time. His nonviolent protests and marches against segregation, as well as his powerful speeches—including his famous "I Have a Dream" speech—motivated people to fight for justice for all.

More than 50 years after his death, Dr. King's dream lives on through a memorial on the National Mall in Washington, D.C. Built in 2011, the memorial features a 30-foot (9-m) statue of Dr. King carved into a granite boulder named the "Stone of Hope."

Today, Dr. King continues to inspire people around the world with his words and his vision for a peaceful world without racism. He will forever be remembered as one of the most prominent leaders of the civil rights movement.

"The time is always right to do what is right."

Martin Luther King, Jr., Memorial in Washington, D.C.

JOHN LEWIS: GETTING IN GOOD TROUBLE

On March 7, 1965, a 25-year-old man linked arms with five other people, including Dr. Martin Luther King, Jr., as they led hundreds in a march across the Edmund Pettus Bridge in Selma, Alabama, U.S.A. It was a simple act, but it carried a very loud message: Those marching along the bridge were marching for racial justice and equality during a time when black people were treated unjustly by many and were denied the same basic rights as white people, including the right to vote.

That young man was John Lewis. And, after crossing the bridge, Lewis was attacked by state troopers and beaten badly. The scene was so shocking that it made national news and created a public outcry. An act that prevented Blacks from being denied the right to vote was passed just five months later. From then on, Lewis, who survived the attack, became a legend in the civil rights movement for his quiet yet powerful ability to create change. He called it getting in "good trouble": standing up for what you believe is right and just, even if it means ruffling feathers along the way.

Lewis went on to serve in the U.S. House of Representatives for 33 years until his death in 2020. Before he passed, he was able to speak about the Black Lives Matter movement, once again encouraging people to fight for justice. "We must use our time and our space on this little planet that we call Earth to make a lasting contribution, to leave it a little better than we found it," said Lewis. "And now that need is greater than ever before."

John Lewis joins hands with President Barack Obama as they lead a commemorative march across the Edmund Pettus Bridge in Selma, Alabama, in 2015.

WOMEN
FIGHTING FOR EQUALITY

Women in New York City cast their votes for the first time in November 1920.

Today, women make up about half of the workforce in the United States. But a little over a century ago, less than 20 percent worked outside the home. In fact, they didn't even have the right to vote!

That began to change in the mid-1800s when women, led by pioneers like Elizabeth Cady Stanton and Susan B. Anthony, started speaking up about inequality. They organized public demonstrations, gave speeches, published documents, and wrote newspaper articles to express their ideas. In 1848, about 300 people attended the Seneca Falls Convention in New York State to address the need for equal rights. By the late 1800s, the National American Woman Suffrage Association had made great strides toward giving women the freedom to vote. One by one, states began allowing women to vote. By 1920, the U.S. Constitution was amended, giving women across the country the ability to cast a vote during any election.

But the fight for equality did not end there. In the 1960s and 1970s, the women's rights movement experienced a rebirth, as feminists protested against injustices in areas such as the workplace and in education.

While these efforts enabled women to make great strides in our society, the efforts to even the playing field among men and women continue today.

New Zealand gave women the right to vote in 1893, becoming the world's first country to do so.

In 2020, Katie Bowers became the first female football coach in Super Bowl history.

248

Women's March in Boston, Massachusetts, U.S.A., on January 21, 2017

Key Events in U.S. Women's History

1848: **Elizabeth Cady Stanton** and **Lucretia Mott** organize the Seneca Falls Convention in New York. Attendees rally for equitable laws, equal educational and job opportunities, and the right to vote.

1920: **The 19th Amendment**, guaranteeing women the right to vote, is ratified.

1964: **Title VII of the Civil Rights Act of 1964,** which prohibits employment discrimination on the basis of sex, is successfully amended.

1971: **Gloria Steinem** heads up the National Women's Political Caucus, which encourages women to be active in government. She also launches *Ms.*, a magazine about women's issues.

1972: Congress approves **the Equal Rights Amendment** (ERA), proposing that women and men have equal rights under the law. It is ratified by 35 of the necessary 38 states, and is still not part of the U.S. Constitution.

1981: President Ronald Reagan appoints **Sandra Day O'Connor** as the first female Supreme Court justice.

2009: President Obama signs **the Lilly Ledbetter Fair Pay Act** to protect against pay discrimination among men and women.

2013: The **ban against women in military combat positions** is removed, overturning a 1994 Pentagon decision restricting women from combat roles.

2016: Democratic presidential nominee **Hillary Rodham Clinton** becomes the first woman to lead the ticket of a major U.S. party.

2017: A crowd of some four million people turned out for the first ever **Women's March**, a protest advocating women's rights. Events were held in locations throughout the country.

FIRST WOMEN-ONLY SPACE WALK

JESSICA MEIR AND CHRISTINA KOCH ON THE INTERNATIONAL SPACE STATION

Call it one giant leap for womankind: On a Friday morning in October 2019, American astronauts Christina Koch and Jessica Meir floated feet-first out of the International Space Station (ISS)—and entered the history books by conducting an all-women space walk.

Though there had been some 200 space walks in support of the ISS prior to this historic one, none had been completed by women only.

So just what does a space walk involve? According to NASA, the astronauts exited the ISS to replace a broken battery unit. It took more than five hours, with Koch and Meir making sure to stay clipped to the ISS with harnesses so they did not float off into space. Space walks aren't easy: In fact, according to NASA, most astronauts consider them to be the most physically demanding part of their job.

Although the space walk was simply a routine part of their mission, the honor of making history was not lost on the astronauts. "In the past, women haven't always been at the table," said Koch, who also set a record for the longest single spaceflight by a woman—with a total of 328 days in space. "Diversity is important, and it is something worth fighting for."

QUIZ WHIZ

Go back in time to seek the answers to this history quiz!

Write your answers on a piece of paper. Then check them below.

1 **True or false?** An 18th-century recipe for homemade cold medicine included the tips of crab claws.

2 Mortar created with _____ was used to hold the Great Wall of China's bricks together.
a. sticky rice flour
b. glue
c. bubble gum
d. dumpling dough

3 Ayutthaya, an ancient capital of the Siamese Kingdom, was known as one of the world's _____ cities.
a. richest
b. smallest
c. tallest
d. largest

4 **True or false?** Legend has it that the Roman goddess Venus was born wearing full battle armor.

5 About how many gems make up the royal collection of crown jewels, housed in the Tower of London?
a. 235
b. 2,350
c. 23,500
d. 230,500

Not **STUMPED** yet? Check out the *NATIONAL GEOGRAPHIC KIDS QUIZ WHIZ* collection for more crazy **HISTORY** questions!

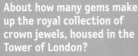

ANSWERS: 1. True; 2. a; 3. d; 4. False. The legend is about the Roman goddess Minerva.; 5. c

HOMEWORK HELP

Brilliant Biographies

Malala Yousafzai

A biography is the story of a person's life. It can be a brief summary or a long book. Biographers—those who write biographies—use many different sources to learn about their subjects. You can write your own biography of a famous person you find inspiring.

How to Get Started

Choose a subject you find interesting. If you think Cleopatra is cool, you have a good chance of getting your readers interested, too. If you're bored by ancient Egypt, your readers will be snoring after your first paragraph.

Your subject can be almost anyone: an author, an inventor, a celebrity, a politician, or a member of your family. To find someone to write about, ask yourself these simple questions:

1. Who do I want to know more about?
2. What did this person do that was special?
3. How did this person change the world?

Do Your Research

- Find out as much about your subject as possible. Read books, news articles, and encyclopedia entries. Watch video clips and movies, and search the internet. Conduct interviews, if possible.
- Take notes, writing down important facts and interesting stories about your subject.

Write the Biography

- Come up with a title. Include the person's name.
- Write an introduction. Consider asking a probing question about your subject.
- Include information about the person's childhood. When was this person born? Where did he or she grow up? Who did he or she admire?
- Highlight the person's talents, accomplishments, and personal attributes.
- Describe the specific events that helped to shape this person's life. Did this person ever have a problem and overcome it?
- Write a conclusion. Include your thoughts about why it is important to learn about this person.
- Once you have finished your first draft, revise and then proofread your work.

Here's a **SAMPLE BIOGRAPHY** of Malala Yousafzai, a human rights advocate and the youngest ever recipient of the Nobel Peace Prize. Of course, there is so much more for you to discover and write about on your own!

Malala Yousafzai

Malala Yousafzai was born in Pakistan on July 12, 1997. Malala's father, Ziauddin, a teacher, made it a priority for his daughter to receive a proper education. Malala loved school. She learned to speak three languages and even wrote a blog about her experiences as a student.

Around the time Malala turned 10, the Taliban—a group of strict Muslims who believe women should stay at home—took over the region where she lived. The Taliban did not approve of Malala's outspoken love of learning. One day, on her way home from school, Malala was shot in the head by a Taliban gunman. Very badly injured, she was sent to a hospital in England.

Not only did Malala survive the shooting—she thrived. She used her experience as a platform to fight for girls' education worldwide. She began speaking out about educational opportunities for all. Her efforts gained worldwide attention, and she was eventually awarded the Nobel Peace Prize in 2014 at the age of 17. She is the youngest person to earn the prestigious prize.

Each year on July 12, World Malala Day honors her heroic efforts to bring attention to human rights issues.

Granite peaks rise above Lake Pehoé in Torres del Paine National Park in Chile's Patagonia region.

GEOGRAPHY
ROCKS

THE POLITICAL WORLD

Earth's land area is made up of seven continents, but people have divided much of the land into smaller political units called countries. Australia is a continent made up of a single country, and Antarctica is used for scientific research. But the other five continents include almost 200 independent countries. The political map shown here depicts boundaries—imaginary lines created by treaties—that separate countries. Some boundaries, such as the one between the United States and Canada, are very stable and have been recognized for many years.

See Europe map for more detail.

Winkel Tripel Projection

0 — miles — 2000
0 — kilometers — 3000

Other boundaries, such as the one between Sudan and South Sudan in northeast Africa, are relatively new and still disputed. Countries come in all shapes and sizes. Russia and Canada are giants; others, such as El Salvador and Qatar, are small. Some countries are long and skinny—look at Chile in South America! Still other countries—such as Indonesia and Japan in Asia—are made up of groups of islands. The political map is a clue to the diversity that makes Earth so fascinating.

OCEAN

Barents Sea
Kara Sea
North Land
New Siberian Islands
Laptev Sea
East Siberian Sea

Svalbard (Norway)
Novaya Zemlya

NORWAY
SWEDEN
FINLAND

R U S S I A

Bering Sea

Sea of Okhotsk

DEN.
GERMANY
EST.
LATV.
LITH.
BELARUS
POLAND

Lake Baikal

UKRAINE
MOLD.
ROMANIA
BULGARIA
GEORGIA

KAZAKHSTAN

MONGOLIA

NORTH KOREA

JAPAN

ITALY
ALBANIA
GREECE
TURKEY
ARM.
AZERB.
UZBEK.
KYRGYZSTAN
TURKMEN.
TAJIKISTAN
SOUTH KOREA

C H I N A

TAIWAN — 30°
The People's Republic of China claims Taiwan as its 23rd province. Taiwan's government (Republic of China) maintains that there are two political entities.

TUNISIA
LEBANON
CYPRUS
SYRIA
IRAQ
IRAN
AFGHAN.
Caspian Sea

Mediterranean Sea

ALGERIA
LIBYA
ISRAEL
JORDAN
KUWAIT
BAHRAIN
QATAR
U.A.E.
SAUDI ARABIA
EGYPT
Red Sea
PAKISTAN
NEPAL
BHUTAN
BANGLADESH
INDIA
MYANMAR (BURMA)
Taiwan

South China Sea

Philippine Sea

Northern Mariana Islands (U.S.)

P A C I F I C

NIGER
CHAD
SUDAN
ERITREA
YEMEN
OMAN
Arabian Sea
Bay of Bengal
LAOS
VIETNAM
THAILAND
CAMBODIA
PHILIPPINES
Guam (U.S.)
OCEAN
MARSHALL ISLANDS

NIGERIA
CAMEROON
C.A.R.
SOUTH SUDAN
ETHIOPIA
DJIBOUTI
SOMALIA
MALDIVES
SRI LANKA
PALAU
FEDERATED STATES OF MICRONESIA
KIRIBATI

TOGO
BENIN
GABON
CONGO
DEM. REP. OF THE CONGO
RWANDA
UGANDA
KENYA
BURUNDI
60°
90°
BRUNEI
MALAYSIA
SINGAPORE
EQUATOR
150°
NAURU
0°

Cabinda (Angola)
TANZANIA
SEYCHELLES
I N D I A N
I N D O N E S I A
New Guinea
PAPUA NEW GUINEA
SOLOMON ISLANDS
TUVALU

ANGOLA
ZAMBIA
COMOROS
MALAWI
MOZAMBIQUE
MADAGASCAR
O C E A N
TIMOR-LESTE (EAST TIMOR)
Coral Sea
VANUATU
FIJI

NAMIBIA
ZIMBABWE
BOTSWANA
MAURITIUS
Réunion (France)
New Caledonia (France)

ESWATINI (SWAZILAND)
SOUTH AFRICA
LESOTHO

A U S T R A L I A

Great Australian Bight
Tasman Sea
North Island
30°

Kerguelen Islands (France)
Tasmania
NEW ZEALAND
South Island

CIRCLE
60°

ANTARCTICA
Ross Sea

⟪THE⟫PHYSICAL WORLD

Earth is dominated by large landmasses called continents—seven in all—and by an interconnected global ocean that is divided into four parts by the continents. More than 70 percent of Earth's surface is covered by oceans, and the rest is made up of land areas.

Different landforms give variety to the surface of the continents. The Rocky Mountains divide North America, the Andes mark the western edge of South America, and the Himalaya tower above South Asia. The Plateau of Tibet forms the rugged core of Asia,

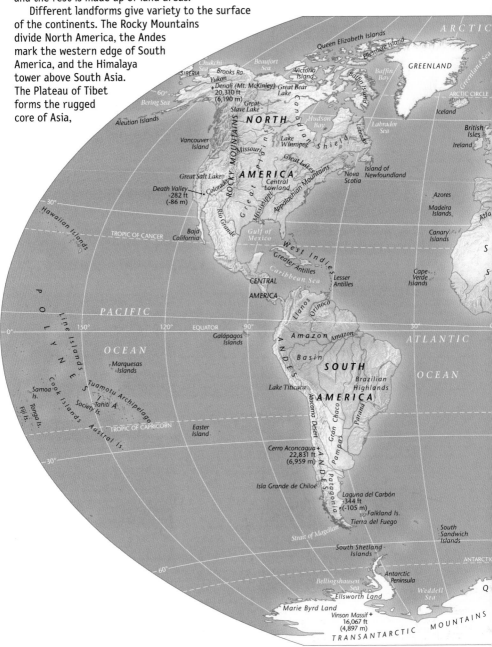

ARCTIC

Queen Elizabeth Islands
Ellesmere Island
GREENLAND
Chukchi
Beaufort Sea
SIBERIA
Brooks Ra.
Victoria Island
Baffin Bay
Baffin Island
Greenland Sea
ARCTIC CIRCLE
Yukon
Denali (Mt. McKinley)
20,310 ft
(6,190 m)
Great Bear Lake
Iceland
60°
Bering Sea
Great Slave Lake
Aleutian Islands
Hudson Bay
Labrador Sea
British Isles
NORTH
Vancouver Island
Lake Winnipeg
Canadian Shield
Ireland
Missouri
Great Lakes
AMERICA
Great Salt Lake
Central Lowland
Appalachian Mountains
Island of Newfoundland
Nova Scotia
Azores
Death Valley
-282 ft
(-86 m)
Colorado
Madeira Islands
30°
Hawaiian Islands
Rio Grande
Atla
TROPIC OF CANCER
Baja California
Gulf of Mexico
West Indies
Canary Islands
S
Greater Antilles
Caribbean Sea
Cape Verde Islands
S
CENTRAL
Lesser Antilles
AMERICA
Llanos
Orinoco
PACIFIC
Line Islands
150°
120°
EQUATOR
90°
Galápagos Islands
Amazon
Amazon
30°
ATLANTIC
OCEAN
Marquesas Islands
Basin
SOUTH
OCEAN
Tuamotu Archipelago
Brazilian Highlands
Samoa Is.
Society Is.
Tahiti
Lake Titicaca
AMERICA
Cook Islands
Tonga Is.
Fiji Is.
Austral Is.
TROPIC OF CAPRICORN
Easter Island
Atacama Desert
Gran Chaco
Paraná
Cerro Aconcagua
22,831 ft
(6,959 m)
Pampas
30°
Isla Grande de Chiloé
ANDES
Patagonia
Laguna del Carbón
-344 ft
(-105 m)
Falkland Is.
Tierra del Fuego
South Sandwich Islands
Strait of Magellan
South Shetland Islands
ANTARCTIC
60°
Antarctic Peninsula
Bellingshausen Sea
Weddell Sea
Q
Ellsworth Land
Marie Byrd Land
Vinson Massif
16,067 ft
(4,897 m)
TRANSANTARCTIC
MOUNTAINS

POLYNESIA

while the Northern European Plain extends from the North Sea to the Ural Mountains. Much of Africa is a plateau, and dry plains cover large areas of Australia. Mountains rise more than 16,000 feet (4,877 m) above Antarctica's massive ice sheets. Mountains and trenches make the ocean floors as varied as any continent. A mountain chain called the Mid-Atlantic Ridge runs the length of the Atlantic Ocean. In the western Pacific, trenches drop deep into the ocean floor.

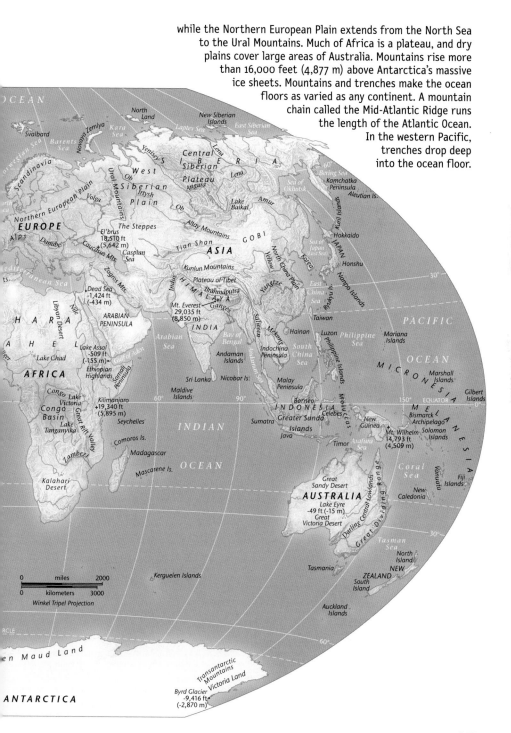

KINDS OF MAPS

Maps are special tools that geographers use to tell a story about Earth. Maps can be used to show just about anything related to places. Some maps show physical features, such as mountains or vegetation. Maps can also show climates or natural hazards and other things we cannot easily see. Other maps illustrate different features on Earth—political boundaries, urban centers, and economic systems.

AN IMPERFECT TOOL

Maps are not perfect. A globe is a scale model of Earth with accurate relative sizes and locations. Because maps are flat, they involve distortions of size, shape, and direction. Also, cartographers—people who create maps— make choices about what information to include. Because of this, it is important to study many different types of maps to learn the complete story of Earth. Three commonly found kinds of maps are shown on this page.

PHYSICAL MAPS. Earth's natural features—landforms, water bodies, and vegetation—are shown on physical maps. The map above uses color and shading to illustrate mountains, lakes, rivers, and deserts of central South America. Country names and borders are added for reference, but they are not natural features.

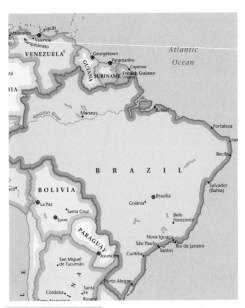

POLITICAL MAPS. These maps represent characteristics of the landscape created by humans, such as boundaries, cities, and place-names. Natural features are added only for reference. On the map above, capital cities are represented with a star inside a circle, while other cities are shown with black dots.

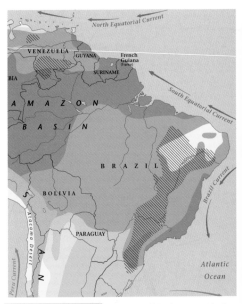

THEMATIC MAPS. Patterns related to a particular topic or theme, such as population distribution, appear on these maps. The map above displays the region's climate zones, which range from tropical wet (bright green) to tropical wet and dry (light green) to semiarid (dark yellow) to arid or desert (light yellow).

MAKING MAPS

Meet a Cartographer!

As a National Geographic cartographer, **Mike McNey** works with maps every day. Here, he shares more about his cool career.

National Geographic staff cartographers Mike McNey and Rosemary Wardley review a map of Africa for the *National Geographic Kids World Atlas.*

What exactly does a cartographer do?

I create maps specifically for books and atlases to help the text tell the story on the page. The maps need to fit into the size and the style of the book, with the final goal being that it's accurate and appealing for the reader.

What kinds of stories have you told with your maps?

Once, I created a map that showed the spread of the Burmese python population in Florida around the Everglades National Park. I've also made maps that show data like farmland, food production, cattle density, and fish catch in a particular location, like the United States.

How do you rely on technology in your job?

All aspects of mapmaking are on the computer. This makes it much quicker to make a map. It also makes it easier to change anything on the map. If you want to change the color of the rivers on the map, you just have to hit one button on the mouse.

How do you create your maps?

I work with geographic information systems (GIS), a computer software that allows us to represent any data on a specific location of the world, or even the entire world. Data can be anything from endangered species, animal ranges, and population of a particular place. We also use remote systems, like satellites and aerial imagery, to analyze Earth's surface.

Satellites in orbit around Earth act as eyes in the sky, recording data about the planet's land and ocean areas. The data are converted to numbers transmitted back to computers that are specially programmed to interpret the data. They record it in a form that cartographers can use to create maps.

What will maps of the future look like?

In the future, you'll see more and more data on maps. I also think more online maps are going to be made in a way that you can switch from a world view to a local view to see data at any scale.

What's the best part of your job?

I love the combination of science and design involved in it. It's also fun to make maps interesting for kids.

259

UNDERSTANDING
MAPS

MAKING A PROJECTION

Globes present a model of Earth as it is—a sphere—
but they are bulky and can be difficult to use and store.
Flat maps are much more convenient, but certain problems
can result from transferring Earth's curved surface to a
flat piece of paper, a process called projection. Imagine a
globe that has been cut in half, like the one to the right. If a
light is shined into it, the lines of latitude and longitude and the
shapes of the continent will cast shadows that can be "projected"
onto a piece of paper, as shown here. Depending on how the paper is
positioned, the shadows will be distorted in different ways.

KNOW THE CODE

Every map has a story to tell, but first you have to know how to read one. Maps represent
information by using a language of symbols. When you know how to read these symbols, you can
access a wide range of information. Look at the scale and compass rose or arrow to understand
distance and direction (see box below).

To find out what each symbol on a map means, you must use the key. It's your secret decoder—
identifying information by each symbol on the map.

There are three main types of map symbols: points, lines, and areas. Points, which can be either
dots or small icons, represent the location or the number of things, such as schools, cities, or
landmarks. Lines are used to show boundaries, roads, or rivers and can vary in color or thickness.
Area symbols use pattern or color to show regions, such as a sandy area or a neighborhood.

SCALE AND DIRECTION

The scale on a map can be shown as a fraction, as words, or as a line or bar. It relates
distance on the map to distance in the real world. Sometimes the scale identifies the
type of map projection. Maps may include an arrow to indicate north on the map or a
compass rose to show all principal directions.

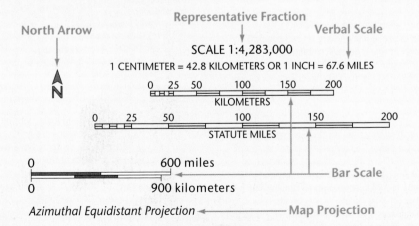

Representative Fraction

North Arrow

Verbal Scale

SCALE 1:4,283,000

1 CENTIMETER = 42.8 KILOMETERS OR 1 INCH = 67.6 MILES

N

0 25 50   100   150   200
KILOMETERS

0   25   50   100   150   200
STATUTE MILES

0   600 miles
0   900 kilometers

Bar Scale

Azimuthal Equidistant Projection ← Map Projection

GEOGRAPHIC FEATURES

rom roaring rivers to parched deserts, from underwater canyons
o jagged mountains, Earth is covered with beautiful and diverse
nvironments. Here are examples of the most common types of
eographic features found around the world.

WATERFALL

Waterfalls form when a river reaches an abrupt change in elevation. At left, the Iguazú waterfall system—on the border of Brazil and Argentina—is made up of 275 falls.

VALLEY

alleys, cut by running water
r moving ice, may be broad
nd flat or narrow and steep,
uch as the Indus River Valley
above) in Ladakh, India.

RIVER

As a river moves through flatlands, it twists and turns. Above, the Rio Los Amigos winds through a rainforest in Peru.

MOUNTAIN

Mountains are Earth's tallest landforms, and Mount Everest (above) rises highest of all, at 29,035 feet (8,850 m) above sea level.

GLACIER

laciers—"rivers" of ice—such
s Hubbard Glacier (above) in
laska, U.S.A., move slowly from
nountains to the sea. Global
varming is shrinking them.

CANYON

Steep-sided valleys called canyons are created mainly by running water. Buckskin Gulch (above) in Utah, U.S.A., is the deepest "slot" canyon in the American Southwest.

DESERT

Deserts are land features created by climate, specifically by a lack of water. Here, a camel caravan crosses the Sahara in North Africa.

AFRICA

In legends from Tanzania, Africa, witches ride on hyenas, not broomsticks.

Hippos sweat an oily red liquid that acts as sunscreen.

Hippopotamus

The massive continent of Africa, where humankind began millions of years ago, is second only to Asia in size. Stretching nearly as far from west to east as it does from north to south, Africa is home to both the longest river in the world (the Nile) and the largest hot desert on Earth (the Sahara).

Luanda, Angola

DRAGON LIZARD SIGHTING

Scientists recently discovered a new species of dragon lizard in southern Africa. Known as the Swazi dragon lizard, the 13-inch (33-cm) lizard has shield-like scales and hides in rock crevices.

ON LOCATION

Nigeria's film industry—also known as Nollywood—is the world's second largest film producer, ahead of Hollywood and behind India's Bollywood. Popular Nollywood films include the romantic comedy *The Wedding Party* and its sequel.

Great Pyramid, Great Numbers
How do the numbers for Earth's biggest pyramid stack up?

Due to erosion the pyramid is **30 feet (9 m)** shorter than it was originally.

Weight of largest stone blocks: **15 tons (14 t)**

Number of stone blocks: **2.3 million**

Angle at which the sides rise: **51°52'**

Number of builders: **20,000**

Height: **451 feet (138 m)**

Average length of each side: **756 feet (230 m)**

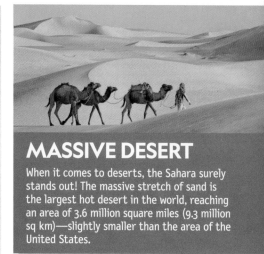

MASSIVE DESERT

When it comes to deserts, the Sahara surely stands out! The massive stretch of sand is the largest hot desert in the world, reaching an area of 3.6 million square miles (9.3 million sq km)—slightly smaller than the area of the United States.

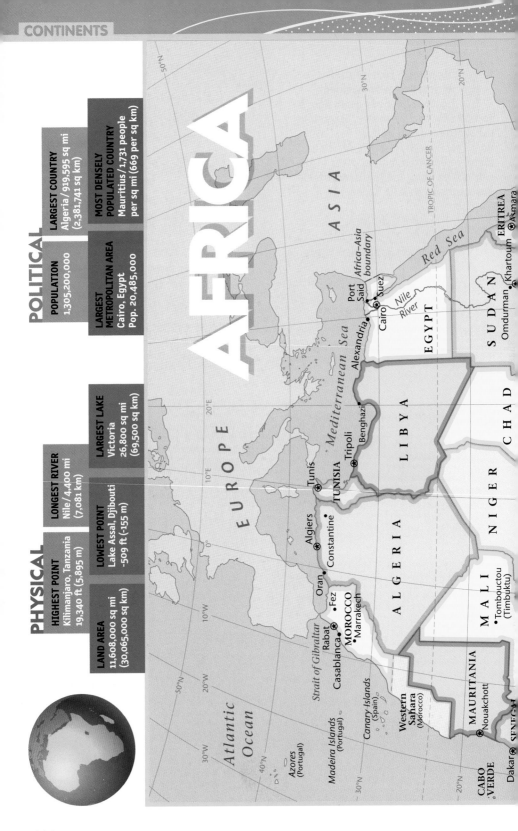

AFRICA

PHYSICAL

HIGHEST POINT	LONGEST RIVER
Kilimanjaro, Tanzania 19,340 ft (5,895 m)	Nile / 4,400 mi (7,081 km)

LAND AREA	LOWEST POINT	LARGEST LAKE
11,608,000 sq mi (30,065,000 sq km)	Lake Assal, Djibouti -509 ft (-155 m)	Victoria 26,800 sq mi (69,500 sq km)

POLITICAL

POPULATION	LARGEST COUNTRY
1,305,200,000	Algeria / 919,595 sq mi (2,381,741 sq km)

LARGEST METROPOLITAN AREA	MOST DENSELY POPULATED COUNTRY
Cairo, Egypt Pop. 20,485,000	Mauritius / 1,731 people per sq mi (669 per sq km)

ASIA

EUROPE

Atlantic Ocean

Azores (Portugal)

Madeira Islands (Portugal)

Canary Islands (Spain)

Strait of Gibraltar

Rabat
Casablanca
Fez
MOROCCO
Marrakech

Oran
Algiers
Constantine

Tunis
TUNISIA
Tripoli
Benghazi

Mediterranean Sea

Alexandria

Cairo
Port Said
Suez

Africa–Asia boundary

Red Sea

TROPIC OF CANCER

ERITREA
Asmara

Omdurman Khartoum

SUDAN

EGYPT

LIBYA

ALGERIA

MALI
Tombouctou (Timbuktu)

NIGER

CHAD

MAURITANIA
Nouakchott

Western Sahara (Morocco)

CABO VERDE

Dakar SENEGAL

Map Key
- ⊛ National capital
- • Other city
- ▲ Highest point (above sea level)
- ▼ Lowest point (below sea level)

Atlantic Ocean

Indian Ocean

Azimuthal Equal-Area Projection

800 Miles
800 Kilometers

SOMALIA
ETHIOPIA
SOUTH SUDAN
DJIBOUTI
Djibouti
Addis Ababa
Juba
UGANDA
Kampala
KENYA
Nairobi
Mombasa
Kilimanjaro
19,340 ft (5,895 m)
Dar es Salaam
TANZANIA
RWANDA
Kigali
BURUNDI
Gitega
Bujumbura
Dodoma
Lake Victoria
SEYCHELLES
Victoria
COMOROS
Moroni
MADAGASCAR
Antananarivo
MAURITIUS
Port Louis
Réunion (France)
Mozambique Channel
MOZAMBIQUE
Maputo
ESWATINI (SWAZILAND)
Mbabane
Lobamba
LESOTHO
Maseru
Durban
SOUTH AFRICA
Bloemfontein
Johannesburg
Pretoria (Tshwane)
Gaborone
BOTSWANA
Port Elizabeth
Cape Town
NAMIBIA
Windhoek
ANGOLA
Luanda
Cabinda (Angola)
Pointe-Noire
Brazzaville
Kinshasa
DEMOCRATIC REPUBLIC OF THE CONGO
Kananga
Mbuji-Mayi
Kisangani
Kolwezi
Kitwe
Lubumbashi
ZAMBIA
Lusaka
ZIMBABWE
Harare
MALAWI
Lilongwe
CONGO
Libreville
GABON
Yaoundé
Douala
CAMEROON
Bangui
CENTRAL AFRICAN REPUBLIC
N'Djamena
DARFUR
Lake Assal (-155 m) -509 ft
Gulf of Aden
SOMALILAND
Mogadishu

NIGERIA
Kano
Abuja
Ogbomosho
Lagos
Porto-Novo
Cotonou
BENIN
TOGO
Lomé
GHANA
Accra
Abidjan
CÔTE D'IVOIRE (IVORY COAST)
Yamoussoukro
LIBERIA
Monrovia
SIERRA LEONE
Freetown
GUINEA
Conakry
GUINEA-BISSAU
Bissau
THE GAMBIA
Bamako
Niamey
Ouagadougou
BURKINA FASO
Malabo
EQUATORIAL GUINEA
SAO TOME & PRINCIPE
São Tomé
Ascension (U.K.)
St. Helena (U.K.)

EQUATOR
TROPIC OF CAPRICORN

ANTARCTICA

Chinstrap penguin

Chinstrap penguins are named for the narrow black bands under their heads.

Antarctica experiences icequakes, which are like earthquakes that occur within an ice sheet.

This frozen continent may be a cool place to visit, but unless you're a penguin, you probably wouldn't want to hang out in Antarctica for long. The fact that it's the coldest, windiest, and driest continent helps explain why humans never colonized this ice-covered land surrounding the South Pole.

Weddell seal

GOING THE DISTANCE

Each year, a few dozen runners from around the world compete in the Antarctic Ice Marathon, where participants face an average temperature with windchill of -4°F (-20°C).

WARMER THAN EVER

With Antarctica experiencing record-breaking high temperatures, the continent as a whole is getting warmer. Temperatures hovering near 70°F (21°C) in February 2020 make the area one of the fastest-warming regions on Earth. Experts are racing to come up with ways to slow the effects of these dangerously high temps—and to save Antarctica from global warming's wrath.

50	50
40	40
30	30
20	20
10	10
0	0
10	10
20	20
30	30
40	40
50	50

Annual Average Snowfall

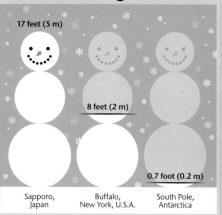

17 feet (5 m)

8 feet (2 m)

0.7 foot (0.2 m)

Sapporo, Japan

Buffalo, New York, U.S.A.

South Pole, Antarctica

SEEING GREEN

Emerald icebergs? Only in Antarctica! Here you can spot these rare and beautiful bergs in a deep green hue. So how do these icebergs acquire their stunning shade? Experts say it could be a combo of the bluish tint of glacial ice and yellow-red glacial dust dredged up from deep below the surface.

PHYSICAL

LAND AREA
5,100,000 sq mi
(13,209,000 sq km)

HIGHEST POINT
Vinson Massif
16,067 ft (4,897 m)

LOWEST POINT
Byrd Glacier
-9,416 ft (-2,870 m)

COLDEST PLACE
Ridge A, annual
average temperature
-94°F (-70°C)

**AVERAGE
PRECIPITATION ON
THE POLAR PLATEAU**
Less than 2 in (5 cm)

POLITICAL

POPULATION
There are no
indigenous inhabitants,
but there are both
permanent and
summer-only staffed
research stations.

**NUMBER OF
INDEPENDENT
COUNTRIES** 0

**NUMBER OF
COUNTRIES
CLAIMING LAND** 7

**NUMBER OF
COUNTRIES
OPERATING YEAR-
ROUND RESEARCH
STATIONS** 21

**NUMBER OF YEAR-
ROUND RESEARCH
STATIONS** 40

Map Key

▲ Highest point (above sea level)
▼ Lowest point (below sea level)
+ Other mountain peak

Atlantic
Ocean

South
Orkney
Islands

South
Shetland
Islands

Antarctic
Peninsula

Graham Land

LARSEN
ICE SHELF

Mount Jackson
10,446 ft (3,184 m)

Alexander
Island

Palmer Land

Weddell
Sea

Coats

FILCHNER
ICE SHELF

RONNE
ICE
SHELF

Berkner
Island

Bellingshausen
Sea

ELLSWORTH LAND

Vinson Massif
▲16,067 ft (4,897 m)

ELLSWORTH MTS.

West

Pacific
Ocean

Amundsen
Sea

MARIE BYRD LAND

Antarctica

ANTARCTIC CIRCLE

Who owns Antarctica?
No one. Seven countries each claim
a piece of this frozen continent.

Atlantic
Ocean

SOUTH
AMERICA

ARGENTINE CLAIM

BRITISH CLAIM

CHILEAN CLAIM

NORWEGIAN
CLAIM

ANTARCTIC CIRCLE

0   600 Miles
0   600 Kilometers

AUSTRALIAN CLAIM

Indian
Ocean

Pacific
Ocean

NEW ZEALAND
CLAIM

FRENCH
CLAIM

AUSTRALIAN
CLAIM

ANTARCTICA

FIMBUL
ICE SHELF

0°

RIISER-LARSEN
ICE SHELF

Q U E E N   M A U D   L A N D

Land

ENDERBY
LAND

60°E

*Indian
Ocean*

Valkyrie
Dome

MacKenzie Bay

75°E

Lambert
Glacier

AMERY ICE SHELF

T
R
A
N
S
A
N
T
A
R
C
T
I
C

M
O
U
N
T
A
I
N
S

AMERICAN

HIGHLAND

WEST
ICE SHELF

Ridge A +

POLAR PLATEAU

East

90°E

★
South Pole

Antarctica

SHACKLETON
ICE SHELF

80°S

105°E

ROSS
ICE
SHELF

Byrd Glacier
-9,416 ft (-2,870 m)

Roosevelt
Island

Taylor
Glacier

Ross Island

Mount Erebus
12,448 ft
(3,794 m)

70°S

W
I
L
K
E
S

L
A
N
D

120°E

*Ross
Sea*

V
I
C
T
O
R
I
A

L
A
N
D

Talos
Dome

180°

60°S

*Indian
Ocean*

0   600 Miles

0   600 Kilometers

Azimuthal Equidistant Projection

150°E

135°E

ASIA

A whirling dervish performs
in Istanbul, Turkey.

Chicken
breast pudding
is a popular
dessert
in Turkey.

China
has only
one time
zone.

Made up of 46 countries, Asia is the world's largest continent. Just how big is it? From western Turkey to the eastern tip of Russia, Asia spans nearly half the globe! Home to more than four billion citizens—that's three out of five people on the planet—Asia's population is bigger than that of all the other continents combined.

Kuala Lumpur, Malaysia

ON THE MOVE

About a third of the population of Mongolia moves seasonally. They live in portable huts called *ger* while traveling up to 70 miles (112 km) on foot to find food sources for their livestock.

FLYING HIGH

Native to Central Asia, the bar-headed goose can soar at altitudes higher than even helicopters can fly. Powerful lungs and strong wings allow these birds to cross over the Himalaya during their annual migration.

SAVING THE SNOW LEOPARDS

Countries with political tensions in Central and South Asia have found something to agree upon. "Peace parks"—protected stretches of the snow leopard's native habitat—will soon appear in border areas shared by countries who have a history of disputes.

World's Deepest Lakes

Lake Baikal (Russia)	Lake Tanganyika (eastern Africa)	Caspian Sea (Central Asia/Europe border)	Lake Malawi (eastern Africa)	Ysyk-Köl (Kyrgyzstan)
			2,316 ft (706 m)	2,297 ft (700 m)
		3,104 ft (946 m)		
	4,708 ft (1,435 m)			
5,369 ft (1,637 m)				

Most of Earth's surface water is stored in lakes. The deepest of all is Asia's Lake Baikal, which contains about 20 percent of Earth's total surface freshwater.

271

PHYSICAL

LAND AREA
17,208,000 sq mi
(44,570,000 sq km)

HIGHEST POINT
Mount Everest,
China–Nepal
29,035 ft (8,850 m)

LOWEST POINT
Dead Sea,
Israel–Jordan
-1,401 ft (-427 m)

LONGEST RIVER
Yangtze, China
3,880 mi (6,244 km)

**LARGEST LAKE
ENTIRELY IN ASIA**
Lake Baikal, Russia
12,200 sq mi
(31,500 sq km)

POLITICAL

POPULATION
4,586,900,000

**LARGEST
METROPOLITAN AREA**
Tokyo, Japan
Pop. 37,435,000

**LARGEST COUNTRY
ENTIRELY IN ASIA**
China
3,705,405 sq mi
(9,596,960 sq km)

**MOST DENSELY
POPULATED COUNTRY**
Singapore
21,814 people
per sq mi
(8,419 per sq km)

A commonly accepted division between Asia and Europe—marked here by a maroon, dashed line—is formed by the Ural Mountains, Ural River, Caspian Sea, Caucasus Mountains, and the Black Sea with its outlets, the Bosporus and Dardanelles.

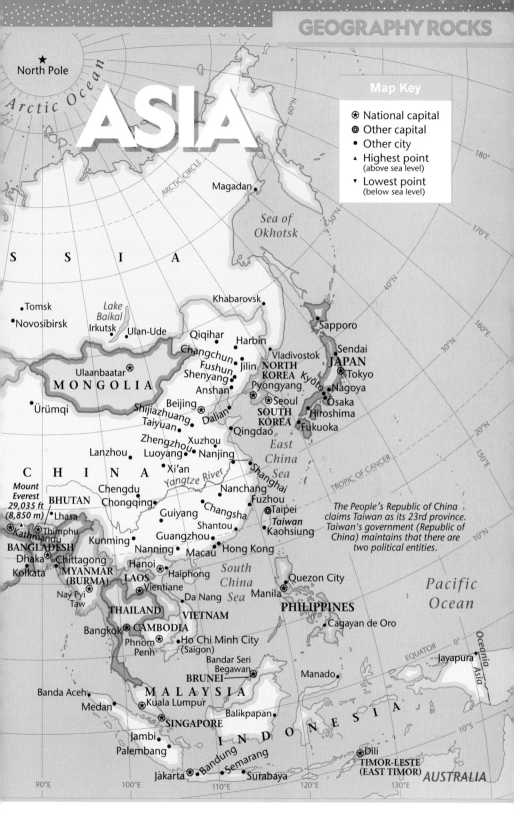

★ North Pole

Map Key

⊗ National capital
◎ Other capital
• Other city
▲ Highest point
(above sea level)
▼ Lowest point
(below sea level)

Arctic Ocean

ASIA

Magadan

Sea of Okhotsk

R U S S I A

Tomsk
Novosibirsk
Irkutsk
Lake Baikal
Ulan-Ude
Khabarovsk

Qiqihar
Harbin
Changchun
Fushun
Jilin
Shenyang
Anshan
Ulaanbaatar
M O N G O L I A
Ürümqi
Beijing
Shijiazhuang
Taiyuan
Dalian
Lanzhou
Zhengzhou
Xuzhou
Luoyang
Nanjing

Vladivostok
NORTH KOREA
Pyongyang
Seoul
SOUTH KOREA
Qingdao

Sapporo
Sendai
JAPAN
Kyoto
Tokyo
Nagoya
Osaka
Hiroshima
Fukuoka

C H I N A
Mount Everest
29,035 ft
(8,850 m)
BHUTAN
Lhasa
Kathmandu
Thimphu
BANGLADESH
Dhaka
Chittagong
Kolkata
MYANMAR
(BURMA)
Nay Pyi Taw

Xi'an
Chengdu
Chongqing
Guiyang
Kunming
Nanning
Guangzhou
Hanoi
Haiphong
LAOS
Vientiane
Da Nang
THAILAND
Bangkok
CAMBODIA
Phnom Penh
VIETNAM
Ho Chi Minh City
(Saigon)

Yangtze River
Nanchang
Changsha
Shantou
Macau
Hong Kong

Shanghai
Fuzhou
Taipei
Taiwan
Kaohsiung

East China Sea

TROPIC OF CANCER

The People's Republic of China claims Taiwan as its 23rd province. Taiwan's government (Republic of China) maintains that there are two political entities.

South China Sea

Quezon City
Manila
PHILIPPINES
Cagayan de Oro

Pacific Ocean

Banda Aceh
Medan
MALAYSIA
Kuala Lumpur
SINGAPORE
Jambi
Palembang
Jakarta
Bandung
Semarang
Surabaya

Bandar Seri Begawan
BRUNEI
Balikpapan
I N D O N E S I A

Manado

EQUATOR
Jayapura
Oceania
Asia

Dili
TIMOR-LESTE
(EAST TIMOR)
AUSTRALIA

90°E   100°E   110°E   120°E   130°E

AUSTRALIA,
NEW ZEALAND, AND OCEANIA

Australia has no native hoofed animals.

At birth, a koala is about the size of a bee.

A koala munches on a eucalyptus leaf in Australia.

274

G'day, mate! This vast region, covering almost 3.3 million square miles (8.5 million sq km), includes Australia—the world's smallest and flattest continent—and New Zealand, as well as a fleet of mostly tiny islands scattered across the Pacific Ocean. Also known as "down under," most of the countries in this region are in the Southern Hemisphere, below the Equator.

Maori children of New Zealand in ceremonial clothing

COLORFUL CRITTER

Almost half of all known peacock spiders on the planet live in Western Australia. This eight-eyed spider, named for the bright blue markings on the males of the species, can jump a distance of more than 20 times its body length.

FLAT LAND

Australia has mountain ranges with low elevations compared to the other continents of the world. This makes it the flattest continent on Earth. Its highest point? Mount Kosciuszko, which is only about one-quarter the height of Mount Everest.

More Animals Than People

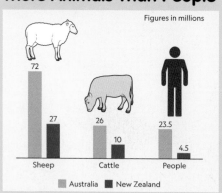

Figures in millions

Sheep	Cattle	People
72	26	23.5
27	10	4.5

■ Australia ■ New Zealand

BEACH IT

Beaches are bountiful in Australia! The continent boasts 10,000 beaches—more than any other country. Whether you're seeking sand, surf, or natural beauty, you'll find a beach for that.

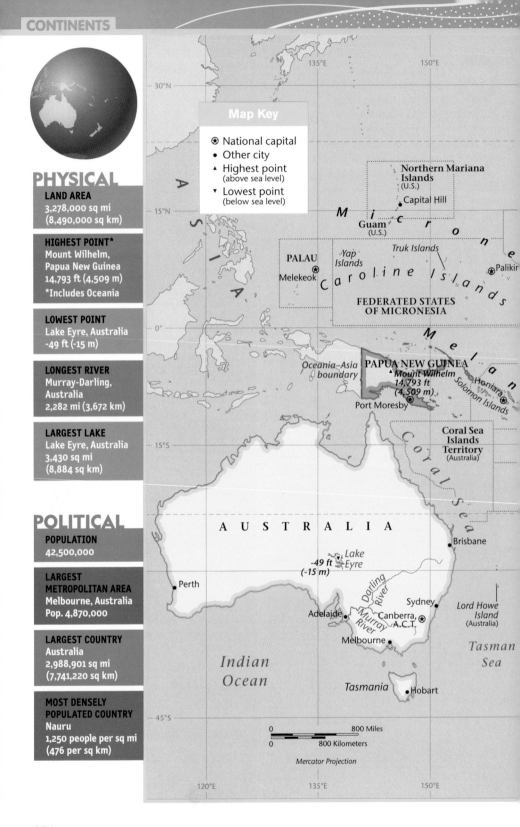

PHYSICAL

LAND AREA
3,278,000 sq mi
(8,490,000 sq km)

HIGHEST POINT*
Mount Wilhelm,
Papua New Guinea
14,793 ft (4,509 m)
*Includes Oceania

LOWEST POINT
Lake Eyre, Australia
-49 ft (-15 m)

LONGEST RIVER
Murray-Darling,
Australia
2,282 mi (3,672 km)

LARGEST LAKE
Lake Eyre, Australia
3,430 sq mi
(8,884 sq km)

POLITICAL

POPULATION
42,500,000

**LARGEST
METROPOLITAN AREA**
Melbourne, Australia
Pop. 4,870,000

LARGEST COUNTRY
Australia
2,988,901 sq mi
(7,741,220 sq km)

**MOST DENSELY
POPULATED COUNTRY**
Nauru
1,250 people per sq mi
(476 per sq km)

Map Key

⊕ National capital
• Other city
▲ Highest point
(above sea level)
▼ Lowest point
(below sea level)

ASIA

Northern Mariana
Islands
(U.S.)
• Capital Hill

Micronesia

Guam
(U.S.)

PALAU
Melekeok ⊛

Yap
Islands

Truk Islands

Caroline Islands

• Palikir

FEDERATED STATES
OF MICRONESIA

Melanesia

Oceania–Asia
boundary

PAPUA NEW GUINEA
▲ Mount Wilhelm
14,793 ft
(4,509 m)

Honiara •
Solomon Islands

Port Moresby

Coral Sea
Islands
Territory
(Australia)

Coral Sea

AUSTRALIA

• Brisbane

-49 ft ▼ Lake
(-15 m)   Eyre

Darling
River

• Perth

Sydney •

Lord Howe
Island
(Australia)

Adelaide •

Murray
River

Canberra, ⊕
A.C.T.

Melbourne •

Indian
Ocean

Tasman
Sea

Tasmania

• Hobart

| 0 | | 800 Miles |
| 0 | | 800 Kilometers |

Mercator Projection

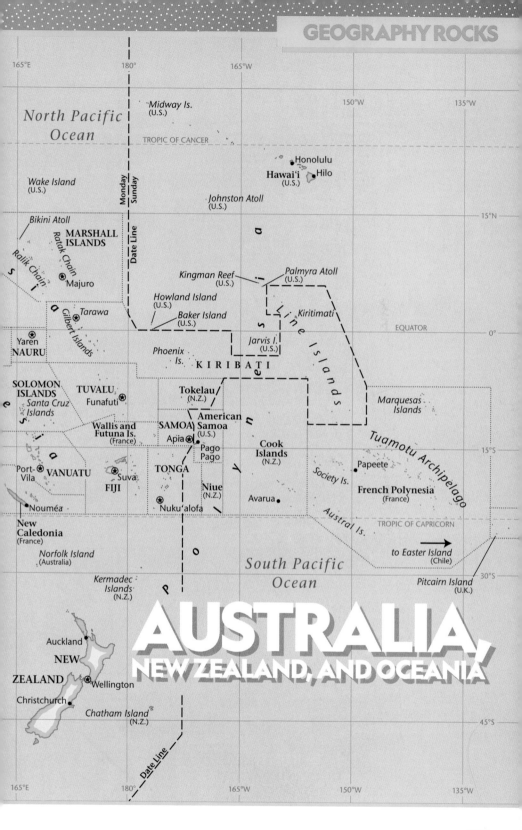

North Pacific
Ocean

Midway Is.
(U.S.)

TROPIC OF CANCER

●Honolulu
Hawai'i ●Hilo
(U.S.)

Wake Island
(U.S.)

Monday Sunday

Date Line

Johnston Atoll
(U.S.)

15°N

Bikini Atoll

MARSHALL
ISLANDS

Ratak Chain

Ralik Chain

✹Majuro

Kingman Reef
(U.S.)

Palmyra Atoll
(U.S.)

Howland Island
(U.S.)

Baker Island
(U.S.)

Line Islands

Kiritimati

EQUATOR   0°

✹Tarawa

Gilbert Islands

Jarvis I.
(U.S.)

✹Yaren
NAURU

Phoenix
Is.

K I R I B A T I

SOLOMON
ISLANDS

Santa Cruz
Islands

TUVALU
Funafuti ✹

Tokelau
(N.Z.)

Marquesas
Islands

15°S

Wallis and
Futuna Is.
(France)

SAMOA
Apia ●✹

American
Samoa
(U.S.)
●Pago
Pago

Polynesia

Cook
Islands
(N.Z.)

Society Is.

●Papeete

Tuamotu Archipelago

Port-
Vila ● **VANUATU**

●Suva
FIJI

TONGA

Niue
(N.Z.)

●Nuku'alofa

Avarua ●

French Polynesia
(France)

●Nouméa

New
Caledonia
(France)

Norfolk Island
(Australia)

Austral Is.

TROPIC OF CAPRICORN

Kermadec
Islands
(N.Z.)

South Pacific
Ocean

to Easter Island
(Chile)

Pitcairn Island
(U.K.)

30°S

AUSTRALIA,
NEW ZEALAND, AND OCEANIA

Auckland ●

NEW

ZEALAND

●Wellington

Christchurch

Chatham Island
(N.Z.)

45°S

Date Line

165°E   180°   165°W   150°W   135°W

EUROPE

The Rubik's Cube was invented in Hungary, a country in Europe.

The national animal of Spain is the bull.

Acrobats build human castles at the La Mercè festival in Barcelona, Spain.

A cluster of peninsulas and islands jutting west from Asia, Europe is bordered by the Atlantic and Arctic Oceans and more than a dozen seas. Here you'll find a variety of scenery, from mountains to countryside to coastlines. Europe is also known for its rich culture and fascinating history, which make it one of the most visited continents on Earth.

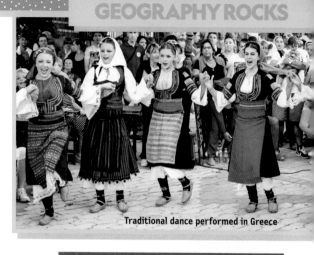

Traditional dance performed in Greece

MORE TREES

Every time a baby is born or adopted in Wales, U.K., a tree is planted to create new woodlands across the country. Since 2008, more than 300,000 trees have been planted, enough to create some 346 acres (140 ha) of new woods.

COOL COMEBACK

Bring back the bison! The European bison's numbers are increasing across the continent, thanks to recent conservation efforts. At one point, the animals' population was about 50, but now it is up to around 7,000 in the wild and captivity.

Europe's Longest Rivers

River	Length
Volga	2,290 mi (3,685 km)
Danube	1,770 mi (2,848 km)
Dnieper	1,420 mi (2,285 km)
Rhine	765 mi (1,230 km)
Elbe	724 mi (1,165 km)

RECYCLING RIGHT

A leader in recycling, Lithuania boasts a rate of 74 percent for recycling plastic packaging—the highest of any European country. Its residents also recycle more than 90 percent of their bottles and cans.

PHYSICAL

LAND AREA
3,841,000 sq mi
(9,947,000 sq km)

HIGHEST POINT
El'brus, Russia
18,510 ft (5,642 m)

LOWEST POINT
Caspian Sea
-92 ft (-28 m)

LONGEST RIVER
Volga, Russia
2,290 mi
(3,685 km)

**LARGEST LAKE
ENTIRELY IN EUROPE**
Ladoga, Russia
6,853 sq mi
(17,749 sq km)

POLITICAL

POPULATION
745,600,000

**LARGEST
METROPOLITAN AREA**
Moscow, Russia
Pop. 12,476,000

**LARGEST COUNTRY
ENTIRELY IN EUROPE**
Ukraine
233,032 sq mi
(603,550 sq km)

**MOST DENSELY
POPULATED COUNTRY**
Monaco
39,000 people per sq
mi (19,500 per sq km)

Map Key

⊛ National capital
◉ Capital of Northern
Ireland, Scotland,
or Wales
• Other city
▫ Small country
▲ Highest point
(above sea level)
▼ Lowest point
(below sea level)

30°W   20°W   10°W   0°

Jan Mayen
(Norway)

Reykjavík
ICELAND

ARCTIC CIRCLE

Norwegian
Sea

PRIME MERIDIAN

Faroe Islands
(Denmark)

Shetland
Islands

Orkney Islands

N O R

Oslo

60°N

SCOTLAND
Glasgow Edinburgh   Göteborg
North
N. IRELAND   Sea   DENMARK
IRELAND   Belfast   Copenhagen ⊛
(ÉIRE)   UNITED KINGDOM
Dublin   Kiel
Liverpool •Manchester
WALES   Birmingham   Hamburg
Cardiff   ENGLAND   The   NETH.
London ⊛   Hague ⊛ Amsterdam   Berlin ⊛
Brussels ⊛   GERMANY
BELGIUM   Frankfurt
⊛ Paris   LUX.   Prague

50°N

Atlantic
Ocean

•Nantes   Munich
LIECH.
Bay of   F R A N C E Zürich•   AUSTRI
Biscay   Bern• SWITZ.   Ljubljana
•Bordeaux Lyon•   Milan   Venice• SLOV.
•Turin   Genoa
Bilbao•   •Toulouse   MONACO   SAN
Oporto•   •Valladolid   •Nice   MARINO
40°N   ANDORRA   Marseille   ITALY
Lisbon•   Madrid⊛ •Zaragoza   Corsica VATICAN
S P A I N   Barcelona (France) CITY⊛
10°W   Valencia•   Sardinia Rome•
•Seville Murcia•   Balearic Is. (Italy)   Naples•
•Málaga   (Spain)   Messina
•Gibraltar (U.K.)   M e d i t e r r a   Palermo•
Catania
Sicily
0   400 Miles   e a l
0   400 Kilometers   A F R I C A   Valletta⊛
Azimuthal Equidistant Projection   ◦ MALTA

0°   10°E

A commonly accepted division between Asia and Europe—marked here by a maroon, dashed line—is formed by the Ural Mountains, Ural River, Caspian Sea, Caucasus Mountains, and the Black Sea with its outlets, the Bosporus and Dardanelles.

Barents Sea

Murmansk

RUSSIA

Archangel

EUROPE

Lake Ladoga

Helsinki

St. Petersburg

Stockholm
Tallinn
ESTONIA

Yaroslavl'
Tver'
Ufa
Kazan'
Volga River

Nizhniy Novgorod

Rīga
LATVIA

Moscow

Samara
Orenburg

Ryazan'

LITHUANIA
Kaliningrad
(Russia)
Vitsyebsk
Vilnius
Smolensk
Penza

Gdańsk
Kaunas
Minsk

POLAND
Warsaw
BELARUS
Homyel'
Bryansk
Saratov

KAZAKHSTAN

Bydgoszcz
Łódź
Kursk

Wrocław
Kraków
Kyiv
Kharkiv
Volgograd

CZECHIA
(CZECH REP.)
L'viv
UKRAINE
Poltava
Donets'k
Astrakhan'

Vienna
SLOVAKIA
Vinnytsya
Dnipropetrovs'k
Rostov

Bratislava
MOLDOVA
Line of
Russian
control
Boundary claimed
by Ukraine
-92 ft ▼
(-28 m)

Budapest
Chișinău

HUNGARY
Odesa
CRIMEA
El'brus
Groznyy

Zagreb
ROMANIA
Simferopol'
(5,642 m) 18,510 ft
Baku

CROATIA
Belgrade
Bucharest
Sevastopol'
Sochi

BOSNIA &
HERZEGOVINA
GEORGIA
AZERBAIJAN

Sarajevo
SERBIA
Black Sea

MONTENEGRO
KOSOVO
Prishtinë
BULGARIA
Varna

Podgorica
Skopje
Sofia

Tirana
N. MACED.

ALBANIA
Thessaloníki
Istanbul

TURKEY

Bosporus

Dardanelles

GREECE

Athens

Sea

Crete

NORTHERN CYPRUS
Nicosia

CYPRUS

Barents Sea
60°E
60°N
50°N
40°N
0°E 20°E 30°E 40°E 50°E
20°E 30°E 40°E

Baltic Sea

Caspian Sea

CRIMEA
Russia invaded Crimea in 2014 and, after secession from Ukraine was approved in a disputed and boycotted referendum held in Crimea, the Russian parliament voted to annex Crimea into the Russian Federation. The United Nations General Assembly subsequently adopted a nonbinding resolution declaring the annexation invalid and affirming Ukraine's territorial jurisdiction. As of 2019, Russia administers and controls all aspects of the peninsula, while Ukraine continues to maintain that Crimea is its sovereign territory.

NORTH AMERICA

Guatemala's national bird is the quetzal, and its money is also called the quetzal.

Wolf eyes glow in the dark.

A gray wolf walking along a forest trail during autumn in Minnesota, U.S.A.

282

From the Great Plains of the United States and Canada to the rainforests of Panama, North America stretches 5,500 miles (8,850 km) from north to south. The third largest continent, North America can be divided into five regions: the mountainous west (including parts of Mexico and Central America's western coast), the Great Plains, the Canadian Shield, the varied eastern region (including Central America's lowlands and coastal plains), and the Caribbean.

Onlookers celebrate the opening of the Panama Canal expansion in 2016.

BIG BONES

Canada was once a hotbed of activity for dinosaurs. In fact, the skeleton of the largest *Tyrannosaurus rex* to date was recently uncovered by researchers at a site in Saskatchewan, Canada. Estimated to weigh more than an elephant, the giant dino—nicknamed "Scotty"—stomped around some 68 million years ago.

BERRY GOOD

The United States is the world's largest producer of strawberries, with some 90 percent of the crops grown in the coastal climates of California. That's about two billion pounds (907 million kg) of strawberries plucked from the state each year! Other top strawberry-producing states? Florida, Oregon, North Carolina, and Washington.

BLOW ON

For the first time in history, wind recently surpassed hydroelectricity as the top source of renewable energy in the United States. Currently, the 60,000 wind turbines in the country can power 32 million homes across 41 states.

World's Longest Coastlines

Country	Coastline
Canada	125,567 miles (202,080 km)
Indonesia	33,998 miles (54,716 km)
Russia	23,397 miles (37,653 km)
Philippines	22,549 miles (36,289 km)
Japan	18,486 miles (29,751 km)

PHYSICAL

LAND AREA	HIGHEST POINT	LARGEST LAKE
9,449,000 sq mi (24,474,000 sq km)	Denali, Alaska, U.S.A. 20,310 ft (6,190 m)	Lake Superior, U.S.–Canada / 31,700 sq mi (82,100 sq km)
LONGEST RIVER	**LOWEST POINT**	
Mississippi-Missouri, United States 3,710 mi (5,970 km)	Death Valley, California, U.S.A. -282 ft (-86 m)	

POLITICAL

POPULATION	LARGEST METROPOLITAN AREA
586,100,000	Mexico City, Mexico Pop. 21,672,000
LARGEST COUNTRY	**MOST DENSELY POPULATED COUNTRY**
Canada 3,855,101 sq mi (9,984,670 sq km)	Barbados / 1,765 people per sq mi (681 per sq km)

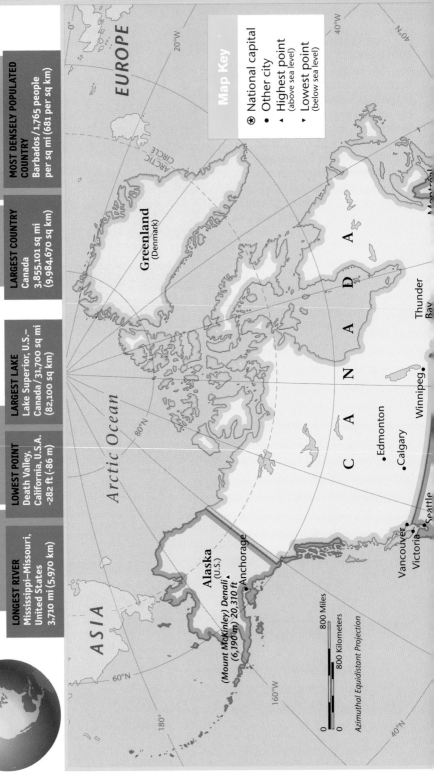

Map Key

⊛ National capital
• Other city
▲ Highest point (above sea level)
▼ Lowest point (below sea level)

EUROPE

Greenland (Denmark)

Arctic Ocean

ASIA

C A N A D A

Thunder Bay

Winnipeg

Edmonton

Calgary

Vancouver

Victoria

Seattle

Alaska (U.S.)

Anchorage

(Mount McKinley) Denali
(6,190m) 20,310 ft

ARCTIC CIRCLE

80°N

60°N

180°

160°W

120°W

40°N

40°N

40°W

20°W

800 Miles

800 Kilometers

Azimuthal Equidistant Projection

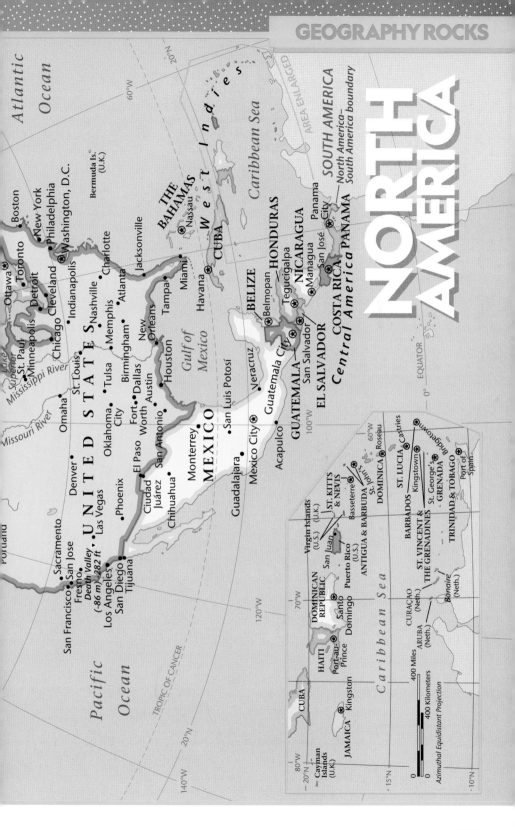

NORTH AMERICA

SOUTH AMERICA

AREA ENLARGED

North America–
South America boundary

Atlantic
Ocean

West Indies

Caribbean Sea

THE BAHAMAS
Nassau

CUBA
Havana

Bermuda Is.
(U.K.)

Boston
New York
Philadelphia
Washington, D.C.
Toronto
Detroit
Cleveland
Indianapolis
Charlotte
Jacksonville
Atlanta
Nashville
Memphis
Birmingham
Tampa
Miami

Ottawa
Minneapolis
St. Paul
Chicago
St. Louis
Nashville

UNITED STATES

Lake Superior

Mississippi River

Missouri River

Omaha
Tulsa
Oklahoma City
Dallas
Fort Worth
Austin
San Antonio
Houston
New Orleans

Gulf of
Mexico

Denver
Las Vegas
Phoenix

Death Valley
(-86 m) -282 ft ▼

Sacramento
San Jose
Fresno
Los Angeles
San Diego
Tijuana

San Francisco

Portland

Pacific
Ocean

El Paso
Ciudad Juárez
Chihuahua

Monterrey

MEXICO

Guadalajara
Mexico City
Acapulco

San Luis Potosí
Veracruz

Guatemala City

BELIZE
Belmopan

GUATEMALA
San Salvador
EL SALVADOR

HONDURAS
Tegucigalpa

NICARAGUA
Managua

COSTA RICA
San José

PANAMA
Panama City

Central America

EQUATOR

TROPIC OF CANCER

20°N

40°N

60°W

100°W

120°W

140°W

0°

Inset map (Caribbean)

Caribbean Sea

CUBA

JAMAICA Kingston
Cayman Islands (U.K.)

HAITI
Port-au-Prince

DOMINICAN REPUBLIC
Santo Domingo

Puerto Rico
(U.S.)
San Juan

Virgin Islands
(U.S.)

ST. KITTS & NEVIS
Basseterre

ANTIGUA & BARBUDA
St. John's

DOMINICA
Roseau

ST. LUCIA
Castries

BARBADOS
Bridgetown

ST. VINCENT & THE GRENADINES
Kingstown

GRENADA
St. George's

TRINIDAD & TOBAGO
Port of Spain

ARUBA
(Neth.)

CURAÇAO
(Neth.)

Bonaire
(Neth.)

400 Miles
0

400 Kilometers
0

Azimuthal Equidistant Projection

80°W
70°W
60°W

20°N
15°N
10°N

285

SOUTH AMERICA

Peru
has more than
3,000 kinds of
potatoes.

Turtles
the size of
compact cars
once roamed
South
America.

A woman sells fruit in Chivay, Peru.

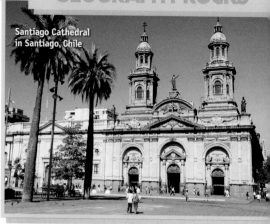

Santiago Cathedral in Santiago, Chile

South America is bordered by three major bodies of water—the Caribbean Sea, Atlantic Ocean, and Pacific Ocean. The world's fourth largest continent extends over a range of climates, from tropical in the north to subarctic in the south. South America produces a rich diversity of natural resources, including nuts, fruits, sugar, grains, coffee, and chocolate.

A HOME FOR ELEPHANTS

When elephants are rescued from circuses, where do they go? In South America, they may head to Elephant Sanctuary Brazil, the only rescue center of its kind on the continent. The center's 2,800 acres (1,130 ha) of lush land offer a peaceful place for the pachyderms to roam.

OCEANS ALL AROUND

South America is surrounded by both the Pacific and Atlantic Oceans. Experts think that the two oceans used to be one massive body of water until North and South America joined together at the Isthmus of Panama some three million years ago. That move, scientists think, divided the original ocean into two. Today, Colombia and Chile are the only two countries in South America with a coastline on each ocean.

Vast Watershed

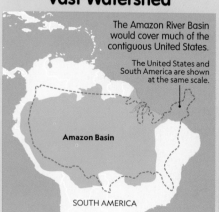

The Amazon River Basin would cover much of the contiguous United States.

The United States and South America are shown at the same scale.

Amazon Basin

SOUTH AMERICA

ANCIENT BRIDGE

Deep in the Peruvian Andes, a suspension bridge made of handwoven grass stretches more than 100 feet (30 m) over a rushing river. Once used to connect two villages on either side of the river, the bridge, which dates back more than 500 years, is now more of a symbolic nod to the past. Each June, the suspension bridge is rebuilt and replaced by the local indigenous community.

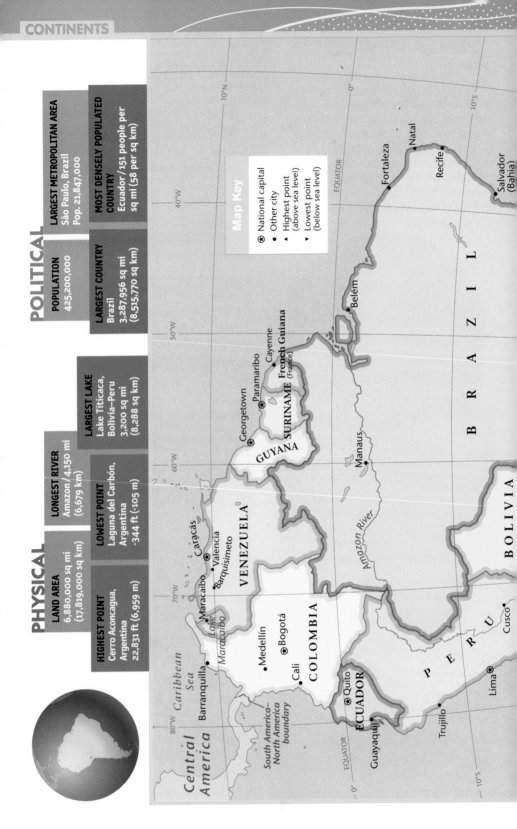

PHYSICAL

HIGHEST POINT
Cerro Aconcagua,
Argentina
22,831 ft (6,959 m)

LAND AREA
6,880,000 sq mi
(17,819,000 sq km)

LOWEST POINT
Laguna del Carbón,
Argentina
-344 ft (-105 m)

LONGEST RIVER
Amazon / 4,150 mi
(6,679 km)

LARGEST LAKE
Lake Titicaca,
Bolivia–Peru
3,200 sq mi
(8,288 sq km)

POLITICAL

POPULATION
425,200,000

LARGEST COUNTRY
Brazil
3,287,956 sq mi
(8,515,770 sq km)

LARGEST METROPOLITAN AREA
São Paulo, Brazil
Pop. 21,847,000

**MOST DENSELY POPULATED
COUNTRY**
Ecuador / 151 people per
sq mi (58 per sq km)

Map Key

⊛ National capital
• Other city
▲ Highest point
(above sea level)
▼ Lowest point
(below sea level)

Central
America

Caribbean
Sea

South America–
North America
boundary

Barranquilla
Maracaibo
Lake
Maracaibo
Caracás
Valencia
Barquisimeto
VENEZUELA
Medellín
Bogotá
Cali
COLOMBIA
Quito
ECUADOR
Guayaquil
Trujillo
Lima
Cusco
P E R U
BOLIVIA
Georgetown
GUYANA
Paramaribo
Cayenne
French Guiana (France)
SURINAME
Manaus
Amazon River
Belém
B R A Z I L
Fortaleza
Natal
Recife
Salvador
(Bahia)

80°W
70°W
60°W
50°W
40°W
10°N
0°
EQUATOR
10°S

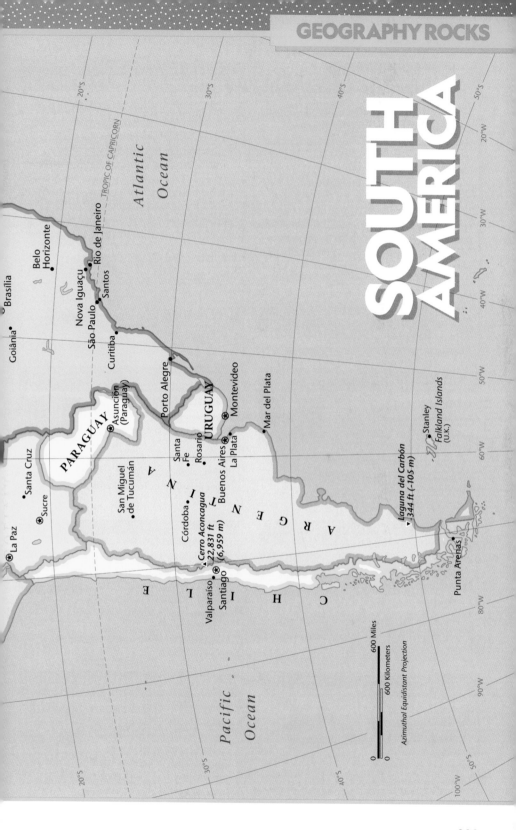

SOUTH AMERICA

Atlantic Ocean

TROPIC OF CAPRICORN

20°S

30°S

40°S

50°S

Brasília

Goiânia

Belo Horizonte

Nova Iguaçu

Rio de Janeiro

São Paulo

Santos

Curitiba

Porto Alegre

PARAGUAY

Asunción (Paraguay)

URUGUAY

Montevideo

Mar del Plata

La Paz

Santa Cruz

Sucre

San Miguel de Tucumán

Santa Fe

Rosario

Córdoba

A R G E N T I N A

Buenos Aires

La Plata

Cerro Aconcagua
22,831 ft
(6,959 m)

Valparaíso

Santiago

C H I L E

Laguna del Carbón
344 ft (–105 m)

Stanley
Falkland Islands
(U.K.)

Punta Arenas

Pacific Ocean

20°S

30°S

40°S

50°S

20°W

30°W

40°W

50°W

60°W

80°W

90°W

100°W

600 Miles

600 Kilometers

Azimuthal Equidistant Projection

0

0

COUNTRIES OF THE WORLD

The following pages present a general overview of all 195 independent countries recognized by the National Geographic Society, including the newest nation, South Sudan, which gained independence in 2011.

The flags of each independent country symbolize diverse cultures and histories. The statistical data cover highlights of geography and demography and provide a brief overview of each country. They present general characteristics and are not intended to be comprehensive. For example, not every language spoken in a specific country can be listed. Thus, languages shown are the most representative of that area. This is also true of the religions mentioned.

A country is defined as a political body with its own independent government, geographical space, and, in most cases, laws, military, and taxes.

Disputed areas such as Northern Cyprus and Taiwan, and dependencies of independent nations, such as Bermuda and Puerto Rico, are not included in this listing.

Note the color key at the bottom of the pages and the locator map below, which assign a color to each country based on the continent on which it is located. Some capital city populations include that city's metro area. All information is accurate as of press time.

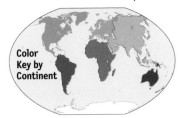

Color Key by Continent

Afghanistan

Area: 251,827 sq mi (652,230 sq km)
Population: 34,941,000
Capital: Kabul, pop. 4,114,000
Currency: afghani
Religions: Sunni Muslim, Shia Muslim
Languages: Afghan Persian (Dari), Pashto, Uzbek, Turkmen

Andorra

Area: 181 sq mi (468 sq km)
Population: 86,000
Capital: Andorra la Vella, pop. 23,000
Currency: euro
Religion: Roman Catholic
Languages: Catalan, French, Castilian, Portuguese

Albania

Area: 11,100 sq mi (28,748 sq km)
Population: 3,057,000
Capital: Tirana, pop. 485,000
Currency: lek
Religions: Muslim, Roman Catholic, Orthodox
Languages: Albanian, Greek

Angola

Area: 481,353 sq mi (1,246,700 sq km)
Population: 30,356,000
Capital: Luanda, pop. 8,045,000
Currency: kwanza
Religions: Roman Catholic, Protestant, indigenous beliefs
Languages: Portuguese, Umbundu, other African languages

Algeria

Area: 919,595 sq mi (2,381,741 sq km)
Population: 41,657,000
Capital: Algiers, pop. 2,729,000
Currency: Algerian dinar
Religion: Sunni Muslim
Languages: Arabic, French, Berber dialects

Antigua and Barbuda

Area: 171 sq mi (443 sq km)
Population: 86,000
Capital: St. John's, pop. 21,000
Currency: East Caribbean dollar
Religions: Anglican, Methodist, other Protestant, Roman Catholic
Languages: English, Antiguan Creole

Argentina

Area: 1,073,518 sq mi
(2,780,400 sq km)
Population: 44,694,000
Capital: Buenos Aires,
pop. 15,057,000
Currency: Argentine peso
Religion: Roman Catholic
Languages: Spanish, Italian, English, German, French

Armenia

Area: 11,484 sq mi
(29,743 sq km)
Population: 3,038,000
Capital: Yerevan,
pop. 1,083,000
Currency: Armenian dram
Religions: Armenian Apostolic, other Christian
Languages: Armenian, Russian

Australia

Area: 2,988,901 sq mi
(7,741,220 sq km)
Population: 23,470,000
Capital: Canberra, A.C.T.,
pop. 452,000
Currency: Australian dollar
Religions: Anglican, Roman Catholic, other Christian
Language: English

Austria

Area: 32,383 sq mi (83,871 sq km)
Population: 8,793,000
Capital: Vienna, pop. 1,915,000
Currency: euro
Religions: Roman Catholic, Protestant, Muslim
Languages: German, Turkish, Serbian, Croatian,
Slovene, Hungarian

Azerbaijan

Area: 33,436 sq mi
(86,600 sq km)
Population: 10,047,000
Capital: Baku, pop. 2,313,000
Currency: Azerbaijani manat
Religions: Muslim, Russian Orthodox
Languages: Azerbaijani (Azeri), Russian, Armenian

Bahamas, The

Area: 5,359 sq mi
(13,880 sq km)
Population: 333,000
Capital: Nassau, pop. 280,000
Currency: Bahamian dollar
Religions: Baptist, Anglican, Roman Catholic,
Pentecostal
Languages: English, Creole

3 cool things about THE BAHAMAS

1. Stretching some 124 miles (200 km),
the Bahamas' Andros Barrier Reef
is the sixth largest coral reef on
the planet.

2. There are 700 islands and islets
that make up the Bahamas—and
only 30 of them are inhabited.

3. The pink sand on Harbour
Island's beach gets its color from
microscopic creatures known as
foraminifera, which have bright
pink or red shells.

Bahrain

Area: 293 sq mi (760 sq km)
Population: 1,443,000
Capital: Manama, pop. 600,000
Currency: Bahraini dinar
Religions: Muslim (Shia and Sunni), Christian
Languages: Arabic, English, Farsi, Urdu

Bangladesh

Area: 57,321 sq mi
(148,460 sq km)
Population: 159,453,000
Capital: Dhaka, pop. 20,284,000
Currency: taka
Religions: Muslim, Hindu
Language: Bangla (Bengali)

Barbados

Area: 166 sq mi (430 sq km)
Population: 293,000
Capital: Bridgetown, pop. 89,000
Currency: Barbadian dollar
Religions: Protestant, Roman Catholic
Languages: English, Bajan

Bhutan

Area: 14,824 sq mi (38,394 sq km)
Population: 766,000
Capital: Thimphu, pop. 203,000
Currencies: ngultrum, Indian rupee
Religions: Lamaistic Buddhist,
Indian- and Nepalese-influenced Hindu
Languages: Sharchhopka, Dzongkha, Lhotshamkha

Belarus

Area: 80,155 sq mi
(207,600 sq km)
Population: 9,528,000
Capital: Minsk, pop. 2,017,000
Currency: Belarusian ruble
Religions: Eastern Orthodox, Roman Catholic
Languages: Russian, Belarusian

Bolivia

Area: 424,164 sq mi (1,098,581 sq km)
Population: 11,306,000
Capitals: La Paz, pop. 1,835,000;
Sucre, pop. 278,000
Currency: boliviano
Religions: Roman Catholic, Protestant
Languages: Spanish, Quechua, Aymara, Guarani

Belgium

Area: 11,787 sq mi (30,528 sq km)
Population: 11,571,000
Capital: Brussels, pop. 2,065,000
Currency: euro
Religions: Roman Catholic, Muslim,
Protestant
Languages: Dutch, French, German

Bosnia and Herzegovina

Area: 19,767 sq mi
(51,197 sq km)
Population: 3,850,000
Capital: Sarajevo, pop. 343,000
Currency: convertible mark
Religions: Muslim, Orthodox, Roman Catholic
Languages: Bosnian, Serbian, Croatian

Belize

Area: 8,867 sq mi (22,966 sq km)
Population: 386,000
Capital: Belmopan, pop. 23,000
Currency: Belize dollar
Religions: Roman Catholic, Protestant
(includes Pentecostal, Seventh-Day Adventist,
Mennonite, Methodist)
Languages: English, Spanish, Creole, Maya

Botswana

Area: 224,607 sq mi
(581,730 sq km)
Population: 2,249,000
Capital: Gaborone, pop. 269,000
Currency: pula
Religions: Christian, Badimo
Languages: Setswana, Sekalanga, Sekgalagadi, English

Benin

Area: 43,484 sq mi (112,622 sq km)
Population: 11,341,000
Capitals: Porto-Novo, pop. 285,000;
Cotonou, pop. 688,000
Currency: Communauté Financière Africaine franc
Religions: Muslim, Roman Catholic, Protestant, Vodoun
Languages: French, Fon, Yoruba, tribal languages

Brazil

Area: 3,287,611 sq mi
(8,514,877 sq km)
Population: 208,847,000
Capital: Brasília, pop. 4,559,000
Currency: Brazilian real
Religions: Roman Catholic, Protestant
Language: Portuguese

COLOR KEY ● Africa ● Australia, New Zealand, and Oceania

Brunei

Area: 2,226 sq mi (5,765 sq km)
Population: 451,000
Capital: Bandar Seri Begawan, pop. 241,000
Currency: Brunei dollar
Religions: Muslim, Christian, Buddhist, indigenous beliefs
Languages: Malay, English, Chinese

Burkina Faso

Area: 105,869 sq mi (274,200 sq km)
Population: 19,743,000
Capital: Ouagadougou, pop. 2,653,000
Currency: Communauté Financière Africaine franc
Religions: Muslim, Catholic, animist
Languages: French, African languages

Bulgaria

Area: 42,811 sq mi (110,879 sq km)
Population: 7,058,000
Capital: Sofia, pop. 1,277,000
Currency: Bulgarian lev
Religions: Eastern Orthodox, Muslim
Languages: Bulgarian, Turkish, Romany

Burundi

Area: 10,745 sq mi (27,830 sq km)
Population: 11,845,000
Capital: Bujumbura, pop. 954,000; Gitega, pop. 120,000
Currency: Burundi franc
Religions: Roman Catholic, Protestant, Muslim
Languages: Kirundi, French, Swahili

SNAPSHOT
Bhutan

A sacred site, Paro Taktsang—or Tiger's Nest Monastery—sits at the edge of a cliff some 3,000 feet (915 m) above Paro, Bhutan.

● Asia ● Europe ● North America ● South America

Cabo Verde

Area: 1,557 sq mi (4,033 sq km)
Population: 568,000
Capital: Praia, pop. 168,000
Currency: Cape Verdean escudo
Religions: Roman Catholic, Protestant
Languages: Portuguese, Crioulo

Cameroon

Area: 183,568 sq mi
(475,440 sq km)
Population: 25,641,000
Capital: Yaoundé, pop. 3,822,000
Currency: Communauté Financière Africaine franc
Religions: Roman Catholic, Protestant, Muslim, animist
Languages: African languages, English, French

Cambodia

Area: 69,898 sq mi (181,035 sq km)
Population: 16,450,000
Capital: Phnom Penh, pop. 2,014,000
Currency: riel
Religion: Buddhist
Language: Khmer

Canada

Area: 3,855,101 sq mi
(9,984,670 sq km)
Population: 35,882,000
Capital: Ottawa, pop. 1,378,000
Currency: Canadian dollar
Religions: Roman Catholic, Protestant
Languages: English, French

SNAPSHOT
Chile

A visitor gazes at the massive "Mano del Desierto" ("Hand of the Desert") sculpture in Antofagasta, Chile.

COLOR KEY ● Africa ● Australia, New Zealand, and Oceania

Central African Republic

Area: 240,535 sq mi
(622,984 sq km)
Population: 5,745,000
Capital: Bangui, pop. 870,000
Currency: Communauté Financière Africaine franc
Religions: Indigenous beliefs, Protestant, Roman Catholic, Muslim
Languages: French, Sangho, tribal languages

Comoros

Area: 863 sq mi (2,235 sq km)
Population: 821,000
Capital: Moroni, pop. 62,000
Currency: Comoran franc
Religion: Sunni Muslim
Languages: Arabic, French, Shikomoro

Chad

Area: 495,755 sq mi
(1,284,000 sq km)
Population: 15,833,000
Capital: N'Djamena, pop. 1,372,000
Currency: Communauté Financière Africaine franc
Religions: Muslim, Protestant, Roman Catholic, animist
Languages: French, Arabic, Sara, indigenous languages

Congo

Area: 132,047 sq mi (342,000 sq km)
Population: 5,062,000
Capital: Brazzaville,
pop. 2,308,000
Currency: Communauté Financière Africaine franc
Religions: Christian, animist, Muslim
Languages: French, Lingala, Monokutuba, Kikongo, local languages

Chile

Area: 291,932 sq mi
(756,102 sq km)
Population: 17,925,000
Capital: Santiago, pop. 6,724,000
Currency: Chilean peso
Religions: Roman Catholic, Protestant
Languages: Spanish, English, indigenous languages

Costa Rica

Area: 19,730 sq mi
(51,100 sq km)
Population: 4,987,000
Capital: San José, pop. 1,379,000
Currency: Costa Rican colón
Religions: Roman Catholic, Evangelical
Languages: Spanish, English

China

Area: 3,705,405 sq mi
(9,596,960 sq km)
Population: 1,384,689,000
Capital: Beijing, pop. 20,035,000
Currency: yuan
Religions: folk religion, Buddhist, Christian
Languages: Standard Chinese or Mandarin, Yue or Cantonese, Wu, Minbei, Minnan, Xiang, Gan, regional

Côte d'Ivoire (Ivory Coast)

Area: 124,504 sq mi
(322,463 sq km)
Population: 26,261,000
Capitals: Abidjan, pop. 5,059,000;
Yamoussoukro, pop. 231,000
Currency: Communauté Financière Africaine franc
Religions: Muslim, Christian, indigenous beliefs
Languages: French, Dioula, native dialects

Colombia

Area: 439,735 sq mi
(1,138,910 sq km)
Population: 48,169,000
Capital: Bogotá, pop. 10,779,000
Currency: Colombian peso
Religions: Roman Catholic, Protestant
Language: Spanish

Croatia

Area: 21,851 sq mi
(56,594 sq km)
Population: 4,270,000
Capital: Zagreb, pop. 685,000
Currency: kuna
Religions: Roman Catholic, Orthodox
Languages: Croatian, Serbian

Cuba

Area: 42,803 sq mi
(110,860 sq km)
Population: 11,116,000
Capital: Havana, pop. 2,138,000
Currencies: Cuban peso, peso convertible
Religion: Roman Catholic
Language: Spanish

Cyprus

Area: 3,572 sq mi (9,251 sq km)
Population: 1,237,000
Capital: Nicosia, pop. 269,000
Currency: euro
Religions: Greek Orthodox, Muslim
Languages: Greek, Turkish, English

Czechia (Czech Republic)

Area: 30,451 sq mi (78,867 sq km)
Population: 10,686,000
Capital: Prague, pop. 1,299,000
Currency: Czech koruny
Religions: Roman Catholic, Protestant
Languages: Czech, Slovak

Democratic Republic of the Congo

Area: 905,354 sq mi
(2,344,858 sq km)
Population: 85,281,000
Capital: Kinshasa, pop. 13,743,000
Currency: Congolese franc
Religions: Roman Catholic, Protestant,
Kimbanguist, Muslim
Languages: French, Lingala, Kingwana, Kikongo, Tshiluba

Denmark

Area: 16,639 sq mi
(43,094 sq km)
Population: 5,810,000
Capital: Copenhagen, pop. 1,334,000
Currency: Danish krone
Religions: Evangelical Lutheran, Muslim
Languages: Danish, Faroese, Greenlandic

Djibouti

Area: 8,958 sq mi
(23,200 sq km)
Population: 884,000
Capital: Djibouti, pop. 569,000
Currency: Djiboutian franc
Religions: Muslim, Christian
Languages: French, Arabic, Somali, Afar

Dominica

Area: 290 sq mi (751 sq km)
Population: 74,000
Capital: Roseau, pop. 15,000
Currency: East Caribbean
dollar
Religions: Roman Catholic, Protestant
Languages: English, French patois

Dominican Republic

Area: 18,792 sq mi
(48,670 sq km)
Population: 10,299,000
Capital: Santo Domingo,
pop. 2,245,000
Currency: Dominican peso
Religion: Roman Catholic
Language: Spanish

Ecuador

Area: 109,483 sq mi
(283,561 sq km)
Population: 16,499,000
Capital: Quito, pop. 1,848,000
Currency: U.S. dollar
Religions: Roman Catholic, Evangelical
Languages: Spanish, Quechua, other
Amerindian languages

Egypt

Area: 386,662 sq mi
(1,001,450 sq km)
Population: 99,413,000
Capital: Cairo, pop. 20,485,000
Currencies: Egyptian pound
Religions: Muslim (mostly Sunni), Coptic Christian
Languages: Arabic, English, French

El Salvador

Area: 8,124 sq mi (21,041 sq km)
Population: 6,187,000
Capital: San Salvador, pop. 1,106,000
Currencies: U.S. dollar, El Salvador colón
Religions: Roman Catholic, Protestant
Languages: Spanish, Nahua

Ethiopia

Area: 426,372 sq mi (1,104,300 sq km)
Population: 108,386,000
Capital: Addis Ababa, pop. 4,592,000
Currency: Ethiopian birr
Religions: Ethiopian Orthodox, Muslim, Protestant
Languages: Oromo, Amharic, Somali

Equatorial Guinea

Area: 10,831 sq mi (28,051 sq km)
Population: 797,000
Capital: Malabo, pop. 297,000
Currency: Communauté Financière Africaine franc
Religions: Roman Catholic, pagan practices
Languages: Spanish, French, Fang, Bubi

3 cool things about ETHIOPIA

1. In an effort to improve deforestation rates, residents across Ethiopia planted more than 350 million trees in 12 hours in 2019, setting a world record.

2. Upon her appointment in 2018, Sahle-Work Zewde became Ethiopia's first female president—and its first female leader in nearly 100 years.

3. A "hidden" population of at least 100 lions was recently discovered in and around Ethiopia's Alatash National Park, an area thought to have lost its lions due to hunting and habitat destruction.

Eritrea

Area: 45,406 sq mi (117,600 sq km)
Population: 5,971,000
Capital: Asmara, pop. 929,000
Currency: nakfa
Religions: Muslim, Coptic Christian, Roman Catholic
Languages: Tigrigna (Tigrinya), Arabic, English, Tigre, Kunama, Afar, other Cushitic languages

Estonia

Area: 17,463 sq mi (45,228 sq km)
Population: 1,244,000
Capital: Tallinn, pop. 441,000
Currency: euro
Religions: Lutheran, Orthodox
Languages: Estonian, Russian

Fiji

Area: 7,056 sq mi (18,274 sq km)
Population: 927,000
Capital: Suva, pop. 178,000
Currency: Fiji dollar
Religions: Protestant, Hindu, Roman Catholic, Muslim
Languages: English, Fijian, Hindustani

Eswatini (Swaziland)

Area: 6,704 sq mi (17,364 sq km)
Population: 1,087,000
Capitals: Mbabane, pop. 68,000; Lobamba, pop. 5,800
Currency: lilangeni
Religions: Christian, Muslim
Languages: English, siSwati

Finland

Area: 130,558 sq mi (338,145 sq km)
Population: 5,537,000
Capital: Helsinki, pop. 1,292,000
Currency: euro
Religion: Lutheran
Languages: Finnish, Swedish

France

Area: 248,573 sq mi
(643,801 sq km)
Population: 67,364,000
Capital: Paris, pop. 10,958,000
Currency: euro
Religions: Roman Catholic, Protestant, Muslim, Jewish
Language: French

Gambia, The

Area: 4,361 sq mi (11,295 sq km)
Population: 2,093,000
Capital: Banjul, pop. 443,000
Currency: dalasi
Religions: Muslim, Christian
Languages: English, Mandinka, Wolof, Fula

Gabon

Area: 103,347 sq mi (267,667 sq km)
Population: 2,119,000
Capital: Libreville, pop. 824,000
Currency: Communauté Financière Africaine franc
Religions: Christian, Muslim
Languages: French, Fang, Myene, Nzebi, Bapounou/Eschira, Bandjabi

Georgia

Area: 26,911 sq mi (69,700 sq km)
Population: 4,003,000
Capital: Tbilisi, pop. 1,077,000
Currency: lari
Religions: Orthodox Christian, Muslim, Armenian Apostolic
Languages: Georgian, Azeri, Armenian

SNAPSHOT
Ghana

A fisherman repairs a net in Accra, Ghana.

COLOR KEY ● Africa ● Australia, New Zealand, and Oceania

Germany

Area: 137,847 sq mi
(357,022 sq km)
Population: 80,458,000
Capital: Berlin, pop. 3,557,000
Currency: euro
Religions: Roman Catholic, Protestant, Muslim
Language: German

Ghana

Area: 92,098 sq mi (238,533 sq km)
Population: 28,102,000
Capital: Accra, pop. 2,475,000
Currency: Ghana cedi
Religions: Christian, Muslim, traditional beliefs
Languages: Asante, Ewe, Fante, Boron (Brong),
Dagomba, Dangme, Dagarte (Dagaba),
Kokomba, English

Greece

Area: 50,949 sq mi (131,957 sq km)
Population: 10,762,000
Capital: Athens, pop. 3,154,000
Currency: euro
Religions: Greek Orthodox, Muslim
Language: Greek

Grenada

Area: 133 sq mi (344 sq km)
Population: 112,000
Capital: St. George's, pop. 39,000
Currency: East Caribbean dollar
Religions: Roman Catholic, Pentecostal,
other Protestant
Languages: English, French patois

Guatemala

Area: 42,042 sq mi (108,889 sq km)
Population: 16,581,000
Capital: Guatemala City,
pop. 2,891,000
Currency: quetzal
Religions: Roman Catholic, Protestant, indigenous
Maya beliefs
Languages: Spanish, Amerindian languages

Guinea

Area: 94,926 sq mi (245,857 sq km)
Population: 11,855,000
Capital: Conakry, pop. 1,889,000
Currency: Guinean franc
Religions: Muslim, Christian, indigenous beliefs
Languages: French, African languages

Guinea-Bissau

Area: 13,948 sq mi
(36,125 sq km)
Population: 1,833,000
Capital: Bissau, pop. 579,000
Currency: Communauté Financière Africaine franc
Religions: Muslim, Christian, indigenous beliefs
Languages: Crioulu, Portuguese, Pular, Mandingo

Guyana

Area: 83,000 sq mi
(214,969 sq km)
Population: 741,000
Capital: Georgetown, pop. 110,000
Currency: Guyanese dollar
Religions: Protestant, Hindu, Roman Catholic, Muslim
Languages: English, Guyanese Creole, Amerindian
languages, Caribbean Hindustani

Haiti

Area: 10,714 sq mi (27,750 sq km)
Population: 10,788,000
Capital: Port-au-Prince,
pop. 2,704,000
Currencies: gourde, U.S. dollar
Religions: Roman Catholic, Protestant, voodoo
Languages: French, Creole

Honduras

Area: 43,278 sq mi
(112,090 sq km)
Population: 9,183,000
Capital: Tegucigalpa,
pop. 1,403,000
Currency: lempira
Religions: Roman Catholic, Protestant
Languages: Spanish, Amerindian dialects

Hungary

Area: 35,918 sq mi (93,028 sq km)
Population: 9,826,000
Capital: Budapest, pop. 1,764,000
Currency: forint
Religions: Roman Catholic, Calvinist, Lutheran
Language: Hungarian, English, German

Iraq

Area: 169,235 sq mi (438,317 sq km)
Population: 40,194,000
Capital: Baghdad, pop. 6,974,000
Currency: Iraqi dinar
Religions: Shia Muslim, Sunni Muslim
Languages: Arabic, Kurdish, Turkmen, Syriac, Armenian

Iceland

Area: 39,769 sq mi (103,000 sq km)
Population: 344,000
Capital: Reykjavík, pop. 216,000
Currency: Icelandic krona
Religions: Lutheran, Roman Catholic
Languages: Icelandic, English, Nordic languages

Ireland (Éire)

Area: 27,133 sq mi (70,273 sq km)
Population: 5,068,000
Capital: Dublin (Baile Átha Cliath), pop. 1,215,000
Currency: euro
Religions: Roman Catholic, Church of Ireland
Languages: English, Irish (Gaelic)

India

Area: 1,269,219 sq mi (3,287,263 sq km)
Population: 1,296,834,000
Capital: New Delhi, pop. 29,399,000
Currency: Indian rupee
Religions: Hindu, Muslim, Christian, Sikh
Languages: Hindi, Bengali, Telugu, Marathi, Tamil, Urdu, Gujarati, Kannada, Malayalam, Oriya, Panjabi, Assamese, English

Israel

Area: 8,019 sq mi (20,770 sq km)
Population: 8,425,000
Capital: Jerusalem, pop. 919,000
Currency: new Israeli sheqel
Religions: Jewish, Muslim
Languages: Hebrew, Arabic, English

Indonesia

Area: 735,358 sq mi (1,904,569 sq km)
Population: 262,787,000
Capital: Jakarta, pop. 10,639,000
Currency: Indonesian rupiah
Religions: Muslim, Protestant, Roman Catholic, Hindu
Languages: Bahasa Indonesia, English, Dutch, Javanese, local dialects

Italy

Area: 116,348 sq mi (301,340 sq km)
Population: 62,247,000
Capital: Rome, pop. 4,234,000
Currency: euro
Religion: Roman Catholic
Languages: Italian, German, French, Slovene

Iran

Area: 636,371 sq mi (1,648,195 sq km)
Population: 83,025,000
Capital: Tehran, pop. 9,014,000
Currency: Iranian rial
Religions: Shia Muslim, Sunni Muslim
Languages: Persian (Farsi), Aziri, Turkic dialects, Kurdish

Jamaica

Area: 4,244 sq mi (10,991 sq km)
Population: 2,812,000
Capital: Kingston, pop. 590,000
Currency: Jamaican dollar
Religions: Protestant, Roman Catholic
Languages: English, English patois

COLOR KEY ● Africa ● Australia, New Zealand, and Oceania

Japan

Area: 145,914 sq mi (377,915 sq km)
Population: 126,168,000
Capital: Tokyo, pop. 37,435,000
Currency: yen
Religions: Shinto, Buddhist
Language: Japanese

Kazakhstan

Area: 1,052,089 sq mi (2,724,900 sq km)
Population: 18,949,000
Capital: Nur-Sultan (Astana), pop. 1,118,000
Currency: tenge
Religions: Muslim, Russian Orthodox
Languages: Kazakh (Qazaq), Russian

Jordan

Area: 34,495 sq mi (89,342 sq km)
Population: 10,458,000
Capital: Amman, pop. 2,109,000
Currency: Jordanian dinar
Religions: Sunni Muslim, Christian
Languages: Arabic, English

Kenya

Area: 224,081 sq mi (580,367 sq km)
Population: 48,398,000
Capital: Nairobi, pop. 4,556,000
Currency: Kenyan shilling
Religions: Protestant, Roman Catholic, Muslim, indigenous beliefs
Languages: English, Kiswahili, indigenous languages

SNAPSHOT
India

Doused in colorful powder and water, friends celebrate Holi, an annual festival in India commemorating spring.

● Asia ● Europe ● North America ● South America

Kiribati

Area: 313 sq mi (811 sq km)
Population: 109,000
Capital: Tarawa, pop. 64,000
Currency: Australian dollar
Religions: Roman Catholic, Protestant
Languages: I-Kiribati, English

Kuwait

Area: 6,880 sq mi (17,818 sq km)
Population: 4,438,000
Capital: Kuwait City, pop. 3,052,000
Currency: Kuwaiti dinar
Religions: Sunni Muslim, Shia Muslim, Christian
Languages: Arabic, English

Kosovo

Area: 4,203 sq mi (10,887 sq km)
Population: 1,908,000
Capital: Prishtinë, pop. 207,000
Currencies: euro, Serbian dinar
Religions: Muslim, Roman Catholic, Serbian Orthodox
Languages: Albanian, Serbian, Bosnian

Kyrgyzstan

Area: 77,201 sq mi (199,951 sq km)
Population: 5,849,000
Capital: Bishkek, pop. 1,017,000
Currency: som
Religions: Muslim, Russian Orthodox
Languages: Kyrgyz, Uzbek, Russian

SNAPSHOT
Kosovo

Kosovo's Old Stone Bridge, in the small town of Prizren, is more than 500 years old.

COLOR KEY ● Africa ● Australia, New Zealand, and Oceania

Laos

Area: 91,429 sq mi
(236,800 sq km)
Population: 7,234,000
Capital: Vientiane, pop. 673,000
Currency: Lao kip
Religions: Buddhist, Christian
Languages: Lao, French, English, ethnic languages

Libya
Area: 679,362 sq mi
(1,759,540 sq km)
Population: 6,755,000
Capital: Tripoli, pop. 1,161,000
Currency: Libyan dinar
Religions: Sunni Muslim, Christian
Languages: Arabic, Italian, English, Berber

Latvia
Area: 24,938 sq mi
(64,589 sq km)
Population: 1,924,000
Capital: Riga, pop. 634,000
Currency: euro
Religions: Lutheran, Orthodox
Languages: Latvian, Russian

Liechtenstein

Area: 62 sq mi (160 sq km)
Population: 39,000
Capital: Vaduz, pop. 5,000
Currency: Swiss franc
Religions: Roman Catholic, Protestant
Languages: German, Italian

Lebanon
Area: 4,015 sq mi (10,400 sq km)
Population: 6,100,000
Capital: Beirut, pop. 2,407,000
Currency: Lebanese pound
Religions: Muslim, Christian
Languages: Arabic, French, English, Armenian

Lithuania

Area: 25,212 sq mi
(65,300 sq km)
Population: 2,793,000
Capital: Vilnius, pop. 538,000
Currency: euro
Religions: Roman Catholic, Russian Orthodox
Languages: Lithuanian, Russian, Polish

Lesotho
Area: 11,720 sq mi (30,355 sq km)
Population: 1,962,000
Capital: Maseru, pop. 202,000
Currencies: loti, rand
Religions: Protestant, Roman Catholic
Languages: Sesotho, English, Zulu, Xhosa

Luxembourg
Area: 998 sq mi (2,586 sq km)
Population: 606,000
Capital: Luxembourg,
pop. 120,000
Currency: euro
Religion: Roman Catholic
Languages: Luxembourgish, German,
French, Portuguese

Liberia

Area: 43,000 sq mi
(111,369 sq km)
Population: 4,810,000
Capital: Monrovia,
pop. 1,467,000
Currency: Liberian dollar
Religions: Christian, Muslim, indigenous beliefs
Languages: English, indigenous languages

Madagascar
Area: 226,658 sq mi
(587,041 sq km)
Population: 25,684,000
Capital: Antananarivo,
pop. 3,210,000
Currency: Malagasy ariary
Religions: Christian, indigenous beliefs, Muslim
Languages: French, Malagasy, English

Malawi

Area: 45,747 sq mi
(118,484 sq km)
Population: 19,843,000
Capital: Lilongwe, pop. 1,075,000
Currency: Malawian kwacha
Religions: Christian, Muslim
Languages: Chichewa, Chinyanja,
other Bantu languages, English

Malaysia

Area: 127,355 sq mi (329,847 sq km)
Population: 31,810,000
Capital: Kuala Lumpur,
pop. 7,780,000
Currency: Malaysian ringgit
Religions: Muslim, Buddhist, Christian, Hindu
Languages: Bahasa Malaysia (Malay), English,
Chinese, Tamil, Telugu, Malayalam

Maldives

Area: 115 sq mi (298 sq km)
Population: 392,000
Capital: Male, pop. 177,000
Currency: rufiyaa
Religion: Sunni Muslim
Languages: Dhivehi, English

Mali

Area: 478,841 sq mi (1,240,192 sq km)
Population: 18,430,000
Capital: Bamako, pop. 2,529,000
Currency: Communauté
Financière Africaine franc
Religions: Muslim, Christian, animist
Languages: French, Bambara, African languages

Malta

Area: 122 sq mi (316 sq km)
Population: 449,000
Capital: Valletta, pop. 213,000
Currency: euro
Religion: Roman Catholic
Languages: Maltese, English

Marshall Islands

Area: 70 sq mi (181 sq km)
Population: 76,000
Capital: Majuro, pop. 31,000
Currency: U.S. dollar
Religions: Protestant, Roman Catholic,
Mormon
Languages: Marshallese, English

3 cool things about the MARSHALL ISLANDS

1. At just 36 years old, the Marshall Islands is one of the world's youngest nations. The chain of some 1,200 islands and atolls gained its independence from the United States in 1986.

2. There are some 47 sunken ships and 270 airplanes dating back to World War II at the bottom of the Pacific Ocean off the coast of the Marshall Islands. This is a popular spot for scuba divers who flock to the tropical waters to explore the submerged ships and planes some 100 feet (30 m) below.

3. First debuted in 1946, the bikini is named for the Marshall Islands' Bikini Atoll. The designer of the two-piece bathing suit gave it the unique name as a nod to the ring-shaped reef, which was in the news at the time during World War II.

Mauritania

Area: 397,955 sq mi
(1,030,700 sq km)
Population: 3,840,000
Capital: Nouakchott, pop. 1,259,000
Currency: ouguiya
Religion: Muslim
Languages: Arabic, Pulaar, Soninke, Wolof,
French, Hassaniya

Mauritius

Area: 788 sq mi (2,040 sq km)
Population: 1,364,000
Capital: Port Louis, pop. 149,000
Currency: Mauritius rupee
Religions: Hindu, Roman Catholic,
Muslim, other Christian
Languages: Creole, Bhojpuri, French, English

Mexico

Area: 758,449 sq mi
(1,964,375 sq km)
Population: 125,959,000
Capital: Mexico City,
pop. 21,672,000
Currency: Mexican peso
Religions: Roman Catholic, Protestant
Languages: Spanish, indigenous languages

Micronesia

Area: 271 sq mi (702 sq km)
Population: 104,000
Capital: Palikir, pop. 7,000
Currency: U.S. dollar
Religions: Roman Catholic, Protestant
Languages: English, Chuukese, Kosrean, Pohnpeian,
Yapese, other indigenous languages

Moldova

Area: 13,070 sq mi
(33,851 sq km)
Population: 3,438,000
Capital: Chisinau,
pop. 504,000
Currency: Moldovan leu
Religion: Eastern Orthodox
Languages: Moldovan, Russian, Gagauz

Monaco

Area: 1 sq mi (2 sq km)
Population: 39,000
Capital: Monaco, pop. 39,000
Currency: euro
Religion: Roman Catholic
Languages: French, English, Italian, Monegasque

Mongolia

Area: 603,908 sq mi
(1,564,116 sq km)
Population: 3,103,000
Capital: Ulaanbaatar,
pop. 1,553,000
Currency: tugrik
Religions: Buddhist, Muslim, Shamanist, Christian
Languages: Mongolian, Turkic, Russian

Montenegro

Area: 5,333 sq mi
(13,812 sq km)
Population: 614,000
Capital: Podgorica, pop. 174,000
Currency: euro
Religions: Orthodox, Muslim, Roman Catholic
Languages: Serbian, Montenegrin,
Bosnian, Albanian

Morocco

Area: 172,414 sq mi
(446,550 sq km)
Population: 34,314,000
Capital: Rabat, pop. 1,865,000
Currency: Moroccan dirham
Religion: Muslim
Languages: Arabic, Berber languages,
Tamazight, French

MOROCCO is home to the WORLD'S OLDEST UNIVERSITY, dating back to the NINTH CENTURY.

Mozambique

Area: 308,642 sq mi
(799,380 sq km)
Population: 27,234,000
Capital: Maputo, pop. 1,104,000
Currency: Mozambique metical
Religions: Christian, Muslim
Languages: Emakhuwa, Portuguese, Xichangana,
Cisena, Elomwe, Echuwabo, other local languages

Myanmar (Burma)

Area: 261,228 sq mi
(676,578 sq km)
Population: 55,623,000
Capital: Nay Pyi Taw,
pop. 1,176,000
Currency: kyat
Religions: Buddhist, Christian, Muslim
Languages: Burmese, ethnic languages

Namibia

Area: 318,261 sq mi
(824,292 sq km)
Population: 2,533,000
Capital: Windhoek, pop. 417,000
Currencies: Namibian dollar,
South African rand
Religion: Christian
Languages: Indigenous languages, Afrikaans, English

Nepal

Area: 56,827 sq mi
(147,181 sq km)
Population: 29,718,000
Capital: Kathmandu, pop. 1,376,000
Currency: Nepalese rupee
Religions: Hindu, Buddhist, Muslim, Kirant
Languages: Nepali, Maithali, Bhojpuri, Tharu,
Tamang, Newar, Magar, Bajjika, Awadhi

Nauru

Area: 8 sq mi (21 sq km)
Population: 10,000
Capital: Yaren, pop. 1,000
Currency: Australian dollar
Religions: Protestant, Roman Catholic
Languages: Nauruan, English

Netherlands

Area: 16,040 sq mi
(41,543 sq km)
Population: 17,151,000
Capitals: Amsterdam, pop. 1,140,000;
The Hague, pop. 685,000
Currency: euro
Religions: Roman Catholic, Protestant, Muslim
Languages: Dutch, Frisian

SNAPSHOT Norway

The brightly painted buildings along the Nidelva River in Trondheim, Norway, date back to the 18th century.

COLOR KEY ● Africa ● Australia, New Zealand, and Oceania

New Zealand

Area: 103,799 sq mi
(268,838 sq km)
Population: 4,546,000
Capital: Wellington, pop. 413,000
Currency: New Zealand dollar
Religions: Protestant, Roman Catholic,
Hindu, Buddhist, Maori Christian
Languages: English, Maori

Nicaragua

Area: 50,336 sq mi
(130,370 sq km)
Population: 6,085,000
Capital: Managua, pop. 1,055,000
Currency: córdoba oro
Religions: Roman Catholic, Protestant
Languages: Spanish, Miskito

Niger

Area: 489,191 sq mi (1,267,000 sq km)
Population: 19,866,000
Capital: Niamey, pop. 1,252,000
Currency: Communauté
Financière Africaine franc
Religion: Muslim
Languages: French, Hausa, Djerma

Nigeria

Area: 356,669 sq mi
(923,768 sq km)
Population: 203,453,000
Capital: Abuja, pop. 3,095,000
Currency: naira
Religions: Muslim, Christian, indigenous beliefs
Languages: English, Hausa, Yoruba,
Igbo (Ibo), Fulani

North Korea

Area: 46,540 sq mi
(120,538 sq km)
Population: 25,381,000
Capital: Pyongyang,
pop. 3,061,000
Currency: North Korean won
Religions: Buddhist, Confucianist, some Christian
Language: Korean

North Macedonia

Area: 9,928 sq mi
(25,713 sq km)
Population: 2,119,000
Capital: Skopje, pop. 590,000
Currency: denar
Religions: Macedonian Orthodox, Muslim
Languages: Macedonian, Albanian, Turkish, Romany,
Aromanian, Serbian

Norway

Area: 125,021 sq mi
(323,802 sq km)
Population: 5,372,000
Capital: Oslo, pop. 1,027,000
Currency: Norwegian krone
Religion: Lutheran
Languages: Bokmal Norwegian, Nynorsk
Norwegian, Sami, Finnish

Oman

Area: 119,499 sq mi
(309,500 sq km)
Population: 4,613,000
Capital: Muscat, pop. 1,502,000
Currency: Omani rial
Religions: Muslim, Christian, Hindu
Languages: Arabic, English, Baluchi,
Urdu, Indian dialects

Pakistan

Area: 307,374 sq mi
(796,095 sq km)
Population: 207,863,000
Capital: Islamabad, pop. 1,095,000
Currency: Pakistani rupee
Religions: Sunni Muslim, Shia Muslim
Languages: Punjabi, Sindhi, Saraiki, Pashto, Urdu,
Baluchi, Hindko, Brahui, English, Burushaski

Palau

Area: 177 sq mi (459 sq km)
Population: 22,000
Capital: Ngerulmud
(on Babeldaob), pop. 277
Currency: U.S. dollar
Religions: Roman Catholic, Protestant, Modekngei
Languages: Palauan, Filipino, English

● Asia ● Europe ● North America ● South America

Panama

Area: 29,120 sq mi (75,420 sq km)
Population: 3,801,000
Capital: Panama City, pop. 1,822,000
Currency: U.S. dollar
Religions: Roman Catholic, Protestant
Languages: Spanish, English

Papua New Guinea

Area: 178,703 sq mi (462,840 sq km)
Population: 7,027,000
Capital: Port Moresby, pop. 375,000
Currency: kina
Religions: Protestant, Roman Catholic
Languages: Tok Pisin, English, Hiri Motu, other indigenous languages

Paraguay

Area: 157,048 sq mi (406,752 sq km)
Population: 7,026,000
Capital: Asunción (Paraguay), pop. 3,279,000
Currency: guaraní
Religions: Roman Catholic, Protestant
Languages: Spanish, Guarani

Peru

Area: 496,224 sq mi (1,285,216 sq km)
Population: 31,331,000
Capital: Lima, pop. 10,555,000
Currency: sol
Religions: Roman Catholic, Evangelical
Languages: Spanish, Quechua, Aymara

Philippines

Area: 115,831 sq mi (300,000 sq km)
Population: 105,893,000
Capital: Manila, pop. 13,699,000
Currency: Philippine peso
Religions: Roman Catholic, Protestant, Muslim
Languages: Filipino (Tagalog), English

Poland

Area: 120,728 sq mi (312,685 sq km)
Population: 38,421,000
Capital: Warsaw, pop. 1,776,000
Currency: zloty
Religion: Roman Catholic
Language: Polish

Portugal

Area: 35,556 sq mi (92,090 sq km)
Population: 10,355,000
Capital: Lisbon, pop. 2,942,000
Currency: euro
Religion: Roman Catholic
Languages: Portuguese, Mirandese

Qatar

Area: 4,473 sq mi (11,586 sq km)
Population: 2,364,000
Capital: Doha, pop. 637,000
Currency: Qatari rial
Religions: Muslim, Christian
Languages: Arabic, English

Romania

Area: 92,043 sq mi (238,391 sq km)
Population: 21,457,000
Capital: Bucharest, pop. 1,812,000
Currency: Romanian leu
Religions: Eastern Orthodox, Protestant, Roman Catholic
Languages: Romanian, Hungarian

Russia

Area: 6,601,665 sq mi (17,098,242 sq km)
Population: 144,478,000
Capital: Moscow, pop. 12,476,000
Currency: Russian ruble
Religions: Russian Orthodox, Muslim
Languages: Russian, Tatar, other local languages
Note: Russia is in both Europe and Asia, but its capital is in Europe, so it is classified here as a European country.

COLOR KEY ● Africa ● Australia, New Zealand, and Oceania

Rwanda

Area: 10,169 sq mi
(26,338 sq km)
Population: 12,187,000
Capital: Kigali, pop. 1,095,000
Currency: Rwandan franc
Religions: Protestant, Roman Catholic, Muslim
Languages: Kinyarwanda, French, English, Kiswahili (Swahili)

San Marino

Area: 24 sq mi (61 sq km)
Population: 34,000
Capital: San Marino, pop. 4,000
Currency: euro
Religion: Roman Catholic
Language: Italian

Samoa

Area: 1,093 sq mi
(2,831 sq km)
Population: 201,000
Capital: Apia, pop. 36,000
Currency: tala
Religions: Protestant, Roman Catholic, Mormon
Languages: Samoan (Polynesian), English

Sao Tome and Principe

Area: 372 sq mi (964 sq km)
Population: 204,000
Capital: São Tomé,
pop. 80,000
Currency: dobra
Religions: Roman Catholic, Protestant
Languages: Portuguese, Forro

SNAPSH⊙T
Samoa

A wooden ladder leads down to the To Sua Ocean Trench swimming hole in Upolo, Samoa.

Asia ● Europe ● North America ● South America

Saudi Arabia

Area: 830,000 sq mi
(2,149,690 sq km)
Population: 33,091,000
Capital: Riyadh, pop. 7,071,000
Currency: Saudi riyal
Religion: Muslim
Language: Arabic

Singapore

Area: 269 sq mi (697 sq km)
Population: 5,996,000
Capital: Singapore,
pop. 5,868,000
Currency: Singapore dollar
Religions: Buddhist, Christian, Muslim, Taoist, Hindu
Languages: English, Mandarin, Malay, Tamil

Senegal

Area: 75,955 sq mi
(196,722 sq km)
Population: 15,021,000
Capital: Dakar, pop. 3,057,000
Currency: Communauté Financière Africaine franc
Religions: Muslim, Roman Catholic
Languages: French, Wolof, Pulaar, Jola, Mandinka

Serbia

Area: 29,913 sq mi (77,474 sq km)
Population: 7,078,000
Capital: Belgrade, pop. 1,394,000
Currency: Serbian dinar
Religions: Serbian Orthodox, Roman Catholic, Protestant
Languages: Serbian, Hungarian, Bosniak, Romany

3 cool things about SINGAPORE

1. Singapore's mascot is the merlion, a half-fish, half-lion mythical creature said to represent Singapore's name in Malay, Singapura, which means "Lion City."

2. The country's Changi Airport features a butterfly garden, an indoor waterfall, a movie theater, and Singapore's tallest slide at four stories high.

3. Singapore's "Night Safari," the world's first nighttime zoo, welcomes guests to check out animals in the dark.

Seychelles

Area: 176 sq mi (455 sq km)
Population: 95,000
Capital: Victoria, pop. 28,000
Currency: Seychelles rupee
Religions: Roman Catholic, Protestant, Hindu, Muslim
Languages: Seychellois Creole, English, French

Slovakia

Area: 18,933 sq mi
(49,035 sq km)
Population: 5,445,000
Capital: Bratislava, pop. 433,000
Currency: euro
Religions: Roman Catholic, Protestant, Greek Catholic
Languages: Slovak, Hungarian, Romany

Sierra Leone

Area: 27,699 sq mi (71,740 sq km)
Population: 6,312,000
Capital: Freetown, pop. 1,168,000
Currency: leone
Religions: Muslim, Christian
Languages: English, Mende, Temne, Krio

Slovenia

Area: 7,827 sq mi
(20,273 sq km)
Population: 2,102,000
Capital: Ljubljana,
pop. 286,000
Currency: euro
Religions: Roman Catholic, Muslim, Orthodox
Languages: Slovene, Serbian, Croatian, Italian, Hungarian

Solomon Islands

Area: 11,157 sq mi
(28,896 sq km)
Population: 660,000
Capital: Honiara, pop. 82,000
Currency: Solomon Islands dollar
Religions: Protestant, Roman Catholic
Languages: Melanesian pidgin, English,
indigenous languages

Somalia

Area: 246,201 sq mi
(637,657 sq km)
Population: 11,259,000
Capital: Mogadishu, pop. 2,180,000
Currency: Somali shilling
Religion: Sunni Muslim
Languages: Somali, Arabic, Italian, English

South Africa

Area: 470,693 sq mi (1,219,090 sq km)
Population: 55,380,000
Capitals: Pretoria (Tshwane),
pop. 2,473,000; Cape Town, pop.
4,524,000; Bloemfontein, pop. 465,000
Currency: rand
Religions: Christian, indigenous religions
Languages: isiZulu, isiXhosa, Afrikaans, Sepedi, Setswana,
English, Sesotho, Xitsonga, siSwati, Tshivenda, isiNdebele

South Korea

Area: 38,502 sq mi
(99,720 sq km)
Population: 51,418,000
Capital: Seoul, pop. 9,962,000
Currency: won
Religions: Christian, Buddhist
Languages: Korean, English

South Sudan

Area: 248,777 sq mi
(644,329 sq km)
Population: 10,205,000
Capital: Juba, pop. 386,000
Currency: South Sudanese pound
Religions: animist, Christian
Languages: English, Arabic, Dinke, Nuer,
Bari, Zande, Shilluk

Spain

Area: 195,124 sq mi (505,370 sq km)
Population: 49,331,000
Capital: Madrid, pop. 6,559,000
Currency: euro
Religion: Roman Catholic
Languages: Castilian Spanish, Catalan,
Galician, Basque

Sri Lanka

Area: 25,332 sq mi
(65,610 sq km)
Population: 22,577,000
Capitals: Colombo, pop. 609,000;
Sri Jayewardenepura Kotte, pop. 103,000
Currency: Sri Lankan rupee
Religions: Buddhist, Muslim, Hindu, Christian
Languages: Sinhala, Tamil

St. Kitts and Nevis

Area: 101 sq mi (261 sq km)
Population: 53,000
Capital: Basseterre, pop. 14,000
Currency: East Caribbean dollar
Religions: Protestant, Roman Catholic
Language: English

St. Lucia

Area: 238 sq mi (616 sq km)
Population: 166,000
Capital: Castries,
pop. 22,000
Currency: East Caribbean dollar
Religions: Roman Catholic, Protestant
Languages: English, French patois

St. Vincent and the Grenadines

Area: 150 sq mi (389 sq km)
Population: 102,000
Capital: Kingstown, pop. 27,000
Currency: East Caribbean dollar
Religions: Protestant, Roman Catholic
Languages: English, Vincentian Creole English,
French patois

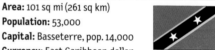

Sudan

Area: 718,723 sq mi
(1,861,484 sq km)
Population: 43,121,000
Capital: Khartoum,
pop. 5,678,000
Currency: Sudanese pound
Religions: Sunni Muslim, Christian
Languages: Arabic, English, Nubian, Ta Bedawie, Fur

Suriname

Area: 63,251 sq mi (163,820 sq km)
Population: 598,000
Capital: Paramaribo, pop. 239,000
Currency: Suriname dollar
Religions: Protestant, Hindu, Roman Catholic, Muslim
Languages: Dutch, English, Sranan Tongo, Caribbean Hindustani, Javanese

Sweden

Area: 173,860 sq mi
(450,295 sq km)
Population: 10,041,000
Capital: Stockholm,
pop. 1,608,000
Currency: Swedish krona
Religion: Lutheran
Languages: Swedish, Sami, Finnish

Some 200 DIFFERENT LANGUAGES are SPOKEN in SWEDEN.

Switzerland

Area: 15,937 sq mi
(41,277 sq km)
Population: 8,293,000
Capital: Bern, pop. 426,000
Currency: Swiss franc
Religions: Roman Catholic, Protestant, Muslim
Languages: German, French, Italian, English, Romansh

Syria

Area: 71,498 sq mi (185,180 sq km)
Population: 19,454,000
Capital: Damascus, pop. 2,354,000
Currency: Syrian pound
Religions: Sunni Muslim, other Muslim (includes Alawite), Christian, Druze
Languages: Arabic, Kurdish, Armenian, Aramaic, Circassian, French

Tajikistan

Area: 55,637 sq mi
(144,100 sq km)
Population: 8,605,000
Capital: Dushanbe,
pop. 894,000
Currency: somoni
Religions: Sunni Muslim, Shia Muslim
Languages: Tajik, Uzbek

Tanzania

Area: 365,754 sq mi (947,300 sq km)
Population: 55,451,000
Capitals: Dar es Salaam, pop. 6,368,000; Dodoma, pop. 262,000
Currency: Tanzanian shilling
Religions: Christian, Muslim, indigenous beliefs
Languages: Kiswahili (Swahili), Kiunguja (Swahili in Zanzibar), English, Arabic, local languages

Thailand

Area: 198,117 sq mi
(513,120 sq km)
Population: 68,616,000
Capital: Bangkok, pop. 10,350,000
Currency: baht
Religions: Buddhist, Muslim, Christian
Languages: Thai, English

Timor-Leste (East Timor)

Area: 5,743 sq mi
(14,874 sq km)
Population: 1,322,000
Capital: Dili, pop. 281,000
Currency: U.S. dollar
Religions: Roman Catholic, Protestant
Languages: Tetum, Portuguese, Indonesian, English

COLOR KEY ● Africa ● Australia, New Zealand, and Oceania

Togo

Area: 21,925 sq mi (56,785 sq km)
Population: 8,176,000
Capital: Lomé, pop. 1,785,000
Currency: Communauté Financière Africaine franc
Religions: Indigenous beliefs, Christian, Muslim
Languages: French, Ewe, Mina, Kabye, Dagomba

Turkey

Area: 302,535 sq mi (783,562 sq km)
Population: 81,257,000
Capital: Ankara, pop. 5,018,000
Currency: Turkish lira
Religion: Muslim
Languages: Turkish, Kurdish, other minority languages

Tonga

Area: 288 sq mi (747 sq km)
Population: 107,000
Capital: Nuku´alofa (on Tongatapu), pop. 27,000
Currency: pa´anga
Religions: Protestant, Church of Latter-day Saints, Roman Catholic
Languages: Tongan, English

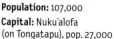

Turkmenistan

Area: 188,456 sq mi (488,100 sq km)
Population: 5,411,000
Capital: Ashgabat, pop. 828,000
Currency: Turkmenistan new manat
Religions: Muslim, Eastern Orthodox
Languages: Turkmen, Russian, Uzbek

There are NO TRAFFIC LIGHTS in TONGA.

The GARAGUM DESERT COVERS some 70 PERCENT of TURKMENISTAN.

Trinidad and Tobago

Area: 1,980 sq mi (5,128 sq km)
Population: 1,216,000
Capital: Port of Spain (on Trinidad), pop. 544,000
Currency: Trinidad and Tobago dollar
Religions: Protestant, Roman Catholic, Hindu, Muslim
Languages: English, Creole, Caribbean Hindustani

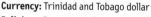

Tuvalu

Area: 10 sq mi (26 sq km)
Population: 11,000
Capital: Funafuti (on Funafuti Atoll), pop. 7,000
Currency: Australian dollar
Religions: Protestant, Baha'i
Languages: Tuvaluan, English, Samoan, Kiribati

Tunisia

Area: 63,170 sq mi (163,610 sq km)
Population: 11,516,000
Capital: Tunis, pop. 2,328,000
Currency: Tunisian dinar
Religion: Muslim
Languages: Arabic, French, Berber (Tamazight)

Uganda

Area: 93,065 sq mi (241,038 sq km)
Population: 40,854,000
Capital: Kampala, pop. 3,318,000
Currency: Ugandan shilling
Religions: Protestant, Roman Catholic, Muslim
Languages: English, Ganda (Luganda), local languages, Swahili, Arabic

● Asia   ● Europe   ● North America   ● South America

Ukraine

Area: 233,032 sq mi
(603,550 sq km)
Population: 41,597,000
Capital: Kyiv, pop. 2,973,000
Currency: hryvnia
Religions: Ukrainian Orthodox, Ukrainian Greek Catholic, Roman Catholic, Protestant, Jewish
Languages: Ukrainian, Russian

United Kingdom

Area: 94,058 sq mi
(243,610 sq km)
Population: 65,105,000
Capital: London, pop. 9,177,000
Currency: pound sterling
Religions: Anglican, Roman Catholic, Presbyterian, Methodist, Muslim, Hindu
Languages: English, Scots, Scottish Gaelic, Welsh, Irish

United Arab Emirates

Area: 32,278 sq mi
(83,600 sq km)
Population: 9,701,000
Capital: Abu Dhabi,
pop. 1,452,000
Currency: United Arab Emirates dirham
Religions: Muslim, Christian, Hindu
Languages: Arabic, Persian, English, Hindi, Urdu

United States

Area: 3,796,741 sq mi
(9,833,517 sq km)
Population: 321,004,000
Capital: Washington, D.C.,
pop. 672,000
Currency: U.S. dollar
Religions: Protestant, Roman Catholic, Jewish
Languages: English, Spanish, Native American

SNAPSHOT
Vietnam

Outdoor market in the streets of Hoi An, Vietnam

COLOR KEY ● Africa ● Australia, New Zealand, and Oceania

Uruguay

Area: 68,037 sq mi
(176,215 sq km)
Population: 3,369,000
Capital: Montevideo, pop. 1,745,000
Currency: Uruguayan peso
Religions: Roman Catholic, Protestant
Language: Spanish

CAPYBARAS— the world's largest RODENT—are native to URUGUAY.

Uzbekistan

Area: 172,742 sq mi
(447,400 sq km)
Population: 30,024,000
Capital: Tashkent,
pop. 2,049,000
Currency: Uzbekistan sum
Religions: Muslim (mostly Sunni), Eastern Orthodox
Languages: Uzbek, Russian, Tajik

Vanuatu

Area: 4,706 sq mi (12,189 sq km)
Population: 288,000
Capital: Port Vila, pop. 53,000
Currency: vatu
Religions: Protestant, Roman Catholic,
indigenous beliefs
Languages: Bislama, English, French, local languages

Vatican City

Area: .17 sq mi (.44 sq km)
Population: 1,000
Capital: Vatican City, pop. 1,000
Currency: euro
Religion: Roman Catholic
Languages: Italian, Latin, French

Venezuela

Area: 352,144 sq mi
(912,050 sq km)
Population: 31,689,000
Capital: Caracas, pop. 2,936,000
Currency: bolívar soberano
Religion: Roman Catholic
Languages: Spanish, numerous indigenous dialects

Vietnam

Area: 127,881 sq mi
(331,210 sq km)
Population: 97,040,000
Capital: Hanoi, pop. 4,480,000
Currency: dong
Religions: Buddhist, Roman Catholic, Hoa Hao, Cao Dai,
Protestant, Muslim
Languages: Vietnamese, English, French, Chinese, Khmer

Yemen

Area: 203,850 sq mi
(527,968 sq km)
Population: 28,667,000
Capital: Sanaa, pop. 2,874,000
Currency: Yemeni rial
Religion: Muslim
Language: Arabic

Zambia

Area: 290,587 sq mi
(752,618 sq km)
Population: 16,445,000
Capital: Lusaka, pop. 2,647,000
Currency: Zambian kwacha
Religions: Protestant, Roman Catholic
Languages: Bemba, Nyanja, Tonga, Lozi, Chewa,
Nsenga, Tumbuka, English

Zimbabwe

Area: 150,872 sq mi
(390,757 sq km)
Population: 14,030,000
Capital: Harare, pop. 1,521,000
Currency: Zimbabwe dollar
Religions: Protestant, Roman Catholic,
indigenous beliefs
Languages: Shona, Ndebele, English

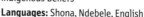

THE POLITICAL UNITED STATES

The United States is made up of 50 states joined like a giant quilt. Each is unique, but together they make a national fabric held together by a constitution and a federal government. State boundaries, outlined in dotted lines on the map, set apart internal political units within the country. The national capital—Washington, D.C.—is marked by a star in a double circle. The capital of each state is marked by a star in a single circle.

11:00 AM
CENTRAL TIME

12:00 NOON
EASTERN TIME

0 ————— 300 miles
0 ————— 300 kilometers
Albers Conic Equal-Area Projection

Lake of the Woods
International Falls
Grand Forks
Fargo
Duluth
Superior
Marquette
Isle Royale
Lake Superior
MINNESOTA
Minneapolis
St. Paul
WISCONSIN
Green Bay
Milwaukee
Madison
Sioux Falls
Cedar Rapids
IOWA
Omaha
Des Moines
Davenport
Lincoln
Rockford
Chicago
Gary
Peoria
ILLINOIS
Springfield
Kansas City
Jefferson City
Topeka
St. Louis
MISSOURI
Springfield
Tulsa
OMA
Fort Smith
Memphis
ARKANSAS
Little Rock
MICHIGAN
Grand Rapids
Lansing
Detroit
Lake Michigan
Lake Huron
Lake Erie
Toledo
Fort Wayne
INDIANA
Dayton
Indianapolis
Cincinnati
Louisville
Frankfort
Evansville
Lexington
KENTUCKY
Paducah
Knoxville
Nashville
TENNESSEE
Chattanooga
Huntsville
Birmingham
MAINE
Bangor
Augusta
Burlington
VT.
Lake Champlain
Montpelier
N.H.
Portland
Concord
Boston
Cape Cod
MASS.
Providence
R.I.
CONN.
Long Island
Albany
Syracuse
Rochester
Lake Ontario
NEW YORK
Buffalo
Hartford
Erie
Newark
New York
Trenton
NEW JERSEY
PENNSYLVANIA
Harrisburg
Pittsburgh
Philadelphia
OHIO
Cleveland
Columbus
Baltimore
Dover
DELAWARE
Annapolis
Washington, D.C.
MARYLAND
WEST VIRGINIA
Charleston
Richmond
VIRGINIA
Chesapeake Bay
Virginia Beach
Roanoke
Norfolk
Greensboro
Raleigh
Cape Hatteras
NORTH CAROLINA
Charlotte
Greenville
Columbia
SOUTH CAROLINA
Charleston
Atlanta
GEORGIA
Macon
Columbus
Savannah
MISSISSIPPI
Jackson
ALABAMA
Montgomery
Natchez
Biloxi
Mobile
Tallahassee
Jacksonville
Gainesville
Dallas
Shreveport
LOUISIANA
Baton Rouge
Beaumont
Lafayette
Houston
New Orleans
Mississippi River Delta
Mobile Bay
Apalachee Bay
Tampa
St. Petersburg
FLORIDA
Orlando
Cape Canaveral
Lake Okeechobee
Fort Lauderdale
The Everglades
Miami
Florida Keys

TIME ZONES: Earth is divided into 24 time zones, each about 15 degrees of longitude wide, reflecting the distance Earth turns from west to east each hour. The U.S. is divided into six time zones, indicated by red dotted lines on the map.

THE PHYSICAL UNITED STATES

Mt. Rainier
14,411 ft
(4,392 m)
Mt. St. Helens
(2,550 m) 8,366 ft
Columbia
Mt. Hood
11,239 ft
(3,425 m)

CASCADE RANGE

Great Sandy
Desert

Columbia Plateau

Blue Mountains

Snake

Bitterroot Range

Salmon River
Mountains

Snake

Snake River Plain

Flathead
Lake

ROCKY

Yellowstone
Lake

Absaroka Range

Milk

Missouri

Fort Peck
Lake

Yellowstone

Bighorn Mts.

Grand
Teton
13,770 ft
(4,197 m)

MOUNTAINS

Front Range

Laramie Mts.

Little Missouri

GREAT

Missouri

Heart

White
Butte
3,506 ft
(1,069 m)

Black
Hills

Harney
Peak
7,242 ft
(2,207 m)

Lake
Sakakawea

Lake
Oahe

Geographical Center
of the 50 United States

White

Niobrara

N. Platte

Sand Hills

James

Missouri

Great
Salt
Lake

Wasatch Range

Uinta Mts.

Great Divide
Basin

Lake
Tahoe

Great

Sierra Nevada

Sacramento Valley

San Joaquin Valley

San Joaquin

Basin

Mt. Whitney
14,494 ft
(4,418 m)

Death
Valley

Mojave

Lowest Point in
North America
(-86 m) -282 ft

Desert

Lake
Powell

Lake
Mead

Grand
Canyon

Painted Desert

Mt. Elbert
(4,399 m) 14,433 ft

Colorado

San Juan Mts.

Colorado

Plateau

Sangre de Cristo

Pikes Peak
14,110 ft
(4,301 m)

S. Platte

PLAINS

Platte

Geographical Center
of the 48
Contiguous United States

Smoky Hill

Arkansas

Red Hills

Cimarron

Channel
Islands

Salton
Sea

Imperial
Valley

Humphreys Peak
12,637 ft
(3,852 m)

Colorado

Gila

Sonoran

Desert

Salt

Black Mesa
4,973 ft
(1,516 m)

Rio Grande

Canadian

Llano
Estacado

Sacramento Mts.

Brazos

Colorado

Guadalupe Peak
8,749 ft
(2,667 m)

Pecos

Edwards
Plateau

Rio Grande

0   400 miles
0   400 kilometers

North Slope

Brooks Range

Yukon

(Mt. McKinley) Denali
(6,190 m) 20,310 ft

Highest Point in
North America

Alaska Range

Alexander
Archipelago

Aleutian Islands

Alaska Peninsula

Kaua'i

Ni'ihau

O'ahu

Moloka'i

Lana'i

Maui

Kaho'olawe

Hawai'i

0   150 miles
0   150 kilometers

Mauna Kea
13,679 ft
(4,169 m)

ALASKA AND HAWAII:
In addition to the states
located on the main landmass,
the U.S. has two states—Alaska
and Hawaii—that are not directly
connected to the other 48 states.
If Alaska and Hawaii were shown in
their correct relative sizes and locations,
the map would not fit on these pages.

Stretching from the Atlantic Ocean in the east to the Pacific Ocean in the west, the United States is the third largest country (by area) in the world. Its physical diversity ranges from mountains to fertile plains and dry deserts. Shading on the map indicates changes in elevation, while colors show different vegetation patterns.

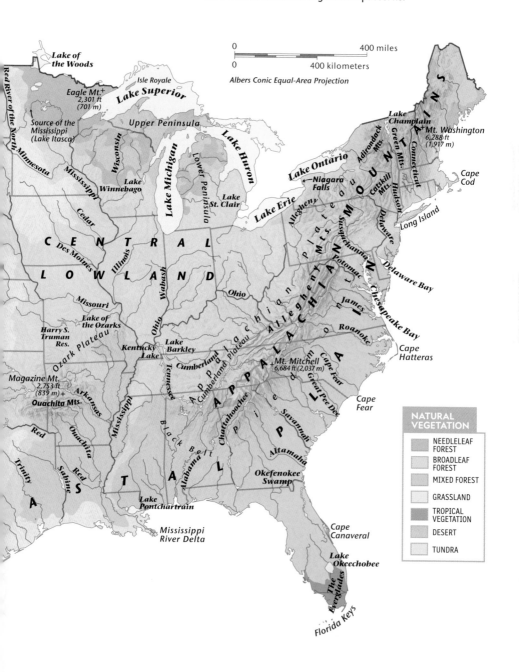

0   400 miles
0   400 kilometers

Albers Conic Equal-Area Projection

Lake of the Woods

Red River of the North

Isle Royale

Eagle Mt. 2,301 ft (701 m)

Lake Superior

Source of the Mississippi (Lake Itasca)

Upper Peninsula

Minnesota

Mississippi

Wisconsin

Lake Winnebago

Cedar

Lake Michigan

Lower Peninsula

Lake Huron

Lake St. Clair

Lake Ontario

Niagara Falls

Lake Erie

Adirondack Mts.

Lake Champlain

Green Mts.

Mt. Washington 6,288 ft (1,917 m)

Connecticut

Cape Cod

APPALACHIAN MOUNTAINS

Allegheny Plateau

Catskill Mts.

Hudson

Delaware

Long Island

Des Moines

Illinois

Wabash

Allegheny

Susquehanna

Potomac

Delaware Bay

C E N T R A L

L O W L A N D

Ohio

Missouri

Lake of the Ozarks

Harry S. Truman Res.

Ozark Plateau

Kentucky Lake

Lake Barkley

Ohio

Tennessee

James

Chesapeake Bay

Roanoke

Cape Hatteras

Appalachian Mts.

Cumberland Plateau

Cumberland

Mt. Mitchell 6,684 ft (2,037 m)

Cape Fear

Great Pee Dee

Magazine Mt. 2,753 ft (839 m)

Ouachita Mts.

Arkansas

Mississippi

A P P A L A C H I A N

Cape Fear

Red

Ouachita

Black Belt

Chattahoochee

Savannah

Altamaha

Trinity

Sabine

Red

T E X A S

Alabama

Okefenokee Swamp

Lake Pontchartrain

Mississippi River Delta

Cape Canaveral

Cape Canaveral

Lake Okeechobee

The Everglades

Florida Keys

NATURAL VEGETATION	
	NEEDLELEAF FOREST
	BROADLEAF FOREST
	MIXED FOREST
	GRASSLAND
	TROPICAL VEGETATION
	DESERT
	TUNDRA

THE STATES

From sea to shining sea, the United States of America is a nation of diversity. In the 244 years since its creation, the nation has grown to become home to a wide range of peoples, industries, and cultures. The following pages present a general overview of all 50 states in the United States.

The country is generally divided into five large regions: the Northeast, the Southeast, the Midwest, the Southwest, and the West. Though loosely defined, these zones tend to share important similarities, including climate, history, and geography. The color key below provides a guide to which states are in each region.

The flag of each state and highlights of demography and industry are also included. These details offer a brief overview of each state.

In addition, each state's official flower and bird are identified.

Color Key by Region

Arizona

Nickname: Grand Canyon State
Area: 113,998 sq mi (295,254 sq km)
Population: 7,172,000
Capital: Phoenix; population 1,574,000
Statehood: February 14, 1912; 48th state
State flower/bird: Saguaro cactus blossom/ cactus wren

Arkansas

Nickname: Natural State
Area: 53,179 sq mi (137,732 sq km)
Population: 3,014,000
Capital: Little Rock; population 198,000
Statehood: June 15, 1836; 25th state
State flower/bird: Apple blossom/ northern mockingbird

You can dig for DIAMONDS in a CRATER in Arkansas and KEEP WHAT YOU FIND.

Alabama

Nickname: Heart of Dixie
Area: 52,419 sq mi (135,765 sq km)
Population: 4,888,000
Capital: Montgomery; population 201,000
Statehood: December 14, 1819; 22nd state
State flower/bird: Camellia/yellowhammer (northern flicker)

Alaska

Nickname: Last Frontier
Area: 663,267 sq mi (1,717,854 sq km)
Population: 737,000
Capital: Juneau; population 32,000
Statehood: January 3, 1959; 49th state
State flower/bird: Forget-me-not/ willow ptarmigan

California

Nickname: Golden State
Area: 163,696 sq mi (423,970 sq km)
Population: 39,557,000
Capital: Sacramento; population 490,000
Statehood: September 9, 1850; 31st state
State flower/bird: California poppy/ California quail

Colorado

Nickname: Centennial State
Area: 104,094 sq mi (269,601 sq km)
Population: 5,696,000
Capital: Denver; population 678,000
Statehood: August 1, 1876; 38th state
State flower/bird: Rocky Mountain columbine/ lark bunting

COLOR KEY ● Northeast ● Southeast

Connecticut

Nickname: Constitution State
Area: 5,543 sq mi (14,357 sq km)
Population: 3,573,000
Capital: Hartford; population 124,000
Statehood: January 9, 1788; 5th state
State flower/bird: Mountain laurel/ American robin

Idaho

Nickname: Gem State
Area: 83,570 sq mi (216,446 sq km)
Population: 1,754,000
Capital: Boise; population 221,000
Statehood: July 3, 1890; 43rd state
State flower/bird: Syringa (mock orange)/ mountain bluebird

Delaware

Nickname: First State
Area: 2,489 sq mi (6,447 sq km)
Population: 967,000
Capital: Dover; population 37,000
Statehood: December 7, 1787; 1st state
State flower/bird: Peach blossom/ blue hen chicken

There is a
POTATO MUSEUM
in **BLACKFOOT,
IDAHO.**

Florida

Nickname: Sunshine State
Area: 65,755 sq mi (170,304 sq km)
Population: 21,299,000
Capital: Tallahassee; population 188,000
Statehood: March 3, 1845; 27th state
State flower/bird: Orange blossom/ northern mockingbird

Illinois

Nickname: Prairie State
Area: 57,914 sq mi (149,998 sq km)
Population: 12,741,000
Capital: Springfield; population 116,000
Statehood: December 3, 1818; 21st state
State flower/bird: Purple violet/ northern cardinal

Georgia

Nickname: Peach State
Area: 59,425 sq mi (153,909 sq km)
Population: 10,519,000
Capital: Atlanta; population 465,000
Statehood: January 2, 1788; 4th state
State flower/bird: Cherokee rose/brown thrasher

Indiana

Nickname: Hoosier State
Area: 36,418 sq mi (94,321 sq km)
Population: 6,692,000
Capital: Indianapolis; population 853,000
Statehood: December 11, 1816; 19th state
State flower/bird: Peony/northern cardinal

Hawaii

Nickname: Aloha State
Area: 10,931 sq mi (28,311 sq km)
Population: 1,420,000
Capital: Honolulu; population 351,000
Statehood: August 21, 1959; 50th state
State flower/bird: Pua aloalo (yellow hibiscus)/ Nene (Hawaiian goose)

Iowa

Nickname: Hawkeye State
Area: 56,272 sq mi (145,743 sq km)
Population: 3,156,000
Capital: Des Moines; population 215,000
Statehood: December 28, 1846; 29th state
State flower/bird: Wild prairie rose/ American goldfinch

Kansas

Nickname: Sunflower State
Area: 82,277 sq mi (213,096 sq km)
Population: 2,012,000
Capital: Topeka; population 127,000
Statehood: January 29, 1861; 34th state
State flower/bird: Sunflower/
western meadowlark

Kentucky

Nickname: Bluegrass State
Area: 40,409 sq mi
(104,659 sq km)
Population: 4,468,000
Capital: Frankfort; population 27,000
Statehood: June 1, 1792; 15th state
State flower/bird: Goldenrod/northern cardinal

Louisiana

Nickname: Pelican State
Area: 51,840 sq mi
(134,264 sq km)
Population: 4,660,000
Capital: Baton Rouge; population 228,000
Statehood: April 30, 1812; 18th state
State flower/bird: Magnolia/brown pelican

Maine

Nickname: Pine Tree State
Area: 35,385 sq mi (91,646 sq km)
Population: 1,338,000
Capital: Augusta; population 19,000
Statehood: March 15, 1820; 23rd state
State flower/bird: White pine cone and tassel/
black-capped chickadee

Maryland

Nickname: Old Line State
Area: 12,407 sq mi (32,133 sq km)
Population: 6,043,000
Capital: Annapolis; population 39,000
Statehood: April 28, 1788; 7th state
State flower/bird: Black-eyed Susan/
Baltimore oriole

Massachusetts

Nickname: Bay State
Area: 10,555 sq mi (27,336 sq km)
Population: 6,902,000
Capital: Boston; population 669,000
Statehood: February 6, 1788; 6th state
State flower/bird: Mayflower/
black-capped chickadee

FENWAY PARK, the Boston Red Sox stadium in Massachusetts, HAS A ROOFTOP VEGETABLE GARDEN.

Michigan

Nickname: Great Lakes State
Area: 96,716 sq mi (250,494 sq km)
Population: 9,996,000
Capital: Lansing; population 115,000
Statehood: January 26, 1837; 26th state
State flower/bird: Apple blossom/
American robin

Minnesota

Nickname: North Star State
Area: 86,939 sq mi (225,171 sq km)
Population: 5,611,000
Capital: St. Paul; population 301,000
Statehood: May 11, 1858; 32nd state
State flower/bird: Showy lady's slipper/
common loon

Mississippi

Nickname: Magnolia State
Area: 48,430 sq mi (125,434 sq km)
Population: 2,987,000
Capital: Jackson; population 170,000
Statehood: December 10, 1817; 20th state
State flower/bird: Magnolia/
northern mockingbird

COLOR KEY Northeast Southeast

Missouri

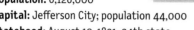

Nickname: Show-Me State
Area: 69,704 sq mi (180,533 sq km)
Population: 6,126,000
Capital: Jefferson City; population 44,000
Statehood: August 10, 1821; 24th state
State flower/bird: Hawthorn blossom/ eastern bluebird

Montana

Nickname: Treasure State
Area: 147,042 sq mi (380,838 sq km)
Population: 1,063,000
Capital: Helena; population 30,000
Statehood: November 8, 1889; 41st state
State flower/bird: Bitterroot/ western meadowlark

Nebraska

Nickname: Cornhusker State
Area: 77,354 sq mi (200,345 sq km)
Population: 1,929,000
Capital: Lincoln; population 277,000
Statehood: March 1, 1867; 37th state
State flower/bird: Goldenrod/ western meadowlark

Nevada

Nickname: Silver State
Area: 110,561 sq mi (286,351 sq km)
Population: 3,034,000
Capital: Carson City; population 54,000
Statehood: October 31, 1864; 36th state
State flower/bird: Sagebrush/ mountain bluebird

New Hampshire

Nickname: Granite State
Area: 9,350 sq mi (24,216 sq km)
Population: 1,356,000
Capital: Concord; population 43,000
Statehood: June 21, 1788; 9th state
State flower/bird: Purple lilac/purple finch

New Jersey

Nickname: Garden State
Area: 8,721 sq mi (22,588 sq km)
Population: 8,909,000
Capital: Trenton; population 85,000
Statehood: December 18, 1787; 3rd state
State flower/bird: Violet/American goldfinch

New Mexico

Nickname: Land of Enchantment
Area: 121,590 sq mi (314,915 sq km)
Population: 2,095,000
Capital: Santa Fe; population 83,000
Statehood: January 6, 1912; 47th state
State flower/bird: Yucca flower/roadrunner

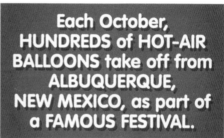

Each October, HUNDREDS of HOT-AIR BALLOONS take off from ALBUQUERQUE, NEW MEXICO, as part of a FAMOUS FESTIVAL.

New York

Nickname: Empire State
Area: 54,556 sq mi (141,299 sq km)
Population: 19,542,000
Capital: Albany; population 98,000
Statehood: July 26, 1788; 11th state
State flower/bird: Rose/eastern bluebird

North Carolina

Nickname: Tar Heel State
Area: 53,819 sq mi (139,389 sq km)
Population: 10,384,000
Capital: Raleigh; population 449,000
Statehood: November 21, 1789; 12th state
State flower/bird: American dogwood/ northern cardinal

North Dakota

Nickname: Peace Garden State
Area: 70,700 sq mi (183,112 sq km)
Population: 760,000
Capital: Bismarck; population 71,000
Statehood: November 2, 1889; 39th state
State flower/bird: Wild prairie rose/
western meadowlark

> At the North Dakota STATE FAIR, visitors have competed in a GREASE-COVERED-WATERMELON RACE.

Ohio

Nickname: Buckeye State
Area: 44,825 sq mi (116,096 sq km)
Population: 11,689,000
Capital: Columbus; population 852,000
Statehood: March 1, 1803; 17th state
State flower/bird: Scarlet carnation/
northern cardinal

Oklahoma

Nickname: Sooner State
Area: 69,898 sq mi (181,036 sq km)
Population: 3,943,000
Capital: Oklahoma City; population 629,000
Statehood: November 16, 1907; 46th state
State flower/bird: Oklahoma rose/
scissor-tailed flycatcher

Oregon

Nickname: Beaver State
Area: 98,381 sq mi (254,805 sq km)
Population: 4,191,000
Capital: Salem; population 164,000
Statehood: February 14, 1859; 33rd state
State flower/bird: Oregon grape/
western meadowlark

Pennsylvania

Nickname: Keystone State
Area: 46,055 sq mi (119,283 sq km)
Population: 12,807,000
Capital: Harrisburg; population 49,000
Statehood: December 12, 1787; 2nd state
State flower/bird: Mountain laurel/
ruffed grouse

Rhode Island

Nickname: Ocean State
Area: 1,545 sq mi (4,002 sq km)
Population: 1,057,000
Capital: Providence; population 180,000
Statehood: May 29, 1790; 13th state
State flower/bird: Violet/
Rhode Island red chicken

South Carolina

Nickname: Palmetto State
Area: 32,020 sq mi (82,932 sq km)
Population: 5,084,000
Capital: Columbia; population 132,000
Statehood: May 23, 1788; 8th state
State flower/bird: Yellow jessamine/
Carolina wren

South Dakota

Nickname: Mount Rushmore State
Area: 77,117 sq mi (199,731 sq km)
Population: 882,000
Capital: Pierre; population 14,000
Statehood: November 2, 1889; 40th state
State flower/bird: Pasque flower/
ring-necked pheasant

Tennessee

Nickname: Volunteer State
Area: 42,143 sq mi (109,151 sq km)
Population: 6,770,000
Capital: Nashville; population 654,000
Statehood: June 1, 1796; 16th state
State flower/bird: Iris/
northern mockingbird

COLOR KEY Northeast Southeast

Texas

Nickname: Lone Star State
Area: 268,581 sq mi (695,621 sq km)
Population: 28,702,000
Capital: Austin; population 917,000
Statehood: December 29, 1845; 28th state
State flower/bird: Texas bluebonnet/ northern mockingbird

Utah

Nickname: Beehive State
Area: 84,899 sq mi (219,887 sq km)
Population: 3,161,000
Capital: Salt Lake City; population 194,000
Statehood: January 4, 1896; 45th state
State flower/bird: Sego lily/California gull

Vermont

Nickname: Green Mountain State
Area: 9,614 sq mi (24,901 sq km)
Population: 626,000
Capital: Montpelier; population 8,000
Statehood: March 4, 1791; 14th state
State flower/bird: Red clover/hermit thrush

3 cool things about VERMONT

1. Billboards have been banned in Vermont since 1968 in an effort to showcase the scenery on the roads and preserve the state's natural beauty.

2. Some 4.5 million acres (1.8 million ha) of Vermont—or 73 percent of the state—are covered in forests. Top trees include beech, birch, maple, pine, spruce, and fir.

3. Sightings of "Champ," Lake Champlain's sea monster, date back hundreds of years and tell of a giant serpent with rows of sharp teeth and silver scales.

Virginia

Nickname: Old Dominion State
Area: 42,774 sq mi (110,785 sq km)
Population: 8,518,000
Capital: Richmond; population 221,000
Statehood: June 25, 1788; 10th state
State flower/bird: American dogwood/ northern cardinal

Washington

Nickname: Evergreen State
Area: 71,300 sq mi (184,665 sq km)
Population: 7,536,000
Capital: Olympia; population 50,000
Statehood: November 11, 1889; 42nd state
State flower/bird: Coast rhododendron/ American goldfinch

West Virginia

Nickname: Mountain State
Area: 24,230 sq mi (62,755 sq km)
Population: 1,806,000
Capital: Charleston; population 49,000
Statehood: June 20, 1863; 35th state
State flower/bird: Rhododendron/ northern cardinal

Wisconsin

Nickname: Badger State
Area: 65,498 sq mi (169,639 sq km)
Population: 5,814,000
Capital: Madison; population 249,000
Statehood: May 29, 1848; 30th state
State flower/bird: Wood violet/ American robin

Wyoming

Nickname: Equality State
Area: 97,814 sq mi (253,336 sq km)
Population: 578,000
Capital: Cheyenne; population 63,000
Statehood: July 10, 1890; 44th state
State flower/bird: Indian paintbrush/ western meadowlark

 Midwest Southwest West

THE TERRITORIES

The United States has 14 territories— political divisions that are not states. Three of these are in the Caribbean Sea, and the other 11 are in the Pacific Ocean.

St. John, U.S. Virgin Islands

Convention Center, San Juan, Puerto Rico

Talofofo Falls, Guam

U.S. CARIBBEAN TERRITORIES

Puerto Rico
Area: 5,324 sq mi (13,790 sq km)
Population: 3,195,000
Capital: San Juan; population 342,000
Languages: Spanish, English

U.S. Virgin Islands
Area: 134 sq mi (346 sq km)
Population: 107,000
Capital: Charlotte Amalie; population 52,000
Languages: English, Spanish, Spanish French

U.S. PACIFIC TERRITORIES

American Samoa
Area: 77 sq mi (199 sq km)
Population: 51,000
Capital: Pago Pago; population 49,000
Language: Samoan, English, Tongan

Guam
Area: 210 sq mi (544 sq km)
Population: 168,000
Capital: Hagåtña (Agana); population 147,000
Languages: English, Filipino, Chamorro, other Pacific island and Asian languages

Northern Mariana Islands
Area: 179 sq mi (464 sq km)
Population: 52,000
Capital: Capital Hill; population 51,000
Languages: Philippine languages, Chinese, Chamorro, English

Other U.S. Territories
Baker Island, Howland Island, Jarvis Island, Johnston Atoll, Kingman Reef, Midway Islands, Palmyra Atoll, Wake Island, Navassa Island (in the Caribbean)

Figures for capital cities vary widely between sources because of differences in the way the area is defined and other projection methods.

THE U.S. CAPITAL

District of Columbia

Area: 68 sq mi (177 sq km)
Population: 672,000

Abraham Lincoln, who was president during the Civil War and a strong opponent of slavery, is remembered in the Lincoln Memorial, located at the opposite end of the National Mall from the U.S. Capitol Building.

The Lincoln Memorial celebrates its 100th anniversary in 2022.

COLOR KEY ● Territories ● Northeast

Check out these outrageous U.S.A. facts.

A ball of **twine** in Kansas **weighs more** than **19,000 pounds** (8,618 kg) and could stretch **halfway across** the **United States.**

The state **"FLOWER"** of Maine is the **WHITE PINE CONE.**

There is a place called **Roach, Missouri.**

Legend says that **PIRATE TREASURE** might be buried near **THE STATUE OF LIBERTY.**

IN ONE SECOND A WATER PIPE **FROM THE HOOVER DAM** COULD FILL **960,000** SODA CANS.

THERE ARE 100-foot (30-m)-tall SAND DUNES IN ALASKA.

THE **BRIGHTEST LIGHT** ON A HOTEL IS IN LAS VEGAS, NEVADA, AND CAN BE SEEN FROM AIRPLANES **250 MILES** (402 KM) **AWAY.**

THE CITY OF **PORTLAND, OREGON,** WAS NAMED IN A **COIN TOSS** —IT HAD A **FIFTY-FIFTY CHANCE** OF BECOMING BOSTON, OREGON.

NIGHTTIME RAINBOWS are common at **Yosemite National Park.**

10 TOWERING FACTS ABOUT UNUSUAL BUILDINGS

Dog lovers visiting Cottonwood, Idaho, U.S.A., can check into a beagle-shaped residence called the **Dog Bark Park Inn.**

LOCATED ON ONE OF BOLIVIA'S SALT FLATS, THE PALACIO DE SAL HOTEL IS MADE ALMOST ENTIRELY OUT OF SALT.

India's National Fisheries Development Board is headquartered in a three-story building shaped like a fish swimming in midair.

THE OUTSIDE OF THE **RIPLEY'S BELIEVE IT OR NOT! MUSEUM** IN NIAGARA FALLS, CANADA, INCLUDES A **COLORFUL SIDEWAYS SCULPTURE** OF THE **EMPIRE STATE BUILDING** TOPPED WITH **KING KONG.**

The inspiration for the **warped shape** of the **Crooked House** in Sopot, Poland, came from Polish fairy-tale illustrations.

BONHOMME'S ICE PALACE WAS CONSTRUCTED FROM NEARLY **2,000 300-POUND** (135-KG) FROZEN BLOCKS FOR THE 2018 QUEBEC WINTER CARNIVAL.

Visitors flock to **HUAINAN, CHINA,** to see a **BUILDING** shaped like a massive **GRAND PIANO** and **VIOLIN.**

The parking garage of the **Kansas City Public Library** in Missouri, U.S.A., is decorated with **two-story-tall book spines showcasing 42 titles.**

A THREE-STORY DONUT atop Randy's Donuts in Inglewood, California, U.S.A., has been GREETING CUSTOMERS for more than SIX DECADES.

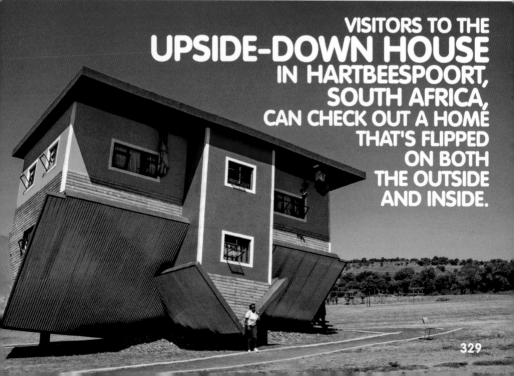

VISITORS TO THE **UPSIDE-DOWN HOUSE** IN HARTBEESPOORT, SOUTH AFRICA, CAN CHECK OUT A HOME THAT'S FLIPPED ON BOTH THE OUTSIDE AND INSIDE.

THE ORIGINAL 7 WONDERS of the WORLD

More than 2,000 years ago, many travelers wrote about sights they had seen on their journeys. Over time, seven of those places made history as the "wonders of the ancient world." There are seven because the Greeks, who made the list, believed the number seven to be magical.

THE NEW 7 WONDERS of the WORLD

Why name new wonders of the world? Most of the original ancient wonders no longer exist. To be eligible for the new list, the wonders had to be human-made before the year 2000 and in preservation. They were selected through a poll of more than 100 million voters!

THE PYRAMIDS OF GIZA, EGYPT
BUILT: ABOUT 2600 B.C.
MASSIVE TOMBS OF EGYPTIAN PHARAOHS LIE INSIDE THIS ANCIENT WONDER—THE ONLY ONE STILL STANDING TODAY.

TAJ MAHAL, INDIA
COMPLETED: 1648
THIS LAVISH TOMB WAS BUILT AS A FINAL RESTING PLACE FOR THE BELOVED WIFE OF EMPEROR SHAH JAHAN.

HANGING GARDENS OF BABYLON, IRAQ
BUILT: DATE UNKNOWN
LEGEND HAS IT THAT THIS GARDEN PARADISE WAS PLANTED ON AN ARTIFICIAL MOUNTAIN, BUT MANY EXPERTS SAY IT NEVER REALLY EXISTED.

PETRA, SOUTHWEST JORDAN
COMPLETED: ABOUT 200 B.C.
SOME 30,000 PEOPLE ONCE LIVED IN THIS ROCK CITY CARVED INTO CLIFF WALLS.

TEMPLE OF ARTEMIS AT EPHESUS, TURKEY
BUILT: SIXTH CENTURY B.C.
THIS TOWERING TEMPLE WAS BUILT TO HONOR ARTEMIS, THE GREEK GODDESS OF THE HUNT.

MACHU PICCHU, PERU
COMPLETED: ABOUT 1450
OFTEN CALLED THE "LOST CITY IN THE CLOUDS," MACHU PICCHU IS PERCHED 7,710 FEET (2,350 M) HIGH IN THE ANDES.

STATUE OF ZEUS, GREECE
BUILT: FIFTH CENTURY B.C.
THIS 40-FOOT (12-M) STATUE DEPICTED THE KING OF THE GREEK GODS.

THE COLOSSEUM, ITALY
COMPLETED: A.D. 80
WILD ANIMALS—AND HUMANS—FOUGHT EACH OTHER TO THE DEATH BEFORE 50,000 SPECTATORS IN THIS ARENA.

MAUSOLEUM AT HALICARNASSUS, TURKEY
BUILT: FOURTH CENTURY B.C.
THIS ELABORATE TOMB WAS BUILT FOR KING MAUSOLUS.

CHRIST THE REDEEMER STATUE, BRAZIL
COMPLETED: 1931
TOWERING ATOP CORCOVADO MOUNTAIN, THIS STATUE IS TALLER THAN A 12-STORY BUILDING AND WEIGHS ABOUT 2.5 MILLION POUNDS (1.1 MILLION KG).

COLOSSUS OF RHODES, RHODES (AN ISLAND IN THE AEGEAN SEA)
BUILT: FOURTH CENTURY B.C.
A 110-FOOT (34-M) STATUE HONORING THE GREEK SUN GOD HELIOS.

CHICHÉN ITZÁ, MEXICO
COMPLETED: 10TH CENTURY
ONCE THE CAPITAL CITY OF THE ANCIENT MAYA EMPIRE, CHICHÉN ITZÁ IS HOME TO THE FAMOUS PYRAMID OF KUKULCÁN.

LIGHTHOUSE OF ALEXANDRIA, EGYPT
BUILT: THIRD CENTURY B.C.
THE WORLD'S FIRST LIGHTHOUSE, IT USED MIRRORS TO REFLECT SUNLIGHT FOR MILES OUT TO SEA.

GREAT WALL OF CHINA, CHINA
COMPLETED: 1644
THE LONGEST HUMAN-MADE STRUCTURE EVER BUILT, IT WINDS OVER AN ESTIMATED 4,500 MILES (7,200 KM).

MORE MUST-SEE SITES

Time and Space

The famous astronomical clock, built in 1410 in Prague, Czechia (Czech Republic), has an astronomical dial on top of a calendar dial. Together, they keep track of time, as well as the movement of the sun, moon, and stars.

Cathedral on the Square

The onion-dome-topped towers of St. Basil's are a key landmark on Moscow's Red Square in Russia. Built between 1554 and 1560 to commemorate military campaigns by Ivan the Terrible, the building is rich in Christian symbolism.

The Upright Stuff

The Tower of Pisa in Italy started tilting soon after its construction began more than 800 years ago. It was built on an ancient riverbed, which proved to be a foundation too soft to support a structure weighing 21 million pounds (9,525 t)! By 1990, Italy's famously tilted landmark leaned so much that officials closed it to visitors, fearing it might fall over. But after years of repair work, the marble monument is again open. And although you can't see the difference, it now leans 19 inches (48 cm) less. To straighten it, some 80 tons (73 t) of soil were dug from below the side opposite the lean. When the ground underneath settled, the tower corrected itself slightly. Officials say it should be safe for tourists to walk up for another 200 years. That gives you plenty of time to plan a visit!

A WORKER REPAINTS A SECTION OF THE BRIDGE.

COLOR CONFUSION

The Golden Gate Bridge was almost given the same colors as a bumblebee! Originally the U.S. Navy wanted to coat the overpass with black and yellow stripes to make it extra visible to sailors. Designers ultimately chose to paint the bridge a bold orange to complement the landscape.

GOLDEN GATE BRIDGE TOWER

TOWER TIME

When the bridge was completed, it had the world's tallest bridge towers. Both columns are about 746 feet (227 m) high—more than twice the height of the Statue of Liberty. Divers helped build the base of the column that sits in the open ocean. First they swam up to 110 feet (34 m) below the water's surface. Using explosives, they then blasted a hole in the seafloor's bedrock where concrete would be poured to create a foundation for the tower. Because the waters were so murky, the divers did all of this in almost total darkness. Sounds like a towering task.

IT TOOK EIGHT YEARS FOR WORKERS TO BUILD FORT POINT.

FORT

HIDDEN FORT

Built during California's gold rush in the mid-1800s, Fort Point is tucked into the bridge's south side. It was designed to protect the region and its gold fields from foreign invaders, although it has never seen battle.

SECRETS OF THE
GOLDEN GATE BRIDGE

THIS GROUNDBREAKING STRUCTURE HAS JAW-DROPPING FEATURES.

The Golden Gate Bridge in San Francisco, California, U.S.A., is a real trailblazer! Finished in 1937, it was the world's largest suspension bridge at the time. Get the inside scoop on this innovative bridge.

HIGHS AND LOWS

Travelers crossing the Golden Gate Bridge aren't the only ones on the move. The overpass is often in motion too! It was designed to sway up to 27 feet (8.2 m) in each direction in high winds. And its length expands and contracts by as much as three feet (0.9 m) as the temperatures go from warm to cool and back again. None of this damages the structure or puts people at risk, because the bridge was built to be flexible.

WHALE OF A VIEW

Scientists hold stakeouts on the bridge's overpass, observing and photographing marine life like gray and humpback whales and dolphin-like mammals called harbor porpoises, who munch on anchovies that thrive in San Francisco Bay.

UNITED STATES
— CALIFORNIA
PACIFIC OCEAN
ATLANTIC OCEAN

★Sacramento
NEVADA
•San Francisco
CALIFORNIA
PACIFIC OCEAN
•Los Angeles

Bizarre Beaches

THE WORLD'S COOLEST COASTLINES OFFER SO MUCH MORE THAN SANDY SHORES.

BLACK-OUT

WHAT: Punaluʻu Black Sand Beach
WHERE: Big Island, Hawaii, U.S.A.
WHY IT'S BIZARRE: The jet-black sand on this skinny stretch of beach is made up of tiny bits of hardened lava, produced over centuries by the nearby (and still active) Kilauea volcano. This cool spot is also a popular nesting place for hawksbill and green sea turtles.

GLASS FROM THE PAST

WHAT: Glass Beach
WHERE: Fort Bragg, California, U.S.A.
WHY IT'S BIZARRE: Decades ago, the water along this beach was a dumping ground for glass bottles and other debris. Now what was once tossed in the ocean has washed up as a rainbow of shimmering sea glass covering the coves.

FOR THE BIRDS

WHAT: Boulders Beach
WHERE: Harbour Island, Bahamas
WHY IT'S BIZARRE: You might expect to see penguins on an icy coast. But these birds like it hot! African penguins splash in the warm waters of this national park next to 540-million-year-old granite boulders.

TIP-OFF

WHAT: Zlatni Rat
WHERE: Bol, Croatia
WHY IT'S BIZARRE: This narrow beach is a real shape-shifter. Its tip—which sticks out as much as 1,640 feet (500 m) into the crystal blue water—shifts in different directions as a result of wind, waves, and currents.

WILD VACATION

EAT ON TABLES AND CHAIRS MADE OF SALT!

SLEEP ON BEDS MADE OF SALT

Salt Hotel
HOTEL TAYKA DE SAL

WHERE Tahua, Bolivia

HOW MUCH About $130 a night

WHY IT'S COOL You've stayed at hotels made of brick or wood. But salt? Hotel Tayka de Sal is made mostly of salt (*sal* means "salt" in Spanish), including some beds—though you'll sleep with regular mattresses and blankets. The hotel sits on the border of Salar de Uyuni, a dried-up prehistoric lake that's the world's biggest salt flat. Builders use the salt from the more than 4,000-square-mile (10,500-sq-km) flat to make the bricks, and then glue them together with a paste of wet salt that hardens when it dries. When rain starts to dissolve the hotel, it's no problem: The owners just mix up more salt paste to strengthen the bricks.

COOL THINGS ABOUT BOLIVIA

During rainy summer months, Bolivia's Salar de Uyuni salt flat looks like a giant mirror.

The bus station in La Paz was designed by Gustave Eiffel, the same architect who built the Eiffel Tower and the Statue of Liberty.

Every August in Bolivia, dogs are honored during the Feast of St. Roch.

THINGS TO DO IN BOLIVIA

Snag a *salteña*—a baked pastry filled with spicy meat—from a street vendor in Cochabamba.

Take a boat to Isla del Sol, an island in Lake Titicaca, where motorized vehicles aren't allowed.

Dance with thousands of masked and costumed performers at the Carnaval de Oruro.

QUIZ WHIZ

Is your geography knowledge off the map? Quiz yourself to find out!

Write your answers on a piece of paper. Then check them below.

1 The Elephant Sanctuary Brazil takes in elephants rescued from _____.

a. construction zones
b. circuses
c. zoos
d. amusement parks

2 Singapore's mascot is which mythical creature?

a. a merlion
b. a unicorn
c. a pegasus
d. a dragon

3 Where was the skeleton of the largest *Tyrannosaurus rex* to date uncovered?

a. Sasebo, Japan
b. Sasaram, India
c. Saskatchewan, Canada
d. Sassari, Italy

4 **True or false?** Australia has no native hoofed animals.

5 Which of the following is not considered a geographic feature?

a. glacier
b. canyon
c. river
d. cloud

Not STUMPED yet? Check out the *NATIONAL GEOGRAPHIC KIDS QUIZ WHIZ* collection for more crazy GEOGRAPHY questions!

ANSWERS: 1. b; 2. a; 3. c; 4. True; 5. d

HOMEWORK HELP

Finding Your Way Around

LATITUDE AND LONGITUDE lines help us determine locations on Earth. Every place on Earth has a special address called absolute location. Imaginary lines called lines of latitude run west to east, parallel to the Equator. These lines measure distance in degrees north or south from the Equator (0° latitude) to the North Pole (90° N) or to the South Pole (90° S). One degree of latitude is approximately 70 miles (113 km).

Lines of longitude run north to south, meeting at the poles. These lines measure distance in degrees east or west from 0° longitude (prime meridian) to 180° longitude. The prime meridian runs through Greenwich, England.

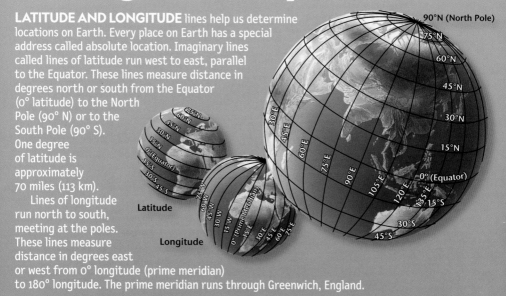

ABSOLUTE LOCATION. Suppose you are using latitude and longitude to play a game of global scavenger hunt. The clue says the prize is hidden at absolute location 30° S, 60° W. You know that the first number is south of the Equator, and the second is west of the prime meridian. On the map at right, find the line of latitude labeled 30° S. Now find the line of longitude labeled 60° W. Trace these lines with your fingers until they meet. Identify this spot. The prize must be located in central Argentina (see arrow, right).

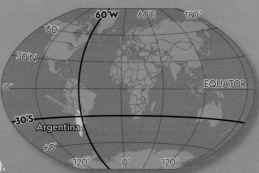

CHALLENGE!

1. Look at the map of Africa on pp. 264–265. Which country can you find at 10° S, 20° E?

2. Look at the map of Asia on pp. 272–273. Which country can you find at 20° N, 80° E?

3. On the map of Europe on pp. 280–281, which country is found at 50° N, 30° E?

4. Look at the map of North America on pp. 284–285. Which country can you find at 20° N, 100° W?

ANSWERS: 1. Angola; 2. India; 3. Ukraine; 4. Mexico

GAME ANSWERS

Green Scene
page 140

Litter is shown in yellow; recycling and compost bins are blue.

What in the World?
page 141

Top row: basketball net, Hula-Hoop, pineapple
Middle row: tree trunk, doughnut, key ring
Bottom row: swim ring, dartboard, Saturn

Find the Hidden Animals
page 142

1. C, 2. A, 3. F, 4. D, 5. E, 6. B

What in the World?
page 145

Top row: paint set, socks, lollipop
Middle row: parrot, cake, crayons
Bottom row: sprinkles, umbrella, Slinky

What in the World?
page 149

Top row: zebra, flamingo, giraffe
Middle row: elephant, mandrill, chameleon
Bottom row: leopard, tortoise, African wild dog

Find the Hidden Animals
page 150

1. E, 2. D, 3. F, 4. B, 5. C, 6. A

What in the World?
page 152

Top row: plums, yarn, sea fan
Middle row: shoelace, sea star, red cabbage
Bottom row: crayons, orchid, amethyst

Signs of the Times
page 153

Signs #1 and #5 are fake.

Want to Learn More?

Find more information about topics in this book in these National Geographic Kids resources.

Brain Candy series

Weird But True! series

Just Joking series

5,000 Awesome Facts (About Everything!) series

Beastly Bionics
Jennifer Swanson
June 2020

Ultimate U.S. Road Trip Atlas, 2nd Edition
Crispin Boyer
April 2020

Fetch! A How to Speak Dog Training Guide
Aubre Andrus
August 2020

Girls Can!
Marissa Sebastian, Tora Shae Pruden, Paige Towler
October 2020

Breaking the News
Robin Terry Brown
October 2020

Cutest Animals on the Planet
National Geographic Kids
March 2021

Top Secret
Crispin Boyer
April 2021

Ultimate Rockopedia
Steve Tomecek
December 2020

Abbreviations:
AL: Alamy Stock Photo
AS: Adobe Stock
DRMS: Dreamstime
GI: Getty Images
IS: iStockphoto
MP: Minden Pictures
NGIC: National Geographic Image Collection
SS: Shutterstock
WHHA: White House Historical Association

All Maps
By National Geographic unless otherwise noted

All Illustrations & Charts
By Stuart Armstrong unless otherwise noted

Front Cover
(orca), Brandon Cole; (volcano), Lucie/AS; (taxi), Grafissimo/IS/GI; (water bottle), Weera Danwilai/SS

Spine
(orca), Brandon Cole

Back Cover
(Earth), ixpert/SS; (chameleon), Vera Kuttelvaserova/AS; (Great Wall), Sean Pavone/SS; (wolf), Gavriel Jecan/GI; (future city), 3000ad/IS/GI; (Holi celebration), ferrantraite/E+/GI; (butterfly), Steven Russell Smith/AL

Front Matter (2-7)
2-3, 500px Prime/GI; 5 (A), Michael Milfeit/500px Prime/GI; 5 (B), ElenaMirage/iStock/GI; 5 (C), pchoui/IS/GI; 5 (D), 3000ad/IS/GI; 6 (A), agefotostock/AL; 6 (B), Photosani/SS; 6 (C), Thomas Sbampato/imageBROKER RF/GI; 6 (D), Dirk Ercken/SS; 6 (E), Coldmoon_photo/IS/GI; 6 (F), Albert Russ/SS; 6 (G), soft_light/AS; 7 (A), tdub_video/IS/GI; 7 (B), Richard T. Nowitz/Corbis; 7 (C), Nick Brundle/Moment Open/GI; 7 (D), Michele Falzone/Stockbyte/GI

Your World 2022 (8-17)
8-9, Michael Milfeit/500px Prime/GI; 10 (UP LE), Caroline Benzel; 10 (UP RT), Stephanie Rousseau/AS; 10 (LO LE), Field Museum of Natural History; 10 (LO RT), Christopher Furlong/GI; 11 (UP), Zero G Kitchen LLC; 11 (LO), Jingmai O'Connor; 12 (UP), Kristian Laine; 12 (LO), Masato Sakai/Yamagata University; 13 (UP), Phil Bex/AL; 13 (CTR), Dmitry Feoktistov/TASS via GI; 13 (LO), Atsushi Tomura/GI; 14 (UP), Ellen Helmke; 14 (CTR), Georgia Institute of Technology; 14 (LO), B Christopher/AL; 15 (UP), Jiraporn Kuhakan/Reuters; 15 (CTR), Sean Viljoen; 15 (LO), Sean Viljoen; 16 (A), SasaStock/SS; 16 (B), Roblan/SS; 16 (C), Magnus Larsson/AS; 16 (D), Patrick Foto/SS; 16 (E), cougarsan/SS; 16 (F), Uryadnikov Sergey/AS; 16 (G), Alhovik/SS; 16 (H), Africa Studio/SS; 16 (I), Jak Wonderly; 17 (UP), Umit Bektas/Reuters; 17 (CTR), Taxon Expeditions; 17 (LO), Jose Angel Astor Rocha/AS

Kids vs. Plastic (18-35)
18-19, ElenaMirage/iStock/GI; 20-21, trial-artinf/AS; 21 (UP), Jacobs Stock Photography Ltd/GI; 21 (CTR RT), SeeCee/SS; 21 (CTR LE), Norbert Pouchain/EyeEm/GI; 22-23, Steve De Neef/NGIC; 23 (RT), Aflo/SS; 23, photka/SS; 23 (LE), Pete Atkinson/GI; 24 (LE), Clearwater Marine Aquarium; 24 (RT), Clearwater Marine

Aquarium; 24-25, Science Faction/GI; 25 (LE), Clearwater Marine Aquarium; 25 (RT), Norbert Wu/MP; 26 (UP RT), Brian J. Skerry/NGIC; 26 (UP LE), Steve De Neef/NGIC; 26 (LO), Brian J. Skerry/NGIC; 27 (A), Levent Konuk/SS; 27 (B), Tory Kallman/SS; 27 (C), Andrea Izzotti/SS; 27 (D), sittipong/SS; 27 (E), Dahlia/SS; 28 (UP LE), KPPWC/AS; 28 (UP RT), Simone/AS; 28 (CTR), eurobanks/AS; 28 (LO LE), Mikhail/AS; 28 (LO RT), Kelpfish/DRMS; 29 (UP), Stephen Coburn/AS; 29 (CTR LE), Brooke BeckerAS; 29 (CTR RT), PaulPaladin/AL; 29 (LO), Lori Epstein/National Geographic Staff; 30 (UP LE), Steven Sanders/Alamy; 30 (UP RT), Fuse/Corbis/GI; 30 (CTR), unkas_photo/IS/GI; 30 (LO-1), ac_bnphotos/IS/GI; 30 (LO-2), yellowdaffs/SS; 30 (LO-3), jenifoto/IS/GI; 30 (LO-4), Shannon Hibberd/National Geographic Staff; 31 (UP LE), Elena Veselova/SS; 31 (LO), Melica/SS; 31 (UP RT), Maks Narodenko/SS; 32-33, Hilary Andrews/National Geographic Staff; 34 (UP LE), Pete Atkinson/GI; 34 (LO LE), Norbert Pouchain/EyeEm/GI; 34 (LO RT), Science Faction/GI; 34 (UP RT), Melica/SS; 35, Albo003/SS

Amazing Animals (36-87)
36-37, pchoui/IS/GI; 38 (CTR), DioGen/SS; 38 (LO), Nick Garbutt; 38 (UP), lifegallery/IS/GI; 39 (UP LE), EyeEm/GI; 39 (UP RT), reptiles4all/SS; 39 (CTR LE), Hiroya Minakuchi/MP; 39 (CTR RT), FP media/SS; 39 (LO), Ziva_K/IS/GI; 40 (UP), Nataliia Melnychuk/SS; 40 (LO), Verena Matthew/AS; 40 (CTR), Suzi Eszterhas/MP; 41 (UP), ZSSD/MP; 41(CTR), Rolf Kopfle/AL; 41 (LO), ZSSD/MP; 42 (UP), Marcel Gross; 42 (CTR), Marcel Gross; 42 (LO), Marcel Gross; 43 (UP), Jasper Doest; 43 (LO LE), Jasper Doest; 43 (LO RT), Karine Aigner/NG Staff; 44 (ALL), From Hen Who Sailed Around the World by Guirec Soudée, copyright © 2018 by Guirec Soudée. Reprinted by permission of Little, Brown an imprint of Hachette Book Group, Inc.; 45 (ALL), Dean MacDam; 46 (UP LE), Steven Kazlowski/Nature Picture Library; 46 (UP RT), Ryan Korpi/IS/GI; 46 (LO), Gary Bell/Oceanwide/MP; 47 (UP LE), Thomas Marent/ARDEA; 47 (UP RT), Mike Hill/AL; 47 (CTR), YAY Media AS/AL; 47 (LO), Cathy Keifer/SS; 48 (UP LE), Klein & Hubert/Nature Picture Library; 48 (UP RT), Kajornyot Krunkitsatien/AS; 48 (LO LE), Juniors Bildarchiv GmbH/AL; 48 (LO RT), Maros Bauer/SS; 49 (UP LE), John Carnemolla/IS; 49 (CTR), Dirk Ercken/SS; 49 (UP RT), Piotr Naskrecki/MP; 49 (LO), Suzi Eszterhas/MP; 50, Cisca Castelijns/MP; 51, Mircea Costina/SS; 52-53, Bornean Sun Bear Conservation Centre; 53 (UP), Siew te Wong/Bornean Sun Bear Conservation Centre; 53 (LO), Bornean Sun Bear Conservation Centre; 54 (LO), Anna Gowthorpe/PA Images via GI; 54 (UP), Abby Wood/Smithsonian's National Zoo; 55 (LO LE), saad315/SS; 55 (UP LE), Andrea Izzotti/SS; 55 (UP RT), Sylvain Cordier/GI; 55 (LO RT), Dr. Axel Gebauer/Nature Picture Library; 56, Staffan Widstrand/Nature Picture Library; 57 (jaguar fur), worldswildlifewonders/SS; 57 (tiger fur), Kesu/SS; 57 (leopard fur), WitR/SS; 57 (lion fur), Eric Isselée/SS; 57 (LE CTR), DLILLC/Corbis/GI; 57 (leopard), Eric Isselée/SS; 57 (tiger), Eric Isselée/SS; 57 (lion), Eric Isselée/SS; 57 (snow leopard fur), Eric Isselee/SS; 57 (snow leopard), Eric Isselee/SS; 58 (RT), Suzi Eszterhas/MP; 58 (CTR), FionaAyerst/GI; 58 (LE), Gerard Lacz/Science Source; 59 (UP),

Felis Images/Nature Picture Library; 59 (LO), Jack Bradley; 60 (UP), Image Source/Corbis; 60 (LO), Juniors/SuperStock; 61 (UP), Tom & Pat Leeson/Ardea; 61 (LO), Lisa & Mike Husar/Team Husar; 62-63, Tony Heald/NPL/MP; 63 (UP), Matthew Tabaccos/Barcroft Media/GI; 63 (LO), Matthew Tabaccos/Barcroft Media/GI; 64 (UP LE), Westend61/GI; 65 (UP RT), Roy L. Caldwell; 65 (LO), Helmut Corneli/Alamy; 66 (UP), Design Pics Inc/Alamy; 66 (LO), mauritius images GmbH/Alamy; 67 (UP LE), Kathryn Jeffs/Nature Picture Library; 67 (LO), Tory Kallman/SS; 67 (CTR RT), Design Pics Inc/Alamy; 67 (UP RT), Tony Wu/Nature Picture Library; 68 (UP), Ian McAllister/NGIC; 68 (LO), Bertie Gregory/MP; 69 (UP), Paul Nicklen/NGIC; 69 (LO LE), Paul Nicklen/NGIC; 69 (LO RT), Paul Nicklen/NGIC; 69 (CTR), Ian McAllister/Pacific Wild; 70, Eric Baccega/NPL/MP; 71 (LO), Jordi Galbany/Dian Fossey Gorilla Fund International; 71 (UP LE), Stone Sub/GI; 71 (CTR RT), courtesy Dallas Zoo; 71 (UP RT), Martin Hale/FLPA/MP; 72 (LO), Heidi & Hans-Juergen Koch/MP; 72 (CTR LE), Stephen Dalton/MP; 72 (UP), Michael D. Kern; 72 (CTR LE), AtSkwongPhoto/SS; 72 (CTR), Hitendra Sinkar Photography/Alamy; 73, gallimaufry/SS; 74 (UP), Norbert Rosing/NGIC; 74-75, David Pike/Nature Picture Library; 74-75, David Hiser/Stone/GI; 74 (CTR), Alaska Stock LLC/Alamy; 75 (LE), Paul Nicklen/NGIC; 75 (RT), Art Wolfe/The Image Bank/GI; 76 (UP), Jane Burton/GI; 76 (LO), Will Hughes/SS; 77 (LO), Brian Kimball/Kimball Stock; 77 (CTR), Ryan Lane/GI; 77 (UP), maljalen/IS; 78 (LO), Justin Siemaszko; 78 (UP), Shai (Asor) Lighter; 79 (CTR), Malia Canann, The Piggy Wiggies; 79 (UP), Joanne Lefson/Farm Sanctuary SA; 79 (LO), Peter Mares; 80 (UP), Chris Butler/Science Photo Library/Photo Researchers, Inc.; 80 (CTR), Publiphoto/Photo Researchers, Inc.; 80 (LO), Pixeldust Studios/NG Creative; 81 (A), Publiphoto/Photo Researchers, Inc.; 81 (B), Laurie O'Keefe/Photo Researchers, Inc.; 81 (C), Chris Butler/Science Photo Researchers, Inc.; 81 (D), Publiphoto/Photo Researchers, Inc.; 81 (E), image courtesy of Project Exploration; 83 (UP LE), Sergey Krasovskiy; 83 (UP RT), Dr. Ashley Poust; 83 (LO), National Park Service; 84 (UP), Franco Tempesta; 84 (LO), Franco Tempesta; 85 (UP), Catmando/SS; 85 (CTR), Franco Tempesta; 85 (LO), Leonello Calvetti/SS; 86 (LO LE), Jane Burton/GI; 86 (UP RT), Tony Heald/NPL/MP; 86 (LO RT), Helmut Corneli/Alamy; 86 (UP LE), Stone Sub/GI; 87, GOLFX/SS

Science and Technology (88-113)
88-89, 3000ad/IS/GI; 90 (UP), C_Eng-Wong Photography/SS; 90 (CTR), Plume Creative/Digital Vision/GI; 90 (LO), Library of Congress Prints and Photographs Division; 91 (UP LE), Rob Stothard/GI; 91 (UP RT), ober-art/SS; 91 (CTR LE), Roman Samokhin/SS; 91 (CTR RT), Chris Ratcliffe/SS; 91 (LO), Naeblys/SS; 92 (LO), Jetpack Aviation; 92 (LO), Solent News/Splash News; 93 (UP LE), Caters News Agency; 93 (LO INSET), REX USA/Aaron Chang/Solent News/Rex; 93, REX USA/Aaron Chang/Solent News/Rex; 93 (UP RT), Bird Photo Booth; 93 (CTR), Bird Photo Booth; 94-95 (ALL), Joe Rocco; 96-99, Mondolithic Studios; 100, Ted Kinsman/Science Source; 101 (A), Sebastian Kaulitzki/SS; 101 (B), Eye of Science/Photo Researchers, Inc.; 101

(C), Volker Steger/Christian Bardele/Photo Researchers, Inc.; 101 (D), ancelpics/GI; 101 (E), puwanai/SS; 101 (F), sgame/SS; 101 (G), kwest/SS; 102 (UP), FotografFFF/SS; 102 (LO), Craig Tuttle/Corbis/GI; 103 (earthworm), Kzww/SS; 103 (mushrooms), Ovydyborets/DRMS; 103-139 (background), Fer Gregory/SS; 103 (seedling), Mathom/DRMS; 104 (UP), SciePro/SS; 104 (LO), R. Gino Santa Maria/DRMS; 105 (LO), cobalt88/SS; 105 (UP), Cynthia Turner; 106 (A), Creator: Odua Images/SS; 106 (B), Creator: Hong Vo/SS; 106 (C), Africa Studio/SS; 106 (D), Sebastian Kaulitzki/SS; 106 (E), Creator: grebcha/SS; 106 (F), Brian Maudsley/SS; 107 (UP RT), AFP/GI; 107 (UP LE), juan moyano/AL; 107 (LO LE), VikramRaghuvanshi/GI; 107 (LO RT), Pasieka/Science Source; 108 (UP LE), Dimarion/SS; 108 (CTR LE), Microfield Scientific Ltd./Science Source; 108 (CTR RT), mrfiza/SS; 108 (LO), iLexx/IS; 108 (UP RT), Eraxion/IS; 109 (UP), Jani Bryson/IS; 109 (CTR), MyImages-Micha/SS; 109 (LO), RapidEye/IS; 110 (LE), Eric Isselee/SS; 110 (RT), sdominick/GI; 111 (UP), Jean-Pierre Clatot/AFP/GI; 111 (CTR), kryzhov/SS; 111 (LO), Lane V. Erickson/SS; 112 (LO RT), iLexx/IS; 112 (UP LE), Mondolithic Studios; 112 (UP RT), Ovydyborets/DRMS.com; 112 (LO LE), kryzhov/SS; 113, Klaus Vedfelt/GI

Culture Connection (114-137)

114-115, agefotostock/AL; 116 (UP LE), CreativeNature.nl/SS; 116 (LO LE), Tubol Evgeniya/SS; 116 (UP), Dave Donaldson/AL; 116 (LO), Pigprox/SS; 116 (LO RT), Stephen Coburn/SS; 117 (LO RT), wacpan/SS; 117 (RT CTR), Zee/Alamy; 117 (CTR), Dinodia/GI; 118 (CTR), 156181766/SS; 119, Chonnanit/SS; 120-121, Rebecca Hale/National Geographic Staff; 122-123, Naeblys/SS; 122 (UP LE), Hemis/AL; 122 (UP RT), E.D. Torial/AL; 122 (LO LE), John Kellerman/AL; 122 (LO RT), Jorgen Udvang/AL; 123 (UP), Roman Babakin/SS; 123 (CTR LE), Clarence Holmes Photography/AL; 123 (CTR RT), George Oze/AL; 123 (LO), Roy Conchie/AL; 124 (CTR LE), iStock/Mlenny; 124 (UP CTR), maogg/GI; 124 (UP RT), Paul Poplis/GI; 124 (LO LE), Glyn Thomas/Alamy; 124 (UP LE), Radomir Tarasov/DRMS; 124 (LO RT), Brian Hagiwara/GI; 125 (LO RT), Kelley Miller/National Geographic Staff Staff; 125 (LO LE), 'Money Dress' with 'Colonial Dress' behind. Paper currency and frame, Lifesize ©Susan Stockwell 2010. ©photo Colin Hampden-White 2010.; 125 (UP CTR LE), Igor Stramyk/SS; 125 (UP RT), Joe Pepler/Rex USA/SS; 125 (UP LE), Georgios Kollidas/Alamy; 125 (CTR RT), Mohamed Osama/DRMS; 125 (CTR RT), Daniel Krylov/DRMS; 126, Rebecca Hale/National Geographic Staff; 127, Mark Thiessen/National Geographic Staff; 127, Danny Smythe/SS; 128 (A), Nguyen Dai Duong; 128 (B), Ho Trung Lam; 128 (C), Mark Thiessen/National Geographic Staff; 128 (D), Randall Scott/NGIC; 129 (A), Mark Thiessen/NGIC; 129 (B), Jeremy Fahringer; 129 (C), Robert Massee; 129 (D), Catherine Cofré; 129 (E), K. Bista; 129 (F), Mark Thiessen/National Geographic Staff; 129 (G), Jeevan Sunuwar Kirat; 129 (H), Jeevan Sunuwar Kirat; 130 (UP LE), liquidlibrary/GI Plu/GI; 130 (UP RT), Jose Ignacio Soto/SS; 130 (LO), Photosani/SS; 131 (UP LE), Corey Ford/DRMS; 131 (RT), IS; 132-133, Christina Balit; 133, Christina Balit; 134 (UP), Randy Olson; 134 (LO LE), Martin Gray/NG

Creative; 134 (LO RT), Sam Panthaky/AFP/GI; 135 (LO LE), Reza/NationalGeographicStock.com; 135 (LO RT), Richard Nowitz/NG Creative; 135 (UP), Thierry Falise/LightRocket/GI; 137 (UP LE), spatuletail/SS; 137 (UP RT), PictureLake/E+/GI; 137 (CTR), cifotart/SS; 137 (LO), zydesign/SS; 137, Danevski/SS

Fun and Games (138-157)

138-139, Thomas Sbampato/imageBROKER RF/GI; 140, Jeff Hendricks and Viktoriya Tsoy (green city), James Yamasaki (litter, bins), image digitally composed; 141 (UP LE), Corbis; 141 (UP RT), Max Power/Corbis; 141 (UP RT), Supapics/Alamy; 141 (CTR LE), Zoom (192) Time/Imagemore/GI; 141 (CTR), Demkat/SS; 141 (CTR RT), Corbis/Jupiterimages; 141 (LO LE), ViewofAmelie/IS; 141 (LO CTR), Simple Stock Shots; 141 (LO RT), hideto999/SS; 142 (A), Gerard Soury/GI; 142 (B), Constantinos Petrinos/Nature Picture Library; 142 (D), Art Wolfe; 142 (E), Andy Rouse/MP; 142 (F), Christopher MacDonald/SS; 143 (A), Jim Brandenburg/MP; 143 (frog in profile), Photolukacs/SS; 143 (frog facing forward), Dirk Ercken/SS; 143 (agouti facing left), Jaymi Heimbuch/MP; 143 (kinkajou sitting), Roland Seitre/MP; 143 (toucan eating), Visuals Unlimited, Inc./Gregory Basco/GI; 143 (kinkajou portrait), Ali Atmaca/Anadolu Agency/GI; 143 (kinkajou hanging), Roland Seitre/MP; 143 (frog from above), Christian Ziegler/MP; 143 (agouti facing right), Thomas Hertwig/Alamy; 143 (toucan) Eduardo Rivero/SS; 144, Jason Tharp; 145 (CTR LE), Pete Turner/GI; 145 (LO RT), Garry Gay/Alamy; 145 (UP RT), Jeffrey Hamilton/Digital Vision/GI; 145 (UP CTR), Elena Schweitzer/SS; 145 (UP LE), EldoradoSuperVector/SS; 145 (LO CTR), Andriy Bondarev/GI; 145 (CTR RT), botulinum21/SS; 145 (LO LE), Shannon Alexander/SS; 145 (CTR), Oleksandra Naumenko/SS; 146 (ALL), Gary Fields; 147 (UP), Bullstar/SS; 147 (CTR RT), Greer & Associates, Inc./SuperStock; 147 (CTR LE), Penny Boyd/Alamy; 147 (LO), Stone Sub/GI; 148, Jim Paillot; 149 (LO CTR), Peter Steyn/Ardea; 149 (UP LE), Alexey Petrunin/DRMS; 149 (UP CTR), Bandersnatch/SS; 149 (UP RT), PhotoDisc; 149 (CTR LE), jeep2499/SS; 149 (CTR), ElisabethAardema/IS; 149 (CTR RT), For Out/SS; 149 (LO LE), Volodymyr Burdiak/SS; 149 (LO RT), Ondrej Prosicky/SS; 150 (C), B&S Draker/Nature Picture Library; 150 (B), Adegsm/IS/GI; 150 (C), Steven Kazlowski/Nature Picture Library; 150 (D), Taja Planinc/IS/GI; 150 (E), Don Paulson Photography/Purestock/Superstock; 150 (F), Roy Toft/NGIC; 151, Dan Sipple; 152 (UP LE), Bill Boch/Foodpix/Jupiterimages; 152 (UP CTR), Ingram Publishing/SuperStock; 152 (UP RT), Darryl Torckler/GI; 152 (CTR RT), Francisco Cruz/Superstock; 152 (CTR RT), Firstlight/GI; 152 (LO CTR), William Thomas Cain/Reportage/GI; 152 (LO CTR), Wendell Webber/Botanica/Jupiterimages; 152 (CTR), Ferenc Cegledi/SS; 153 (1), Paul Souders/Stone/GI; 153 (2), Yagil Henkin/Alamy; 153 (3), robertharding/Alamy; 153 (4), Jonathan Blair/NGIC; 153 (5), Jonathan Tourtellot/NGIC; 153 (6), Danita Delimont/GI; 153 (7), Peter Dazeley/The Image Bank/GI; 154 (UP), otsphoto/SS; 154 (CTR LE), Cosmin Manci/SS; 154 (LO), Helena Queen/SS; 154 (CTR RT), cynoclub/SS; 155, Dan Sipple; 156, Strika Entertainment, Inc.

Space and Earth (158-179)

158-159, Coldmoon_photo/IS/GI; 160 (UP), NGIC; 160 (LO), Joe Rocco; 161 (UP), Ralph Lee Hopkins/NGIC; 161 (UP LE and RT), Visuals Unlimited/GI; 161 (CTR LE), Visuals Unlimited/Corbis; 161 (CTR RT), Dirk Wiersma/Photo Researchers, Inc.; 161 (LO LE), Charles D. Winters/Photo Researchers, Inc.; 161 (LO RT), Theodore Clutter/Photo Researchers, Inc.; 162 (UP LE), raiwa/IS; 162 (LO LE), Albert Russ/SS; 162 (UP RT), MarcelC/IS; 162 (CTR RT), Anatoly Maslennikov/SS; 162 (LO RT), IS; 163 (UP LE), didyk/IS; 163 (UP RT), Mark A. Schneider/Science Source; 163 (LO LE), Ben Johnson/Science Source; 163 (LO CTR LE), Kazakovmaksim/DRMS; 163 (LO RT), oldeez/DRMS; 163 (LO CTR RT), Ingemar Magnusson/DRMS; 163 (UP CTR RT), Joel Arem/Science Source; 163 (UP LE), Meetchum/DRMS; 163 (UP CTR LE), Albertruss/DRMS; 163 (UP RT), 123dartist/DRMS; 163 (UP CTR RT), Igorkali/DRMS; 164 (LO CTR), ODM/SS; 165, Mark Shneider/Visuals Unlimited/Corbis; 165 (UP FAR LE), Dzarek/SS; 165 (UP CTR), Kevin Hewitt Photography Inc.; 165 (UP CTR), photolibrary.com; 165 (UP CTR RT), Danny Smythe/SS; 165 (UP CTR RT), Trinacria Photo/SS; 165 (UP RT), Smit/SS; 165 (LO LE), John Madden/IS; 165 (LO RT), Dai Haruki/IS/GI; 166, Frank Ippolito; 167 (UP LE), All Canada Photos/Alamy; 167 (CTR LE), NASA; 167 (CTR RT), Diane Cook & Len Jenshel/NGIC; 167 (LO LE), Image Science and Analysis Laboratory, NASA-Johnson Space Center. "The Gateway to Astronaut Photography of Earth."; 167 (LO RT), Douglas Peebles Photography/Alamy; 167, NG Maps; 168 (UP LE), Florian Neukirchen/AL; 168 (UP RT), Victoria Chekalina/AS; 168 (LO LE), Franco Tempesta; 168 (LO RT), Keystone Press/AL; 169 (UP), Image courtesy of New Zealand American Submarine Ring of Fire 2007 Exploration, NOAA Vents Program, NOAA-OE; 169 (CTR LE), iofoto/SS; 169 (CTR RT), Derek G. Humble/SS; 169 (LO), Sean Pavone/SS; 170-171 (CTR), Mark Garlick/Science Photo Library; 170 (LO), NASA/CXC/IOA/A FABIAN ETAL/Science Photo Library; 171 (UP), NASA, ESA and M.J. Jee (Johns Hopkins University); 171 (LO), M. Markevitch/CXC/CFA/NASA/Science Photo Library; 172-173, David Aguilar; 174, David Aguilar; 174 (LO), NASA/JHUAPL/SwRI; 175, David Aguilar; 176 (UP), EHT Collaboration/NASA; 177 (A), Allexxandar/IS/GI; 177 (B), Walter Myers/Stocktrek Images/Corbis/GI; 177 (C), Tony & Daphne Hallas/Photo Researchers, Inc.; 177 (D), Don Smith/Photolibrary/GI; 178 (UP), John Madden/IS; 178 (LO), Image courtesy of New Zealand American Submarine Ring of Fire 2007 Exploration, NOAA Vents Program, NOAA-OE; 178 (CTR), NASA/CXC/IOA/A FABIAN ETAL/Science Photo Library; 179 (UP), pixhook/E+/GI

Awesome Exploration (180-197)

180-181, soft_light/AS; 182 (UP), Mark Thiessen/National Geographic Staff; 182 (CTR LE), Steffen Foerster/SS; 182 (CTR RT), Nick Dale/AS; 182 (surfboard), Steve Collender/SS; 182 (LO), Jeff Mauritzen; 183 (UP), Alize Bouriat; 183 (CTR LE), Jeff Mauritzen; 183 (CTR RT), Salome Buglass/Charles Darwin Foundation; 183 (LO), Tomas Kotouc/SS; 184 (UP), Tyler Roemer; 184 (LO LE), Tyler Roemer; 185 (LO LE), Randall

Scott/NGIC; 185 (UP LE), Jacqueline Faherty/ NGIC; 185 (LO), National Geographic Channels/ Michael Stankevich; 186-187 (ALL), Joel Sartore, National Geographic Photo Ark/NGIC; 188-189, Wes C. Skiles/NGIC; 188 (LO), Wes C. Skiles/ NGIC; 188 (UP), Wes C. Skiles/NGIC; 189, Andrew Hounslea/GI; 190 (UP), Agustín Fuentes; 190 (LO), Frans Lanting/Frans Lanting Stock; 191, Arctic-Images/Corbis; 191 (LO LE), Arctic Images/AL; 191 (LO RT), Arctic Images/AL; 192, Thomas Cabotiau/SS; 193 (UP), Tony Campbell/ SS; 193 (LO), SS; 194, Mattias Klum/NGIC; 195 (UP), Brian J. Skerry/NGIC; 195 (LO), Michael Nichols/NGIC; 196 (UP RT), Steffen Foerster/SS; 196 (LO RT), Arctic Images/AL; 196 (UP LE), Wes C. Skiles/NGIC; 196 (LO LE), National Geographic Channels/Michael Stankevich; 197, Grady Reese/IS.com

Wonders of Nature (198-219)

198-199, tdub_video/IS/GI; 200 (LE), AVTG/ IS.com; 200 (RT), Brad Wynnyk/SS; 201 (UP LE), Rich Carey/SS; 201 (UP RT), Richard Walters/ IS.com; 201 (LO LE), Karen Graham/IS.com; 201 (LO RT), Michio Hoshino/MP/NG Creative; 202 (UP), Dobermaraner/SS; 202 (LO LE), guenter-manaus/SS; 202 (LO RT), Pete Oxford; 203 (UP), duangnapa_b/SS; 203 (CTR LE), Thawisak/AS; 203 (CTR RT), snaptitude/AS; 203 (LO), Janne Hamalainen/SS; 204 (LE), cbpix/SS; 204 (RT), Mike Hill/Photographer's Choice/GI; 204-205, Chris Anderson/SS; 205 (LE), Wil Meinderts/ Buiten-beeld/MP; 205 (RT), Paul Nicklen/ NGIC; 206, Steve Mann/SS; 207 (UP), Chasing Light-Photography by James Stone/GI; 207 (LO), James Balog/NGIC; 208 (UP), Stuart Armstrong; 208 (LO), Franco Tempesta; 209 (Statue of Liberty), Chris Parypa Photography/ SS; 209 (bus), Rob Wilson/SS; 209 (paper boat), Nadiia Ishchenko/SS; 209 (orca), Christian Musat/SS; 210 (LO RT), Eric Nguyen/Corbis; 210 (LO LE), Alan and Sandy Carey/GI; 210 (CTR RT), Brand X; 210 (UP LE), Richard T. Nowitz/Corbis; 210 (UP RT), gevende/IS/GI; 211 (LO), Richard Peterson/SS; 211 (1), Leonid Tit/SS; 211 (2), Frans Lanting/NG Creative; 211 (3), Daniel Loretto/ SS; 211 (4), Lars Christensen/SS; 212, Digital Vision/GI; 213 (UP LE), Lori Mehmen/Associated Press; 213 (LO LE), Jim Reed; 213 (EFo), Susan Law Cain/SS; 213 (EF1), Brian Nolan/IS.com; 213 (EF2), Susan Law Cain/SS; 213 (EF3), Judy Kennamer/SS; 213 (EF4), jam4travel/SS; 213 (EF5), jam4travel/SS; 214-215, 3dmotus/SS; 216, Galen Rowell/Corbis/GI; 217 (UP LE), Aikman/ Newspix/GI; 217 (UP RT), Australian Reptile Park; 217 (LO), Xinhua/Stringer via GI; 217 (LO INSET), Banaras Khan/AFP via GI; 218 (CTR RT), duangnapa_b/SS; 218 (UP), cbpix/SS; 218 (LO), Alan and Sandy Carey/GI; 218 (LE), Aikman/ Newspix/GI

History Happens (220-251)

220-221, Nick Brundle/Moment Open/GI; 222 (LO), Fengling/SS; 222 (UP LE), DeAgostini/ GI; 222 (UP RT), LibraryTuul/Robert Harding Picture; 223 (LO RT), Yoshio Tomii/SuperStock; 223 (LO LE), Kenneth Garrett/NGIC; 223 (UP), Adam Woolfitt/Robert Harding Picture Library; 224-225, Mondolithic Studios; 224 (UP RT), Seamas Culligan/Zuma/Corbis; 224 (LO), Roger Ressmeyer/Corbis; 226 (UP LE), Andrey Burmakin/SS; 226 (UP RT), Sean Pavone/SS;

226 (LO LE), Edwin Remsberg/AL; 226 (LO RT), Wong Chi Chiu/AS; 227 (UP), Johnstocker/ AS; 227 (CTR LE), Artokoloro/AL; 227 (CTR RT), Frederic J. Brown/AFP via GI; 227 (LO), Caoerlei/ DRMS; 228 (treasure map paper), EcOasis/SS; 228 (gold frame), Iakov Filimonov/SS; 228-229 (old paper), val lawless/SS; 228, Matjaz Slanic/ E+/GI; 228 (LO), Mari Lobos; 229 (gold oval frame), Winterling/DRMS; 229 (UP), Mari Lobos; 229 (LO), Mari Lobos; 230 (UP LE), Metropolitan Museum of Art, Munsey Fund, 1932; 230 (UP RT), DEA/A. De Gregorio/De Agostini/GI; 230 (LO), Look and Learn/Bridgeman Images; 231 (UP LE), Purchase, Arthur Ochs Sulzberger Gift, and Rogers, Acquisitions and Fletcher Funds, 2016/Metropolitan Museum of Art; 231 (UP RT), Metropolitan Museum of Art; 231 (LO), Heritage Images/GI; 232-233, CTON; 234, U.S. Air Force photo/Staff Sgt. Alexandra M. Boutte; 235, 2nd Lt. D McLellan/IWM/GI; 236, Scott Rothstein/SS; 237 (LO), Gary Blakely/ SS; 237 (CTR), Zack Frank/SS; 237 (UP), SS; 238, Adrian Lubbers; 239 (coins), Asaf Eliason/ SS; 239 (50 dollar bill), Brian McEntire/SS; 239 (20 dollar bill), Robynrg/SS; 239 (2 dollar bill), CreativeWay/Alamy; 239 (10 dollar bill), CreativeWay/Alamy; 239 (coins), Asaf Eliason/ SS; 240 (LO), Education Images/UIG/GI; 240 (CTR), AFP/GI; 240 (UP), grandriver/E+/GI; 241 (A), WHHA; 241 (B), WHHA; 241 (C), WHHA; 241 (D), Steve Byland/DRMS; 241 (E), WHHA; 241 (F), WHHA; 241 (G), WHHA; 241 (H), WHHA; 241 (I), WHHA; 242 (A), WHHA; 242 (B), WHHA; 242 (C), WHHA; 242 (D), WHHA; 242 (E), WHHA; 242 (F), WHHA; 242 (G), WHHA; 242 (H), WHHA; 242 (I), Duda Vasilii/SS; 242 (J), WHHA; 243 (A), WHHA; 243 (B), WHHA; 243 (C), WHHA; 243 (D), WHHA; 243 (E), WHHA; 243 (F), WHHA; 243 (G), WHHA; 243 (H), WHHA; 243 (I), WHHA; 243 (J), WHHA; 244 (A), WHHA; 244 (B), WHHA; 244 (C), WHHA; 244 (D), WHHA; 244 (E), WHHA; 244 (F), WHHA; 244 (G), WHHA; 244 (H), WHHA; 244 (I), WHHA; 244 (J), Artbox/SS; 245 (A), WHHA; 245 (B), WHHA; 245 (C), WHHA; 245 (D), WHHA; 245 (E), MPI/GI; 245 (F), WHHA; 245 (G), The White House; 245 (H), Pete Souza/The White House; 245 (I), Shealah Craighead/The White House; 245 (J) David Lienemann/The White House; 246 (UP), Bettmann/Corbis/GI; 246 (INSET), Science Source/GI; 247 (UP), Charles Kogod/ NGIC; 247 (LO), Saul Loeb/AFP via GI; 248, Bettmann Archive/GI; 249 (UP LE), Scott Eisen/ GI; 249 (UP RT), AP/SS; 249 (LO), AP/SS; 250 (UP), Sean Pavone/SS; 250 (CTR RT), LibraryTuul/ Robert Harding Picture; 250 (CTR LE), DEA/A. De Gregorio/De Agostini/GI; 251, Christopher Furlong/GI

Geography Rocks (252-337)

252-253, Michele Falzone/Stockbyte/GI; 259 (LO), NASA; 259 (UP), Mark Thiessen/National Geographic Staff; 261 (UP CTR), Maria Stenzel/ NG Creative; 261 (LO CTR), Bill Hatcher/ NG Creative; 261 (LO RT), Carsten Peter/ NG Creative; 261 (UP RT), Gordon Wiltsie/ NG Creative; 261 (LO LE), James P. Blair/NG Creative; 261 (UP LE), Thomas J. Abercrombie/ NG Creative; 261 (BACK), Fabiano Rebeque/ Moment/GI; 262, iStock/GI; 263 (UP), AdemarRangel/GI; 263 (CTR RT), Iko/SS; 263 (CTR LE), Edward Stanley; 263 (LO), eAlisa/ SS; 266, Klein & Hubert/Nature Picture Library; 267 (CTR), Mark Conlon, Antarctic

Ice Marathon; 267 (UP), Achim Baque/SS; 267 (LO), Stephen Nicol; 267 (CTR RT), Flipser/SS; 270, P Deliss/The Image Bank/GI; 271 (UP), Jon Arnold Images/Danita Delimont.com; 271 (CTR RT), Nancy Brown/Photographer's Choice/GI; 271 (CTR LE), John Downer/MP; 271 (LO), slowmotiongli/AS; 274, Arun Roisri/ Moment RF/GI; 275 (UP), Andrew Watson/John Warburton-Lee Photography Ltd/GI; 275 (CTR LE), Adam Fletcher/MP; 275 (CTR RT), David Wall Photo/GI; 275 (LO), Martin Valigursky/AS; 278, Guillem Lopez/Cavan Images; 279 (UP), Roy Pedersen/SS; 279 (CTR LE), Thomas Lohnes/ GI; 279 (CTR RT), Richard Becker/AL; 279 (LO), Aleksandr Volkov/AL; 282, Gavriel Jecan/GI; 283 (UP), Rodrigo Arangua/GI; 283 (CTR LE), Beth Zaiken; 283 (CTR RT), Neirfy/SS; 283 (LO), Mint Images RF/GI; 286, hadynyah/IS/GI; 287 (CTR RT), DC_Colombia/GI; 287 (UP), Soberka Richard/hemis.fr/GI; 287 (LO), Keren Su/GI; 287, Eraldo Peres/AP/SS; 293, Kelly Cheng/GI; 294, Uros Ravbar/DRMS; 298, Renate Wefers/ EyeEm/GI; 301, ferrantraite/E+/GI; 302, DaveLongMedia/IS/GI; 306, Nikolai Sorokin/ DRMS; 309, Michael Runkel/AL; 314, Steve Lovegrove/SS; 326 (UP), SeanPavonePhoto/IS/ GI; 326 (CTR LE), TexPhoto/E+/SS; 326 (CTR RT), Harold G Herradura/SS; 326 (LO), PhotoDisc; 327 (UP LE), Mint Images Limited/AL; 327 (LO RT), Oku Okoko Photography/SS; 327 (LO LE), photka/SS; 327 (CTR LE), DmitrySerbin/SS; 327 (CTR RT), Doug Demarest/Design Pics/GI; 327 (UP RT), Ian Cook/Image Source/Superstock; 327 (CTR), North Wind Picture Archives/Alamy; 328 (UP LE), M L Pearson/AL; 328 (UP RT), Exotica/AL; 328 (LO LE), Kenishirotie/AL; 328 (LO RT), Oleksandr Prykhodko/AL; 329 (UP), Rubens Abboud/AL; 329 (CTR), Angela Hampton Picture Library/AL; 329 (LO), Themba Hadebe/AP/SS; 330 (A), David Sutherland/The Image Bank/ GI; 330 (B), Ferdinand Knab/The Bridgeman Art Library/GI; 330 (C), Ferdinand Knab/The Bridgeman Art Library/GI; 330 (D), Ferdinand Knab/The Bridgeman Art Library/GI; 330 (E), Wilhelm van Ehrenberg/The Bridgeman Art Library/GI; 330 (F), Ferdinand Knab/The Bridgeman Art Library/GI; 330 (G), DEA Picture Library/GI; 330 (H), Holger Mette/SS; 330 (I), Holger Mette/SS; 330 (J), Jarno Gonzalez Zarraonandia/SS; 330 (K), David Iliff/SS; 330 (L), ostill/SS; 330 (M), Hannamariah/SS; 330 (N), Jarno Gonzalez Zarraonandia/SS; 331 (UP RT), Taylor S. Kennedy/NGIC; 331 (LO), Iourii Tcheka/SS; 331 (UP LE), Gilmanshin/SS; 332 (LO), S.Borisov/SS; 332-333, Justin Sullivan/ GI; 332 (CTR), Justin Sullivan/GI; 332 (UP), Andy Freeberg; 333, Nick Ut/AP Photo; 334 (UP LE), Danita Delimont/AL; 334 (LO RT), Gardel Bertrand/GI; 334 (UP RT), ArtyAlison/IS/GI; 334 (LO LE), Ian Cumming/ZUMApress/Newscom; 335 (ALL), Red De Hoteles Tayka; 336 (LO), Maria Stenzel/NG Creative; 336 (CTR), Beth Zaiken; 336 (UP), Eraldo Peres/AP/SS

NATIONAL GEOGRAPHIC and Yellow Border Design are trademarks of the
National Geographic Society, used under license.

Since 1888, the National Geographic Society has funded more than 12,000 research,
exploration, and preservation projects around the world. The Society receives
funds from National Geographic Partners, LLC, funded in part by your purchase.
A portion of the proceeds from this book supports this vital work.
To learn more, visit natgeo.com/info.

For more information, visit nationalgeographic.com, call 1-877-873-6846,
or write to the following address:

National Geographic Partners, LLC
1145 17th Street N.W.
Washington, DC 20036-4688 U.S.A.

For librarians and teachers:
nationalgeographic.com/books/librarians-and-educators

More for kids from National Geographic: natgeokids.com

National Geographic Kids magazine inspires children to explore their world
with fun yet educational articles on animals, science, nature, and more.
Using fresh storytelling and amazing photography, *Nat Geo Kids* shows kids
ages 6 to 14 the fascinating truth about the world—and why they should care.
kids.nationalgeographic.com/subscribe

For rights or permissions inquiries, please contact National Geographic Books
Subsidiary Rights: bookrights@natgeo.com

Designed by Kathryn Robbins and Ruthie Thompson

**National Geographic supports K–12 educators with ELA Common Core Resources.
Visit natgeoed.org/commoncore for more information.**

The publisher would like to thank everyone who worked to make this book come
together: Angela Modany, associate editor; Mary Jones, project editor;
Sarah Wassner Flynn, writer; Michelle Harris, researcher;
Lori Epstein, photo director; Mike McNey, map production; Chris Philpotts,
illustrator; Anne LeongSon and Gus Tello, design production assistants; Joan
Gossett, editorial production manager; and Molly Reid, production editor.

Trade paperback ISBN: 978-1-4263-7202-5
Reinforced library binding ISBN: 978-1-4263-7203-2

Printed in the United States of America
21/WOR/1